MY 60 MEMORABLE GAMES

My **60** Memorable Games

Selected and fully annotated
by Bobby Fischer

with Introductions to the games
by International Grandmaster **Larry Evans**

BATSFORD

This edition first published in the United Kingdom in 2008 by

B T Batsford
Old West London Magistrates' Court
10 Southcombe Street
London
W14 0RA
www.batsford.com

An imprint of Pavilion Books Group Ltd

First published in the United Kingdom by Faber and Faber, 1969
Revised edition published by Batsford, 1995

ISBN 978 1 9063 8830 0

A CIP catalogue record for this book is available from the British Library.

17 16 15 14
10 9

Reproduction by Spectrum Colour Ltd, Ipswich

Printed and bound by CPI Group (UK) Ltd, Croydon, CR0 4YY

This book can be ordered direct from the publisher at the website:
www.anovabooks.com

Or try your local bookshop

Contents

(B and W refer to Black and White)

Preface

Author's Preface

The 60 games annotated in this volume were all played during 1957 through '67 and, with the exception of nos. 44 and 50, under strict tournament conditions. The notes frequently include references to additional games, occasionally presenting them in full. An interested reader will find 34 of my earlier efforts in Bobby Fischer's Games of Chess *(Simon and Schuster, 1959).*

All of the 60 here offered contain, for me, something memorable and exciting – even the 3 losses. I have tried to be both candid and precise in my elucidations in the hope that they would offer insights into chess that will lead to fuller understanding and better play.

Finally, I wish to express my gratitude to Larry Evans, friend and colleague, for his invaluable aid in the preparation of the text as well as for his lucid introductions.

ROBERT J. FISCHER
New York City

On the chessboard lies and hypocrisy do not survive long.
The creative combination lays bare the presumption of a lie;
the merciless fact, culminating in a checkmate, contradicts the hypocrite.

— EMANUEL LASKER

1 Fischer - Sherwin *[U.S.A.]*

NEW JERSEY OPEN CHAMPIONSHIP 1957
SICILIAN DEFENSE

Too little, too late

Although Sherwin makes no serious errors in the opening, he misses several equalizing opportunities. Demonstrating the technical virtuosity that is to become his hallmark, Fischer, with astonishing maturity, gradually strengthens his grip by accumulating small advantages: the better center and the two Bishops. Sherwin, meanwhile, attempts to consolidate his position — only to see his 14-year-old opponent shatter it with a thunderbolt (18 ♘xh7). It brings to mind Alekhine's combinations, which also seemed to spring from nowhere. Sherwin, lashing back, refuses to fall. However, his defense finally disintegrates under a series of acute blows to his wobbly King.

1	e4	c5
2	♘f3	e6
3	d3	...

This used to be my favorite. I thought it led to a favorable variation of the King's Indian reversed, particularly after Black has committed himself with ...e6.

3	...	♘c6
4	g3	♘f6

Fischer-Ivkov, Santa Monica 1966 continued *4...d5 5 ♘bd2 ♗d6 6 ♗g2 ♘ge7 7 0-0 0-0 8 ♘h4!* with chances for initiative.

5	♗g2	♗e7
6	0-0	0-0

More usual is *6...d5*; but Black has purposely delayed placing his center Pawns. Has he a new idea in mind?

7	♘bd2	...

After *7* e5 ♘d5 *8* ♘bd2 f6 *9* exf6 ♘xf6 *10* ♖e1 gives White an edge.

7	...	♖b8

Sherwin slid the Rook here with his pinky, as if to emphasize the cunning of this mysterious move. *7*...d5 *8* ♖e1 b5 *9* e5 ♘d7 *10* ♘f1 b4 *11* h4 a5 *12* ♗f4 a4 *13* a3! Fischer-Mjagmasuren, Sousse Interzonal 1967, leads to double-edged play where Black's chances on the Q-side countervail White's K-side attack – but White usually comes first.

8	♖e1	d6
9	c3	b6

Not bad. But I had expected *9*...b5 *10* d4 cxd4! (if *10*...b4 *11* e5! bxc3? [*11*...dxe5 *12* dxe5 ♘d7 *13* c4 holds the advantage] *12* exf6 cxd2 *13* ♘xd2! wins a piece) *11* cxd4 d5 with equality.

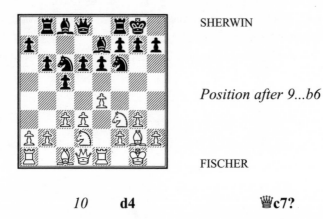

SHERWIN

Position after 9...b6

FISCHER

10	d4	♛c7?

This leads to trouble. Black should strive for counterplay by opening the c-file: *10*...cxd4 *11* cxd4 d5 *12* e5 ♘d7, etc.

11	e5!	♘d5

Worse is *11*...♘d7 *12* exd6 ♗xd6 *13* ♘e4 cxd4 *14* ♘xd6 ♛xd6 *15* ♗f4 e5 *16* ♘xe5! ♘dxe5 *17* cxd4 winning a Pawn. The best try is *11*...dxe5 *12* dxe5 ♘d7 *13* ♛e2 ♗b7 *14* h4 with a bind, but Black's game may be tenable.

12	exd6	♗xd6

13	♘e4!	c4

An unpleasant choice, since it releases the pressure in the center and gives White a free hand to start operations on the K-side. However, other moves lose material:

A] *13...♗e7 14 c4 ♘f6 15 ♗f4*, etc.

B] *13...cxd4 14 ♘xd6 ♕xd6 15 c4! ♘f6 16 ♗f4* and again the lineup on this diagonal is unfortunate.

14	♘xd6	♕xd6
15	♘g5!	♘ce7?

A bad mistake. Black's game is still tenable after *15...h6 16 ♘e4 ♕d8.*

16	♕c2!	♘g6

On *16...f5? 17 ♕e2* picks off a Pawn. Had Sherwin seen what was coming, however, he might have chosen *16...g6 17 ♘e4 ♕c7 18 ♗h6 ♖d8*, though *19 ♕d2* prepares to exploit his weakened dark squares.

17	h4	♘f6

Apparently everything's defended now. Unappetizing is *17...♖d8 (17...h6 18 h5 hxg5 19 hxg6 f6? 20 ♕e2-h5) 18 ♘xh7! ♔xh7 19 h5 f5 20 hxg6+ ♔xg6 21 ♖e5!* with a bind.

SHERWIN

Position after 17...♘f6

FISCHER

18	♘xh7!	...

Throwing a monkey wrench into Black's carefully contrived setup! As usual, tactics flow from a positionally superior game.

18	...	♘xh7

Not *18...*♔xh7? *19* ♗f4.

19	h5	♘h4!

The best fighting chance. Not *19...*♘e7 *20* ♗f4 wins a clear exchange.

20	♗f4	♕d8
21	gxh4	...

21 ♗xb8? ♘xg2 *22* ♔xg2 ♗b7+ *23* f3 ♕xb8.

21	...	♖b7!
22	h6!	...

He's hoping for *22* ♗xb7 ♗xb7 and, suddenly, the initiative passes to Black despite his material deficit.

22	...	♕xh4

Once again, time-pressure had Sherwin burying his thumbs in his ears. Instead of trying to mix it up, Black should keep his King sheltered as long as possible with *22...*g6 *23* h5! g5 (if *23...*gxh5 *24* ♕e2), but *24* ♗e5 stays a Pawn ahead with two Bishops. It might still be a fight, though.

23	hxg7	♔xg7?

Suicidal. The last hope would have been *23...*♖d8 *24* ♗g3 ♕h6, though *25* ♕e2 is hard to meet (if *25...*b5 *26* a4 a6 *27* axb5 axb5 *28* ♖a8).

SHERWIN

Position after 23...♔xg7?

FISCHER

24	♖e4!	...

Threatening 25 ♗e5+.

| 24 | ... | ♕h5 |
| 25 | ♖e3! | ... |

Now the Rook joins the King hunt – and it's murder. The immediate threat is 26 ♖h3 ♕g6 27 ♖g3.

| 25 | ... | f5 |
| 26 | ♖h3 | ♕e8 |

26...♕g6? 27 ♖g3.

| 27 | ♗e5+ | ... |

White can pick off a couple of exchanges with 27 ♗h6+ ♔g8 28 ♗xf8 ♕xf8 29 ♗xb7, etc. But by now I felt there was more in the offing.

| 27 | ... | ♘f6 |

27...♔g8? 28 ♖g3+ ♔f7 29 ♖g7 mate.

| 28 | ♕d2! | ♔f7 |
| 29 | ♕g5 | ♕e7 |

On 29...♔e7 30 ♖h7+ is devastating.

30	♗xf6	♕xf6
31	♖h7+	♔e8
32	♕xf6	♖xh7

On 32...♖xf6 33 ♗xb7 nets a whole Rook.

| 33 | ♗c6+ | Black resigns |

SHERWIN

Final Position after 33 ♗c6+

FISCHER

If 33...♗d7 34 ♕xe6+.

2 Fischer - Larsen *[Denmark]*

PORTOROZ 1958

SICILIAN DEFENSE

Slaying the dragon

Although the Sicilian, as a whole, is still the best fighting defense at Black's disposal, much of the steam has been taken out of the time-honored Dragon Variation. This is one of the key games which helped to batter its reputation.

   In a laudable attempt to create complications, Larsen deviates from the book on move 15. That proves to be disastrous, since his counterattack never gets started. Mechanically, routinely, Fischer pries open the h-file, sacrificing first a Pawn and then the exchange. There is an aura of the inevitable about the outcome. Here the notes are as instructive and lucid as the text, which is an object lesson in how to mount an assault against the fianchettoed King.

1	e4	c5
2	♘f3	d6
3	d4	cxd4
4	♘xd4	♘f6
5	♘c3	g6

Larsen was one of the diehards who refused to abandon the Dragon until recently. White's attack almost plays itself ... weak players even beat Grandmasters with it. I once thumbed through several issues of *Shakhmatny Bulletin*, when the Yugoslav Attack was making its debut, and found the ratio was something like nine wins out of ten in White's favor. Will Black succeed in reinforcing the variation? Time will tell.

6	♗e3	♗g7

6...♘g4? still loses to 7 ♗b5+.

7	f3	0-0
8	♕d2	♘c6
9	♗c4	...

This refinement supersedes the old 0-0-0. The idea is to prevent ...d5.

9	...	♘xd4

Just how Black can attempt to thread his way to equality is not clear. Interesting is Donald Byrne's *9...a5*. The strongest reply is *10 g4* and if *10...♘e5 11 ♗e2 d5? 12 g5!* wins a Pawn.

10	♗xd4	♗e6

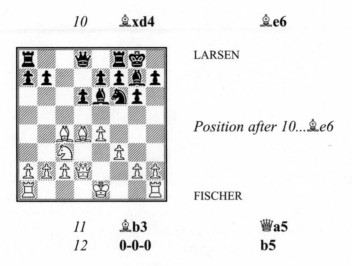

LARSEN

Position after 10...♗e6

FISCHER

11	♗b3	♕a5
12	0-0-0	b5

After *12...♗xb3 13 cxb3!* Black cannot make any attacking headway against this particular Pawn configuration. White is lost in the King and Pawn ending, it's true, but Black usually gets mated long before then. As Tarrasch put it: "Before the endgame the gods have placed the middle game."

13	♔b1	b4
14	♘d5	...

Weaker is *14 ♘e2 ♗xb3 15 cxb3 ♖fd8*.

14	...	♗xd5

Bad judgment is *14...♘xd5? 15 ♗xg7 ♔xg7 16 exd5 ♗d7 17 ♖de1* with a crushing bind. (Suetin-Korchnoi, USSR Championship prelims 1953.)

15	♗xd5	...

Stronger is *15 exd5! ♕b5 16 ♖he1 a5 17 ♕e2!* (Tal-Larsen, Zurich 1959) where White abandons the attack and plays for pressure along the e-file instead.

| 15 | ... | ♖ac8? |

The losing move. After the game Larsen explained he was playing for a win, and therefore rejected the forced draw with *15...♘xd5 16 ♗xg7 ♘c3+ 17 bxc3 (17 ♗xc3 bxc3 18 ♕xc3 ♕xc3 19 bxc3 ♖fc8* renders White's extra Pawn useless.) *17...♖ab8! 18 cxb4 ♕xb4+! 19 ♕xb4 ♖xb4+ 20 ♗b2 ♖fb8*, etc. After *15...♘xd5*, however, I intended simply *16 exd5 ♕xd5 17 ♕xb4*, keeping the game alive.

| 16 | ♗b3! | ... |

He won't get a second chance to snap off the Bishop! Now I felt the game was in the bag if I didn't botch it. I'd won dozens of skittles games in analogous positions and had it down to a science: pry open the h-file, sac, sac ... mate!

| 16 | ... | ♖c7 |

This loss of time is unfortunately necessary if Black is ever to advance his a-Pawn. *16...♕b5?* is refuted by *17 ♗xa7*.

| 17 | h4 | ♕b5 |

There's no satisfactory way to impede White's attack. If *17...h5 18 g4! hxg4 (18...♖fc8 19 ♖dg1 hxg4 20 h5! gxh5 21 fxg4 ♘xe4 22 ♕f4 e5 23 ♕xe4 exd4 24 gxh5 ♔h8 25 h6 ♗f6 26 ♖g7! wins) 19 h5! gxh5 (on 19...♘xh5 20 ♗xg7 ♔xg7 21 fxg4 ♘f6 22 ♕h6+ mates) 20 fxg4 ♘xe4 (on 20...hxg4 21 ♖dg1 e5 22 ♗e3 ♖d8 23 ♗h6; or 20...♘xg4 21 ♖dg1 ♗xd4 22 ♖xg4+! hxg4 23 ♕h6 leads to mate) 21 ♕e3 ♘f6 (21...♗xd4 22 ♕xe4 ♗g7 23 ♖xh5) 22 gxh5 e5 23 h6* wins.

LARSEN

Position after 17...♕b5

FISCHER

Now Black is threatening to get some counterplay with ...a5-a4.

18	**h5!**	...

There's no need to lose a tempo with the old-fashioned g4.

18	...	**⊡fc8**

On *18...gxh5 19 g4! hxg4 20 fxg4!* ♘xe4 *21* ♕h2 ♘g5 *22* ♗xg7 ♔xg7 *23* ♖d5 ♖c5 *24* ♕h6+ ♔g8 *25* ♖xg5+ ♖xg5 *26* ♕xh7 mate.

19	**hxg6**	**hxg6**
20	**g4**	...

Not the impatient *20* ♗xf6? ♗xf6 *21* ♕h6 e6! (threatening ...♕e5) and Black holds everything.

20	...	**a5**

Now Black needs just one more move to get his counterattack moving. But for the want of a nail the battle was lost...

21	**g5**	**♘h5**

Vasiukov suggests *21...*♘e8 as a possible defense (not *21...a4? 22 gxf6 axb3 23 fxg7! bxc2+ 24* ♕xc2! e5 *25* ♕h2 wins); but White crashes through with *22* ♗xg7 ♘xg7 (*22...*♔xg7? *23* ♕h2) *23* ♖h6! e6 (if *23...a4 24* ♕h2 ♘h5 *25* ♖xg6+) *24* ♕h2 ♘h5 *25* ♗xe6! fxe6 (*25...*♕xg5 *26* ♖xg6+! ♕xg6 *27* ♗xc8, threatening ♖g1) *26* ♖xg6+ ♘g7 *27* ♖h1, etc.

LARSEN

Position after 21...♘h5

FISCHER

22	**♖xh5!**	...

Fine wrote: "In such positions, combinations are as natural as a baby's smile."

22	...	gxh5

No better is *22...♗xd4 23 ♕xd4 gxh5 24 g6 ♕e5* (if *24...e6 25 ♕xd6*) *25 gxf7+ ♔h7* (if *25...♔f8 26 ♕xe5 dxe5 27 ♖g1 e6 28 ♗xe6 ♔e7 29 ♗xc8 ♖xc8 30 ♖g5* wins) *26 ♕d3!* (intending f4) should be decisive.

23	g6	e5

On *23...e6 24 gxf7+ ♔xf7* (if *24...♖xf7 25 ♗xe6*) *25 ♗xg7 ♔xg7 26 ♖g1+ ♔h7 27 ♕g2 ♕e5 28 ♕g6+ ♔h8 29 ♖g5 ♖g7 30 ♖xh5+ ♔g8 31 ♗xe6+ ♔f8 32 ♖f5+ ♔e7 33 ♖f7+* wins.

24	gxf7+	♔f8
25	♗e3	d5!

A desperate bid for freedom. On *25...a4* (if *25...♖d8 26 ♗h6*) *26 ♕xd6+ ♖e7 27 ♕d8+! ♖xd8 28 ♖xd8+ ♖e8 29 ♗c5+* mates.

26	exd5!	...

Not *26 ♗xd5 ♖xc2!*

26	...	♖xf7

On *26...a4 27 d6! axb3 28 dxc7* wins.

27	d6	♖f6

On *27...♖d7* White can either regain the exchange with *28 ♗e6* or try for more with *28 ♗h6*. And on *27...♖xf3 28 d7*, threatening ♕d6 mate.

28	♗g5	♕b7

On *28...♕d7 29 ♕d5! ♕f7* (if *29...♖f7 30 ♗e7+!*) *30 ♗xf6* wins material.

29	♗xf6	♗xf6
30	d7	♖d8
31	♕d6+	...

A mistake! *31 ♕h6+!* forces mate in three.

31	...	**Black resigns**

3 Petrosian *[U.S.S.R.]* - Fischer

PORTOROZ 1958

KING'S INDIAN DEFENSE

Bear hug

In what appear to be perfectly equal positions, Petrosian consistently finds seemingly innocuous moves which gradually overwhelm his opponent. He accomplishes his objective simply by exchanging pieces and maneuvering for victory without taking unnecessary risks.
This essentially defensive technique has the virtue, when it doesn't utterly succeed, of producing a draw. Fischer, by contrast, generally chooses the sharpest course, however precipitous it may become. Occasionally he overreaches himself, but it makes for interesting chess.

In this game, replete with errors on both sides, Petrosian succeeds in pinning his opponent for a time to a static endgame. But Fischer manages to burst his bonds, only to blunder on the very next move (51...♔d6). Petrosian, however, by blundering in his turn, restores the balance. The ensuing Rook and Pawn ending produces a thrilling draw.

1	c4	♘f6
2	♘c3	g6
3	g3	♗g7
4	♗g2	0-0
5	♘f3	d6
6	0-0	♘c6
7	d3	...

On 7 d4 I intended 7...e5. Petrosian is striving for an English Opening formation, a slow system for which he is temperamentally suited.

7	...	♘h5
8	d4	...

Reckoning he can afford this loss of time in view of Black's misplaced KN. On 8 ♖b1 f5! 9 ♕c2 a5 10 a3 f4 (Petrosian-Vasiukov, Moscow 1956) Black obtains an excellent aggressive setup. I was as impressed by that game as Petrosian must have been, since he got crushed.

8	...	e5
9	**d5**	...

9 dxe5 dxe5 *10* ♕xd8 ♖xd8 *11* ♘d5 ♖d7 *12* ♗h3 f5 *13* g4 ♘f6!
If *14* gxf5 (*14* ♘xf6+ ♗xf6 *15* gxf5 gxf5 *16* ♗xf5?? ♖g7+ wins)
14...♘xd5 *15* cxd5 ♖xd5.

9	...	♘e7
10	**e4**	...

FISCHER

Position after 10 e4

PETROSIAN

This is the right time to get in *10*...c5! Petrosian-Boleslavsky, USSR
Championship prelims 1957, continued: *11* ♘e1 ♔h8 *12* ♘d3 f5
13 ♖b1 ♘f6=.

10	...	f5
11	**exf5**	gxf5

Tempting but unsound is *11*...♘xf5 *12* g4 ♘d4 *13* gxh5 ♗g4
14 ♘xd4! ♗xd1 *15* ♘e6, etc. And on *11*...♗xf5 *12* ♘g5 ♕d7 *13* ♘e6!
♗xe6 *14* dxe6 ♕xe6 *15* ♗xb7 ♖ab8 *16* ♗g2 ♕xc4 *17* ♘d5! White
comes out on top.

12	**♘xe5!**	♘xg3

A "desperado" combination: this Knight (which is doomed anyway)
sells its life as dearly as possible.

13	**hxg3**	...

Simple and good. I had expected *13* fxg3, but Petrosian eschews the
K-side attack and plays for control of the center squares instead. His
judgment turns out to be right.

| 13 | ... | ♗xe5? |

13...dxe5, keeping a fluid Pawn center, offers more play. I was unduly worried about White's passed d-Pawn after *14* c5.

14	f4!	♗g7
15	♗e3	♗d7
16	♗d4	...

Forcing the trade of Black's most active piece. White soon obtains a firm grip on the position.

| 16 | ... | ♘g6 |
| 17 | ♖e1? | ... |

A careless transposition. Now by *17*...♗xd4+ *18* ♕xd4 h5! followed by ...h4, Black could exchange his isolated h-Pawn for White's g-Pawn and the game would be dead equal. Correct was *17* ♗f3.

| 17 | ... | ♖f7? |
| 18 | ♗f3! | ... |

Black doesn't get a second chance.

FISCHER

Position after 18 ♗f3!

PETROSIAN

18	...	♕f8
19	♔f2	♖e8
20	♖xe8	♕xe8
21	♗xg7	♖xg7
22	♕d4	b6
23	♖h1	...

White has effortlessly achieved a plus and now he wants to improve his position before embarking on a committal course. *23* b4!, threatening c5, is much sharper, and poses more immediate problems.

| 23 | ... | a5 |

My first free breath!

| 24 | ♘d1 | ♕f8 |
| 25 | ♘e3 | ... |

Petrosian keeps building without getting sidetracked – even by good moves. I was more afraid of *25* ♗h5! tying me up completely. Then the Rook can't move because of ♗xg6 followed by a check on h8.

| 25 | ... | ♖f7! |
| 26 | b3 | ♕g7 |

The exchange of Queens eases the cramp. White can't afford to retreat and cede this important diagonal.

27	♕xg7+	♔xg7
28	a3	♖f8
29	♗e2	...

White constantly finds ways to improve his position. Not *29* b4 axb4 *30* axb4 ♖a8 and Black seizes the open file.

29	...	♘e7
30	♗d3	h6
31	♖h5	♗e8

FISCHER

Position after 31...♗e8

PETROSIAN

| 32 | ♖h2 | ... |

Avoiding a little trap: *32 ♘xf5+?* (or *32 ♖xf5? ♖h8!*) *32...♘xf5 33 ♖xf5 ♖h8!* followed by ...♗g6 winning the exchange.

32	...	♗d7
33	♖h1	♖h8
34	♘c2!	...

Headed for an even stronger post on d4. I was amazed during the game. Each time Petrosian achieved a good position, he managed to maneuver into a better one.

34	...	♔f6
35	♘d4	♔g7
36	♗e2	...

Feigning an invasion with ♗h5 and ♖e1 and ♘e6. White has two wings to operate on: Black must be flexed to react appropriately, and this requires alertness.

36	...	♘g8?

Panicking and giving him the opportunity he's been waiting for to sneak b4 in at a moment when Black can't counter with ...axb4 and ...♖a8. Petrosian likes to play cat-and-mouse, hoping that his opponents will go wrong in the absence of a direct threat. The amazing thing is – they usually do! Witness a case in point. I should just have ignored his "threat" with, say, *36...♖a8 37 ♗h5 ♖c8 38 ♖e1 ♔f6* and if *39 ♘e6 c6.*

37	b4!	♘f6
38	♗d3!	...

38 bxa5 ♘e4+ 39 ♔g2 bxa5 40 ♖b1 ♘c5 holds.

FISCHER

Position after 38 ♗d3!

PETROSIAN

38	...	**axb4**

38...♘e4+? 39 ♗xe4 fxe4 40 bxa5 bxa5 (if 40...♖a8 41 axb6 cxb6 42 ♖b1) 41 ♖b1 followed by ♖b7 wins easily. White also invades after 38...♔g6 39 bxa5 bxa5 40 ♖b1.

39	**axb4**	**♔g6**
40	**♖a1!**	...

White has finally achieved his ideal setup, but Black's game is still tenable.

40	...	**♘g4+**
41	**♔e2**	**♖e8+**
42	**♔d2**	**♘f6**
43	**♖a6**	...

43 ♖a7 ♖c8 transposes to the game.

43	...	**♖b8**
44	**♖a7**	**♖c8**
45	**c5!**	...

This Pawn sac caught me completely by surprise. It's the only line that gives Black any trouble.

45	...	**bxc5**

Not 45...♘xd5? 46 c6.

46	**bxc5**	**dxc5**
47	**♘f3!**	**♔f7!**

47...♘xd5 loses to 48 ♘e5+.

48	**♘e5+**	**♔e7**
49	**♘xd7**	**♘xd7**
50	**♗xf5**	**♖f8!**
51	**g4**	...

51 ♗xd7 ♔xd7 52 ♔e3 (if 52 ♖a6 ♖g8) 52...♔d6 53 ♖a6+ ♔xd5 54 ♖xh6 ♖e8+ 55 ♔f3 c4 should draw.

FISCHER

Position after 51 g4

PETROSIAN

51	...	♚d6?

Should be the losing move! Correct is *51...♘f6! 52 ♗e6 ♘xd5!
53 ♗xd5 ♖xf4* (*53...♖d8* also draws) winning the last Pawn and forcing
a draw.

52	♗xd7!	♚xd7
53	♔e3	♖e8+

On *53...c4 54 ♖a6* wins. The idea is to force his King to the K-side,
away from the passed c-Pawn.

54	♔f3	...

Not *54 ♔d3 ♖g8*.

54	...	♚d6
55	♖a6+	♚xd5
56	♖xh6	c4

FISCHER

Position after 56...c4

PETROSIAN

57	♖h1?	...

As Petrosian points out in the Russian bulletins of the tournament, White can win with the following line: "*57 ♖h7! c6 58 ♖d7+ ♔c5 59 ♖d1 c3 60 g5 ♔c4 61 g6 c2 62 ♖c1 ♔c3 63 f5 ♖g8 64 ♔f4 ♔d2 65 ♖xc2+ ♔xc2 66 ♔g5 c5 67 f6 c4 68 f7 ♖xg6+ 69 ♔xg6 c3 70 f8=♕.*" White is a tempo ahead of the game, where Black's Pawn succeeds in reaching c2, instead of c3 (as here).

What if Black tries to improve? For example, after *57 ♖h7 c5 58 ♖d7+ ♔e6 59 ♖d1 ♖b8*. Now there are two main lines:

A] *60 g5? c3 61 ♔g4* (if *61 ♖c1 ♔f5 62 ♖xc3 c4! 63 ♖xc4 ♖b3+* with a draw by blockade although two Pawns down) *61...♖b4! 62 ♖e1+ ♔f7 63 ♔f5 c2 64 ♖c1 ♖c4 65 g6+ ♔g7 66 ♔g5 ♖c3* draws.

B] *60 f5+! ♔e5 61 ♖e1+ ♔d4* (after *61...♔f6 62 ♔f4 c3 63 g5+ ♔g7 64 g6 c2 65 ♔g5 ♖b1 66 f6+* wins) *62 g5 c3 63 f6 c2 64 ♖c1!* (*64 f7? ♖b1!* draws) *64...♔e5 65 ♔g4!* snuffs out Black's resistance.

57	...	c3
58	g5	c5
59	♖d1+	...

It's tough right down the line. After *59 g6 ♖g8 60 f5 ♔e5! 61 ♔g4 ♔f6 62 ♖c1 c4! 63 ♖xc3 ♖c8!* White can make no headway. Or on *59 ♔g4 ♖e2! 60 g6 ♔e4! 61 ♔g5 ♖g2+ 62 ♔f6 ♔xf4*, etc., as the Russian bulletins also point out.

59	...	♔c4
60	g6	c2
61	♖c1	...

On *61 ♖g1 ♖d8!* the threat of *...♖d1* forces *62 ♖c1* (not *62 g7? ♖g8!* followed by *...♖xg7* and wins).

61	...	♔d3
62	f5	♖g8!
63	♔f4	♔d2
64	♖xc2+	♔xc2
65	♔g5	c4
66	f6	c3
67	f7	

Drawn

FISCHER

Final Position after 67 f7

PETROSIAN

I offered the draw, not realizing it was bad etiquette. It was Petrosian's place to extend the offer after *67...♖xg6+* (if Black wants to get melodramatic *67...♖c8 68* g7 ♔b1 *69* f8=♕ ♖xf8 *70* gxf8=♕ c2 reaches the same position); *68* ♔xg6 ♔b1 *69* f8=♕ c2 with a book draw.

4 Pilnik *[Argentina]* - Fischer

MAR DEL PLATA 1959

SICILIAN DEFENSE

Tact and tactics

*The presence in Argentina of Pilnik, Najdorf, and Eliskases,
who chose to remain there after participating in the Buenos Aires
chess Olympic of 1939, created a chess renaissance, as attested
by the annual event at Mar del Plata which, though not lavish
with prizes, offers an exotic vacation and attracts the world's best.
Fischer tied for 3-4 with Ivkov, a mere half point behind Pachman
and Najdorf in a strong field of fifteen.*

*After a lackluster opening by both sides, and a middle game that,
with the exception of 26...bxa3 can scarcely be described as more
than routine, Fischer pilots the game into an even ending.
Both he and Pilnik then proceed to complicate; but the latter
is drawn into making a false lead, which Fischer exploits
by obtaining a passed center Pawn. From this point on, although
Pilnik does all that can be done to stave off the inevitable,
Fischer is not gulled into making a single wrong step.*

1	e4	c5
2	♘f3	d6
3	d4	cxd4
4	♘xd4	♘f6
5	♘c3	a6
6	♗e2	...

For 6 h3 see games 35, 40, 43. For 6 ♗c4 see games 17, 55, 58.

6	...	e5
7	♘b3	♗e7

For 7...♗e6 see game 42.

| 8 | 0-0 | ... |

Another try is *8* ♗g5 0-0! *(8...*♘bd7? *9* a4! gives a powerful bind) *9* ♘d2 ♘xe4! *10* ♗xe7 ♘xc3 *11* ♗xd8 ♘xd1 *12* ♗e7 ♖e8 *13* ♘c4 ♘xb2! *14* ♘b6 ♖xe7 *15* ♘xa8 ♘a4 *16* 0-0-0 (Fischer-Ghitescu, Leipzig 1960) *16...*♖d7! with the better game.

8	...	**0-0**
9	**♗e3**	**♗e6**
10	**f3**	...

A sharper alternative is *10* a4 ♕c7 *11* a5 ♘bd7 *12* ♘d5 ♘xd5 *13* exd5 ♗f5 *14* c4 ♗g6 *15* ♔h1 ♖ac8 *16* ♕d2 ♕d8 *17* ♖ac1 h6 *18* f4 exf4 *19* ♗xf4 ♗g5=. (Smyslov-Gligorich, Havana 1962.)

10	...	**♕c7**

Premature is *10*...d5 *11* exd5 ♘xd5 *12* ♘xd5 ♕xd5 *13* ♕xd5 ♗xd5 *14* ♖fd1 with a slight edge in the ending.

FISCHER

Position after 10...♕c7

PILNIK

11	**♕e1**	...

Once popular, this whole system is now known to give White nothing. It hinders neither Black's development nor his Q-side expansion.

11	...	**♘bd7**
12	**♖d1**	...

On *12* a4, ...d5 is strong.

12	...	**b5**

| 13 | ♖d2 | ... |

13 a3 is met by *13...*♘b6 *14* ♗xb6! ♕xb6+ =.

| 13 | ... | ♘b6 |

More direct is *13...*b4 *14* ♘d5 ♘xd5 *15* exd5 ♗f5 *16* ♕f2 a5 with good play against White's backward c-Pawn.

| 14 | ♕f2? | ... |

Careless. *14* ♗xb6 is necessary.

| 14 | ... | ♖ab8? |

I figured if he didn't take it off last move he wouldn't take it now; so I wanted to build a little more and keep the option of moving the Knight to a4 as well as c4. But Black should pounce on the chance to play *14...*♘c4! *15* ♗xc4 bxc4 *16* ♗b6 (if *16* ♘a1 ♖ab8 *17* ♖b1 ♖b7 is strong; or *16* ♘c1 ♖ab8 *17* ♘a4 c3! *18* bxc3? ♕c6 *19* ♘b6 ♗d8) *16...*♕c8 *17* ♘a5 ♘d7! and White's in trouble. E.g., *18* ♘d5 (or if *18* ♗e3 ♗d8 *19* ♘d5 ♗xd5 *20* ♖xd5 ♘f6 winning at least the exchange) *18...*♗xd5 *19* ♖xd5 (if *19* exd5 ♘xb6 *20* ♕xb6 ♗d8 *21* ♕b4 ♖b8 *22* ♕a3 ♗xa5 *23* ♕xa5 ♖xb2) *19...*♖b8 winning at least a Pawn.

| 15 | ♗xb6! | ... |

Pilnik hastens to make amends for his omission. Not *15* ♘a5? d5! wins material. (STAHLBERG)

15	...	♖xb6
16	♘d5	♘xd5
17	exd5	♗d7
18	f4	♗f6

I didn't want to weaken my e6 square with *18...*f5 *19* c3 ♗f6 *20* fxe5 dxe5 (if *20...*♗xe5 *21* ♘d4) *21* ♘c5=.

| 19 | c3 | ♖bb8 |
| 20 | fxe5 | ♗xe5 |

On *20...dxe5 21* d6 gives White active play. Black's advantage of the Bishop pair is neutralized by the weakness of his c6, which White can later occupy with his Knight.

21	♘d4	g6
22	a3	...

More to the point was *22* ♗f3 b4 *23* cxb4 ♖xb4 *24* ♘c6=.

22	...	a5
23	♔h1	...

23 ♗f3 should again be played. White starts drifting.

23	...	b4
24	cxb4	...

On *24* axb4 axb4 *25* c4 b3! holds the initiative.

24	...	axb4
25	♖c2	...

On *25* ♗f3 bxa3 *26* bxa3 ♖a8 presents its problems.

25	...	♕b6
26	♘c6	...

FISCHER

Position after 26 ♘c6

PILNIK

This is the position White was playing for. A draw now looks secure.

26	...	bxa3!
27	♕xb6	...

27 bxa3 is also adequate. But not *27* ♘xb8? ♕xf2 *28* ♖xf2 a2 *29* ♖f1 (if *29* ♖c1 ♗xb2) *29*...♗f5 *30* ♖cc1 ♖xb8 wins.

27	...	♖xb6
28	**bxa3**	**♖a8**
29	**♘xe5?**	...

This gives Black a strong passed e-Pawn. Correct is *29* ♖a2 ♖b2 *30* ♖xb2 ♗xb2 *31* ♗b5! ♖xa3 (otherwise a4) *32* ♘e7+ ♔f8 *33* ♘xg6+ with a draw in view. On *33*...hxg6 *34* ♗xd7 produces opposite colored Bishops. Or on *33*...♔e8 *34* ♖e1+! (*34* ♗xd7+ ♔xd7 *35* ♖xf7+? ♔d8 wins a piece) *34*...♔d8 *35* ♗xd7 fxg6 (if *35*...♔xd7 *36* ♘f8+ any *37* ♘xh7) =.

| 29 | ... | **dxe5** |
| 30 | **♖c3** | ... |

30 ♖c7 gets nowhere after *30*...♖d6; and the sacrifice *31* ♗b5?! is refuted by *31*...♗xb5 *32* ♖fxf7 ♖c8! Or on *30* ♖a2 (*30* ♖a1? ♖xa3) *30*...♖a5 *31* ♗c4 (if *31* ♖d1 ♗a4) *31*...♖c5 and the d-Pawn falls.

| 30 | ... | **♖b2!** |
| 31 | **♖c7** | ... |

Desperately striving for counterplay. On *31* ♗c4 (to prevent ...♖a2) *31*...♔g7 *32* d6 f5 *33* ♗d5 ♖a6 again wins the d-Pawn. Or *31* ♗f3 f5 *32* ♖c7 ♗b5 *33* ♖e1 e4 squelches White's play.

| 31 | ... | **♗f5** |

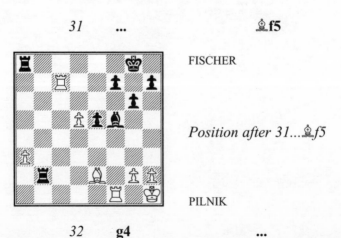

FISCHER

Position after 31...♗f5

PILNIK

| 32 | **g4** | ... |

A wild hope. Hopeless is *32* ♗c4 ♖c2! *33* d6 ♖xc4! *34* ♖xc4 ♗d3 *35* ♖fc1 ♗xc4 *36* ♖xc4 ♖xa3 *37* ♔g1 ♔g7! Black soon picks off the d-Pawn and wins easily.

32	...	♗e4+
33	♗f3	♗d3
34	**d6**	...

Or *34* ♖e1 e4! *35* ♗g2 (if *35* ♗xe4 ♖e8 wins) *35*...♖d8 *36* ♖c5 ♔g7! *37* ♔g1 (if *37* g5 h6 *38* h4 hxg5 *39* hxg5 ♖h8+ *40* ♔g1 ♖h4! wins) *37*...f5 *38* gxf5 gxf5 and the two passed center Pawns should win (if *39* d6 ♔f6!).

34	...	♖d8
35	♖e1	♖xd6

Najdorf chided me after the game for "missing" *35*...e4 *36* ♗xe4! ♖b1! *37* ♖xb1 ♗xe4+ *38* ♔g1 ♗xb1 and wins.

36	♖xe5	...

Falling into the trap. *36* ♖e7 holds out longer, but *36*...♖f6 *37* ♗d5 e4 *38* ♗xe4 ♗xe4+ *39* ♖7xe4 ♖ff2 wins.

36	...	♖f6!
37	♖e3	...

Forced. On *37* ♗g2 ♖b1+ is decisive.

37	...	♖xf3!
38	♖xf3	♗e4
39	♖cxf7	♖f2
40	♖f8+	♔g7
	White resigns	

After *41* ♖8f7+ ♔h6 wins. Or *41* ♖8f4 ♗d5 (*41*...♗xf3+ *42* ♔g1 ♖g2+ *43* ♔f1 ♗c6 *44* ♖c4 ♗b5! also wins) cooks White's goose.

5 Fischer - Rossetto *[Argentina]*

MAR DEL PLATA 1959

SICILIAN DEFENSE

The unpleasant obligation

This game exemplifies most dramatically the German expression zugzwang.

Unable to achieve any workable advantage from the opening or mid-game, Fischer embarks on an equally unpromising ending. He manages, however, after 19 ♘d5, to acquire a Bishop against a Knight. Subsequently he employs an unusual Rook maneuver along the third rank (24 ♖a3) in order to make spatial inroads. Rossetto unwittingly co-operates and soon is faced by a rare predicament: although material is equal, any move he makes must disturb the precarious balance and hasten his own disaster. That is zugzwang – and, appropriately, Rossetto resigns.

1	e4	c5
2	♘f3	e6
3	d4	cxd4
4	♘xd4	a6
5	c4	♕c7

Stronger is 5...♘f6 6 ♘c3 ♗b4 which theory gives as equal for Black.

6	♘c3	♘f6
7	♗d3?	...

Misplacing the Bishop. Right is 7 a3! and if 7...♘c6 8 ♗e3, etc. (if 8...♘e5 9 ♗e2! ♘xc4? 10 ♗xc4 ♕xc4 11 ♖c1 wins).

7 a3!, by preventing ...♗b4 once and for all, forces Black to adopt a kind of Scheveningen formation that keeps him desperately cramped. A Spielmann-Tartakover game proceeded: 7...♗e7 8 ♗e2 0-0 9 0-0 d6 10 ♗e3 ♘bd7 11 ♖c1 b6 12 b4! ♗b7 13 f3 ♖ac8 14 ♕e1 ♕b8 15 ♕f2 "with a beautiful position for White." (From *More Chess Questions Answered*.)

7	...	♘c6
8	♗e3	♘xd4?

Instead of trying to simplify, Black should select the aggressive 8...♘e5! 9 ♖c1 (not 9 0-0 ♘eg4! or if 9 ♗e2 ♘xc4 10 ♗xc4 ♕xc4 11 ♖c1 ♕b4 12 0-0 d6; and if 13 ♘b3? ♘xe4! 14 a3 ♘xc3, etc.) 9...♘fg4! with advantage.

9	♗xd4	♗c5
10	♗c2	d6
11	0-0	♗d7
12	♘a4	...

Forcing a series of exchanges which give White a microscopic edge, at best.

12	...	♗xd4
13	♕xd4	♖d8
14	♖fd1	0-0
15	♖ac1	...

On 15 ♕xd6 ♕xd6 16 ♖xd6 ♗xa4 17 ♖xd8 ♖xd8 18 ♗xa4 ♘xe4=.

15	...	♕a5

15...b5? 16 cxb5 axb5 17 ♘c3 (not 17 e5? dxe5 18 ♗xh7+ ♔xh7) and Black's b-Pawn is weak. 15...♗c6 is solid but cramped.

16	♕b6	♕xb6

Unsound is 16...♕e5 17 ♖xd6 ♘g4 18 g3 ♕h5 19 h4.

17	♘xb6	♗c6
18	f3	♘d7!

Black had relied on this move to get him out of trouble. Now 19 ♘xd7 (or 19 ♘a4 ♘e5 20 ♗b3 g5! holds the balance) 19...♖xd7 20 ♖d2 ♖fd8 21 ♖cd1 ♔f8 is dead equal.

19	♘**d5!**	...

An unexpected reply which throws Black, unjustifiably, into a state of confusion.

ROSSETTO

Position after 19 ♘d5!

FISCHER

19	...	♗**xd5**

Caught by surprise. Rossetto fails to find the most accurate reply: *19...♘e5!* (also tenable is *19...exd5 20 exd5 ♘e5 21 dxc6 bxc6 22 b3 c5 23 ♗e4 ♖fe8) 20 ♘e7+ (if 20 ♘e3 g5!) 20...♔h8 21 ♘xc6 bxc6 22 ♗a4 g5!* followed by *...♔g7-f6-e7=.*

20	**exd5**	**e5**

Safer is *20...♘e5 21 ♗e4 b6* (not *21...f5? 22 dxe6!*).

21	**b4**	...

Playing for the big breakthrough on c5.

21	...	**g6**

On *21...a5 22 a3 axb4 23 axb4 ♖a8 24 ♗f5!* holds the advantage.

22	♗**a4**	**b6**

On *22...♘b6 23 ♗b3* followed by c5.

23	♖**d3**	**f5?**

Oblivious to the danger! The best defense is *23...a5 24 a3* (Black should hold after *24 ♗xd7 ♖xd7 25 bxa5 bxa5 26 c5 dxc5 27 ♖xc5 a4*)

24...f5 and it's hard for White to make progress. Black should never allow c5 without first forcing White to make the concession of exchanging the Bishop for the Knight.

| 24 | ♖a3! | ... |

The threat is simply *25* ♗xd7. The veiled and seemingly insignificant attack on Black's a-Pawn is the means of forcing him to drop the protection of his c5 square.

| 24 | ... | ♘b8 |

Forced. On *24*...♘f6 *25* ♗c6 wins a Pawn. The only other try is *24*...a5 *25* bxa5 bxa5 *26* ♗c6! ♘c5 (on *26*...♘b8 *27* ♗b5! or *26*...♘b6 *27* ♖b1! ♘xc4? *28* ♖c3 ♘d2 *29* ♖b2 traps the Knight) *27* ♖xa5 and White should win.

| 25 | c5! | bxc5 |

On *25*...b5 *26* ♗b3 ♖f7 *27* c6 ♖c7 *28* ♖a5! ♔f7 *29* a4 bxa4 *30* ♖xa4 ♔e7 *31* ♗c4 picks off the a-Pawn.

| 26 | bxc5 | dxc5 |
| 27 | ♖xc5 | ♔g7 |

On *27*...♘d7 (if *27*...♖c8 *28* ♖ac3 keeps the bind) *28* ♖c7 ♘f6 *29* ♗b3 ♔h8 *30* ♖xa6 ♘xd5 *31* ♗xd5 ♖xd5 *32* ♖aa7 wins. Black's game collapses once the heavy guns penetrate.

| 28 | ♖b3 | ♖f7 |
| 29 | d6! | ♘d7 |

The Pawn is obviously immune. So Black attempts to revive his Knight.

| 30 | ♖c7 | ♘f8 |

Also hopeless is *30*...♘f6 *31* ♖bb7 ♖xc7 *32* dxc7 ♖c8 *33* ♗b3 ♘e8 *34* ♖b8 ♘d6 *35* ♖xc8 ♘xc8 *36* ♗e6, etc.

31	♖bb7	♖xc7
32	dxc7	♖c8
33	♗b3!	...

Completely immobilizing Black. He is reduced to Pawn moves.

33	...	a5
34	a4	h6
35	h3	g5
36	g4	fxg4
37	hxg4	**Black resigns**

ROSSETTO

Final Position after 37 hxg4

FISCHER

Zugzwang! Black has run out of satisfactory Pawn moves. On *37...*♔f6 *38* ♖b8 wins a piece. On *37...*♘g6 *38* ♗e6 wins. Or on any Rook move, say *37...*♖e8, *38* c8=♕+.

6 Fischer - Shocron [*Argentina*]

MAR DEL PLATA 1959

RUY LOPEZ

A small oversight

Fischer's opening repertoire has been less extensive than most practicing Grandmasters', yet his contributions to theory have been numerous. 20 g5!? is one of his innovations. However, it is not responsible for Shocron's defeat. Neither is Shocron's response; in retrospect, his system of defense seems surprisingly adequate. Nevertheless, after defending sensibly, Shocron outfoxes himself. Thinking he has seen one move further than his adversary, he provokes a combination. But his vision is one move short. In consequence, though otherwise it had withstood all of Fischer's assaults, his game crumbles.

1	e4	e5
2	♘f3	♘c6
3	♗b5	a6
4	♗a4	♘f6
5	0-0	♗e7
6	♖e1	b5
7	♗b3	d6
8	c3	0-0
9	h3	...

For an immediate *9* d4!? see game 36.

9	...	♘a5
10	♗c2	c5
11	d4	♕c7

For Keres' *11...♘d7* see game 38.

12	♘bd2	♗d7

Some alternatives are *12...♔h8, ...♖e8, ...♖d8, ...♘c6, ...♗b7, ...♘d7, ...cxd4*. I don't think there's any easy way for Black to achieve complete equality – but who knows?

| 13 | ♘f1 | ♖fe8 |
| 14 | ♘e3 | g6 |

The Yugoslav System, popularized by Gligorich and Matanovich. The idea is to strengthen the position, and transfer the Bishop to f8 while awaiting further developments. Black will undertake specific counteraction only after White commits himself.

SHOCRON

Position after 14...g6

FISCHER

| 15 | dxe5 | ... |

This positional approach bares the hole on d5, so that White may gain access to it with his Knight. Alternate plans ensue after *15 ♗d2 ♗f8* and now:

A] The quiet *16 ♖c1 ♗g7?* (after *16...♘c6 17 d5! ♘a5* [on *17...♘d8 18 c4!* robs Black of his normal counterplay with ...c4, Olafsson-Ivkov, Buenos Aires 1960, and now White can leisurely build up a strong attack with ♔h2, g4, ♖g1 and later the stock sac ♘f5] *18 b4 ♘b7 19 a4* with a slight advantage) *17 b4 ♘c6 18 ♘d5! ♘xd5 19 exd5 ♘e7 20 dxc5 ♘xd5* (if *20...dxc5 21 ♗e3 ♕d6 22 ♗xc5 ♕xd5 23 ♗b3!*) *21 ♗b3 ♘f6* (if *21...♗c6 22 ♗g5!*) *22 cxd6 ♕xd6 23 ♘g5! ♖f8 24 ♗e3 ♕xd1 25 ♖exd1 h6 26 ♘e4! ♘xe4 27 ♖xd7 ♖ac8 28 c4 ♘g5 29 ♗xg5 hxg5 30 c5* Black resigns. (Fischer-Rinaldo, US Open 1957.)

B] The sharp *16 b4 cxb4 17 cxb4 ♘c4 18 ♘xc4 bxc4 19 ♖c1 exd4 20 ♘xd4 d5* (not *20...c3 21 ♗b3 ♘xe4 22 ♖xe4! ♖xe4 23 ♕f3 ♗c6 24 ♕xc3* wins) *21 exd5 ♖xe1+?* (better is *21...♕d6*) *22 ♗xe1 ♕d6.* (Fischer-Matanovich, Bled 1961.) And now, as Keres pointed out,

White can retain his extra Pawn with *23 ♘f3!* Not *23...♕xd5? 24 ♗c3!* wins a piece. Or *23...♘xd5 24 ♗e4.*

15	...	dxe5
16	♘h2	...

When examined microscopically, Black has his problems. The hole on d5 might be described as "gaping".

16	...	♖ad8
17	♕f3	♗e6

On *17...h5? 18 ♘d5! ♘xd5 19 exd5* Black's K-side is weakened.

18	♘hg4	♘xg4
19	hxg4	...

Black has a new burden: neutralizing the potential attack along the open h-file.

19	...	♕c6
20	g5!?	...

SHOCRON

Position after 20 g5!?

FISCHER

The old line *20 ♕g3 f6* (better is *20...♗f6*) *21 g5!* is good for White. (Boleslavsky-Tal, USSR 1957.) I'd always thought my line was an improvement (the idea is to clear g4 for the Knight before Black can force an exchange with ...♘c4) but a closer look at this game shows that Black may have resources.

20	...	♘c4

20...♗xg5 puts White's concept to the crucial test. After *21* ♘d5! ♗xc1 (*21...*♗xd5 *22* ♗xg5 wins the exchange) *22* ♘f6+ ♔h8! (if *22...*♔f8 *23* ♖axc1 ♖e7 *24* ♘xh7+ ♔g8 *25* ♖cd1! ♖a8 [*25...*♖xd1 *26* ♘f6+ ♔g7 *27* ♖xd1 ♘b7 *28* g4! followed by g5 with a strong attack] *26* ♘f6+ ♔g7 *27* ♘d5 ♗xd5 *28* ♖xd5 White's better) *23* ♖axc1 (*23* ♘xe8 ♗g5 *24* ♘f6 ♘c4! Black has good play for the exchange) *23...*♖f8 (not *23...*♖e7 *24* ♕g3 threatening either ♕xe5 or ♕h4) *24* ♕g3 ♕c7! *25* ♕g5 ♔g7 and now White can force a draw with *26* ♘h5+, etc., or try for more with either *26* f4 or ♖e3.

21	♘g4	♗xg4

Black can't allow ♘f6+. As a consequence, White obtains the Bishop pair and attacking prospects along the open h-file.

22	♕xg4	♘b6!

To prevent a4 and, as will be seen, to swing the Knight to f8 in order to defend the vulnerable h7 Pawn. For Unzicker's *22...*f6 see game 10.

23	g3	c4!

The right timing. He's careful to see that a4 is restrained. Wrong, for example, is *23...*♘d7 *24* a4 b4 *25* cxb4 cxb4 *26* ♗b3! and this Bishop comes crashing back into the game via the open diagonal.

24	♔g2	♘d7
25	♖h1	♘f8

Phase one is over. Having seen his K-side threats neatly parried, White is compelled to start some action on the opposite wing.

SHOCRON

Position after 25...♘f8

FISCHER

| 26 | **b4** | .... |

26 b3 leads to trouble after *26...b4! 27* cxb4 c3 *28* a3? ♘e6 *29* ♕h3 h5 *30* gxh6 *e.p.* ♘d4! and wins. On *26* a4 b4! *27* cxb4 ♗xb4 *28* a5 (threatening ♗a4) *28...*♕c7 is satisfactory.

| 26 | ... | **♕e6** |

Sharper is *26...*a5! *27* a3 (if *27* bxa5 ♕a6 *28* a4 ♕xa5) *27...*♖a8=.
Bad, however, is *26...*cxb3 *e.p. 27* ♗xb3 ♕xc3 *28* ♗e3 (*28* ♗b2!? ♕xb2 *29* ♕f3 ♘e6 *30* ♗xe6 ♖f8! holds. But not *30...*fxe6? *31* ♖xh7! ♖f8 *32* ♖ah1! ♕xf2+ *33* ♕xf2 ♖xf2+ *34* ♔xf2 ♖d2+ *35* ♔f3 ♗xg5 *36* ♖h8+ mates) *28...*♖d7 (not *28...*♕c8? *29* ♕f3 ♘e6 *30* ♖xh7! wins) *29* ♖xh7! should win.

27	**♕e2**	**a5**
28	**bxa5**	**♕a6**
29	**♗e3**	**♕xa5**
30	**a4**	**♖a8**

30...♕xc3! *31* axb5 leads to equal play.

| 31 | **axb5** | **♕xb5** |

More active is *31...*♕xc3! (if *32* ♖ac1 ♗a3!). But not *31...*♕xa1? *32* ♖xa1 ♖xa1 *33* ♕xc4, resigns.

32	**♖hb1**	**♕c6**
33	**♖b6!**	**♕c7**
34	**♖ba6**	...

Obtaining control of the a-file.

34	...	**♖xa6**
35	**♖xa6**	**♖c8**
36	**♕g4**	**♘e6**

Bringing the Knight back into the game. Wrong would be an attempt to simplify with *36...*♗c5 *37* ♗xc5 ♕xc5 *38* ♗a4! and Black has trouble finding a move. If *38...*♘e6 *39* ♗d7. Or *38...*♖d8 *39* ♖c6 ♕a7 *40* ♖xc4 ♖d2 *41* ♕f3 staying a Pawn ahead.

37	♗a4	♖b8
38	♖c6	♕d8?

Up to here Shocron has defended coolly, but now he makes a fatal miscalculation. Correct is *38...♕d7!* and it's not clear how White can improve his position any further. If *39 ♔h2* (not *39 ♖xc4 ♕d3! 40 ♖c6 ♖b1* with a strong attack) *39...♖b1! 40 ♖b6* (if *40 ♖xc4 ♕d3 41 ♖c8+ ♔g7 42 ♕h4 ♗xg5! 43 ♗xg5 ♖h1+! 44 ♔xh1 ♕f1+* with a perpetual) *40...♕d3 41 ♖xb1* (not *41 ♖xe6? ♕f1!*) *41...♕xb1 42 ♗d7 ♘c7!* (on *42...♘c5 43 ♗c6* followed by *♗d5* should win) *43 ♗c6 ♕d3!* with drawing chances.

39	♖xe6!	♕c8!

Blow for blow! Apparently Shocron was prepared for this trick, having seen that *39...fxe6? 40 ♕xe6+ ♔f8 41 ♕xe5* is crushing.

SHOCRON

Position after 39...♕c8!

FISCHER

Now how does White avoid losing material?

40	♗d7!	**Black resigns**

This is the shot he overlooked. On *40...♕xd7 41 ♖xg6+* wins his Queen.

7 Olafsson *[Iceland]* - Fischer

ZURICH 1959

KING'S INDIAN DEFENSE

Pride goeth

Miscalculating, as he explains in his notes, Fischer rapidly gets into trouble and is thrown on the defensive. Olafsson quietly strengthens his attacking prospects and seems well on the road to victory. But he tries, prematurely, to force the issue (21 ♘b1) and, as the game opens up, loses the initiative, although he seems to be blissfully unaware of it. He fails to foresee the power of the riposte to his 24 ♕d2. Still blind to the danger, while seeking a forced win, he misses several opportunities to equalize. In extreme time pressure, he is compelled to exchange Queens under particularly unfavorable circumstances. The resulting endgame holds no further surprises.

1	c4	♘f6
2	♘c3	g6
3	d4	♗g7
4	e4	d6
5	♘f3	0-0
6	♗e2	e5
7	d5	♘bd7
8	♗g5	...

Steinitz automatically gave this pin a question mark. Since there is no real threat involved (because the Bishop is worth more than the Knight) Black can now gain time by kicking it around.

Petrosian has had some success with this treatment. The idea is to restrain ...♘e8 and the subsequent ...f5.

8	...	h6
9	♗h4	a6

This slow system has never been refuted. But better is *9...g5! 10 ♗g3* (Black's break with ...f5 has now been blunted, but on the other hand White's Bishop on g3 is deadwood), *10...♘h5! 11 h4*, the latest wrinkle

(*11* ♘d2 ♘f4 *12* 0-0 ♘xe2+ *13* ♕xe2 f5 *14* exf5 ♘f6 *15* c5 ♗xf5 *16* ♖ac1 ♖f7! *17* ♘c4 ♗f8 is better for Black. Wexler-Reshevsky, Buenos Aires 1960), *11*...♘xg3! *12* fxg3 gxh4! *13* ♖xh4 (if *13* ♘xh4 ♕g5 *14* ♘f5 ♘f6; or *13* gxh4 f5 *14* exf5 ♘f6 *15* 0-0 ♗xf5) *13*...f5 *14* ♕c2 ♘c5 *15* ♗d3 ♕f6 with advantage. (Damyanovich-Hort, Sarajevo 1964.)

	10	♘d2	♕e8

FISCHER

Position after 10...♕e8

OLAFSSON

The idea is to free the Knight and thus make possible the break with ...f5. In some variations, the Queen may help to support ...b5 also, particularly if White elects to castle long.

	11	g4!?	...

In the Candidates' Tournament, 1959, Tal essayed against me the quieter *11* 0-0 ♘h7 *12* b4 ♘g5 (later I tried *12*...♗f6!? against him) *13* f3 f5 with chances for both sides. The text is risky and commits White to Q-side castling.

	11	...	♘h7
	12	♕c2	♘g5?

Intending ...♘h3-f4, but White's simple reply brands it as a mistaken plan. Correct is *12*...♘c5 *13* 0-0-0 (*13* b4 ♘d7 leaves White with a shaky game) *13*...f5=.

	13	h3!	♘c5
	14	0-0-0	♗d7

Weak is *14*...f5 *15* ♗xg5! hxg5 *16* gxf5 gxf5 *17* ♖dg1.

15	f3	♘a4

15...b5!? *16* b4 ♘b7 may not be too bad.

16	♘xa4	♗xa4
17	b3	♗d7
18	♗f2	c5!
19	h4	...

Black's game springs to life after *19* dxc6 *e.p.*? bxc6 *20* ♘b1 d5!
21 exd5 (or *21* ♗c5 d4 *22* ♗xf8 ♗xf8 with a juicy position) *21*...cxd5
22 ♖xd5 ♗c6, etc.

19	...	♘h7
20	♗e3	b5
21	♘b1?	...

Intending ♕d2. But correct is *21* ♗d3! (if *21* h5 ♘g5), maintaining
the bind by restraining ...f5.

21	...	f5!

Ready or not – here we come! Olafsson was sure that this break was
impossible, or he wouldn't have allowed it.

22	gxf5	gxf5
23	exf5	...

To prevent ...f4 which would seal the K-side and neutralize White's
attack.

23	...	♗xf5
24	♕d2	...

This is the position White played for.

24	...	e4!

The game turns on this shot. *24*...♖f6 or *24*...h5 cedes the initiative.

25	♖dg1	...

25 ♗xh6 loses to *25*...e3! *26* ♗xe3 (if *26* ♕xe3 ♗xb1! *27* ♔xb1
♕g6+ wins a piece) *26*...♗xb1 *27* ♔xb1 ♕e5.

25	...	exf3?

Correct is *25*...♖a7! and if *26* ♗xh6 exf3 transposing to the game.

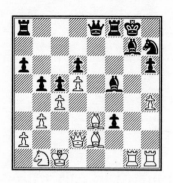

FISCHER

Position after 25...exf3?

OLAFSSON

26	♗xh6?	...

26 ♖xg7+! (STAHLBERG) 26...♔xg7 27 ♗xh6+ ♔h8 28 ♗xf8 ♕xf8 29 ♗xf3 wins a Pawn (if 29...♗xb1 30 ♕c3+).

26	...	♖a7!

Olafsson later told me he had underestimated the strength of this defensive move.

27	♗xg7	♖xg7
28	♖xg7+	♔xg7
29	♗d3	...

An admission of defeat since Black's f-Pawn now becomes dangerously potent. But not 29 ♗xf3? (or 29 ♕c3+ ♕e5 30 ♕xf3 ♗xb1 31 ♕g4+ ♗g6) 29...♗xb1 30 ♔xb1 ♖xf3 31 ♕g2+ ♕g6+ (the saving resource) and Black hangs on to his extra piece. My game hinges on this defense, on the fact that the f-Pawn has such divine protection.

29	...	bxc4
30	♖g1+	♔h8
31	♕c3+	...

Now Black gets another passed center Pawn, but White's defense is difficult anyway. 31 bxc4 f2 32 ♖f1 ♗xd3 33 ♕xd3 ♕e1+ 34 ♔c2 ♘f6 35 ♘d2 ♘g4 wins.

31	...	♕e5

32	♕xe5+	...

After *32 ♗xf5 ♖xf5 33 bxc4 ♘f6* White has nothing better than to transpose into the actual game with *34 ♕xe5.*

32	...	dxe5
33	♗xf5	♖xf5
34	bxc4	...

34 d6 ♘f6 35 ♘d2! offers no better: e.g., *35...cxb3 36 axb3 e4 37 ♘c4! f2 38 ♖f1 ♘g4!* (threatening ...e3) *39 ♔d1 ♘h2! 40 d7 ♖d5+* is decisive.

34	...	♘f6
35	♘d2	f2
36	♖h1	...

White must keep his f1 square open for the Knight.

36	...	e4

FISCHER

Position after 36...e4

OLAFSSON

37	♔d1

A better chance is offered by *37 ♘f1 ♘g4! 38 ♔d2* (if *38 d6 ♖f6 39 d7 ♖d6*) but *38...♖f3!* squelches all counterplay.

37	...	e3
38	♘f1	♖e5
39	♔e2	♘h5!
40	♔f3	e2
	White resigns	

One of the Black Pawns must reincarnate.

8 Fischer - Keres [U.S.S.R.]

ZURICH 1959

RUY LOPEZ

Meat and potatoes

*Alekhine said, in his prime, that to wrest a point from him it was
necessary to win the same game three times: once at the beginning,
once in the middle, once at the end. No less a tribute may be paid
to Keres.*

*Each phase of this game is fascinating and hard-fought. Even the
errors, and there are more than a few, contribute to making it an
unusually complete exhibition of two master craftsmen using all the
tools of their trade. While perhaps unglamorous, there is meat here,
and potatoes too. And it is likely that as a result of this victory Fischer
came to be regarded as a serious contender by the leading Soviet
Grandmasters — this was the first time he had defeated one.*

1	e4	e5
2	♘f3	♘c6
3	♗b5	a6
4	♗a4	♘f6
5	0-0	♗e7
6	♖e1	b5
7	♗b3	0-0
8	c3	d6
9	h3	♘a5
10	♗c2	c5
11	d4	♕c7
12	♘bd2	cxd4

Keres has abandoned *12...♖d8 13 ♘f1 d5? 14 dxe5! dxe4 (if
14...♘xe4 15 ♕e2 ♗b7 16 ♘e3 threatening ♘xd5) 15 ♘1d2! exf3
16 exf6 ♗xf6 17 ♕xf3 ♗e6 18 ♘e4 with a winning attack.*

13	cxd4	♗b7
14	♘f1	♖ac8
15	♗d3	♘c6

Keres later played *15...♘d7* against Smyslov at the Candidates' 1959. The game continued *16 ♘e3* (better is *16 d5 f5 17 ♘e3! f4 18 ♘f5 ♗d8 19 ♗d2!*) *16...exd4 17 ♘xd4 ♗f6 18 ♘df5 g6=*.

| 16 | ♘e3 | ♖fe8 |

Black already has difficulties. On *16...♘xd4 17 ♘xd4 exd4 18 ♘f5 ♖fe8 19 ♗g5* is strong. Not *16...♘b4? 17 ♗b1 ♗xe4?? 18 ♗xe4 ♘xe4 19 a3 ♘c6 20 ♘d5*, etc.

| 17 | ♘f5? | ... |

A superficial plan. Correct is *17 d5! ♘b4* (if *17...♘b8 18 a4!*) *18 ♗b1 a5 19 ♕e2! ♘d7* (if *19...♕b6 20 ♘f5!*) *20 ♗d2 ♕b6 21 a3 ♘a6 22 b4* followed by *♗d3* with a bind.

17	...	♗f8
18	♗g5	♘d7
19	♖c1	♕b8

To get out of the pin.

| 20 | ♗b1 | ♘xd4 |
| 21 | ♘3xd4 | ♖xc1? |

Overlooking White's follow-up. After *21...exd4 22 ♖xc8 ♕xc8 23 ♕xd4 ♘c5!* White has precisely nothing.

| 22 | ♗xc1 | exd4 |

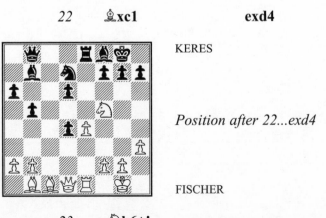

KERES

Position after 22...exd4

FISCHER

| 23 | ♘h6+! | ... |

Keres probably expected *23* ♕xd4 ♘c5=.

23	...	gxh6
24	♕g4+	♔h8
25	♕xd7	...

Regaining the piece. Black's extra Pawn is meaningless in view of his mangled Pawn formation.

| 25 | ... | ♗d5! |

An energetic maneuver! This Bishop is headed, if circumstances permit, toward the defense of Black's weakened K-side.

| 26 | ♕f5 | ♖e5! |
| 27 | ♕f3 | f5! |

Aggressive defense!

| 28 | ♗f4! | ♖e8 |

On *28...♖e7 29 ♕d1 ♗xe4 30 ♗xe4 fxe4 31 ♕xd4+ ♗g7 32 ♕d5!* maintains pressure against the weak Pawns.

29	♕h5!	♗xe4
30	f3	♗c6
31	♖c1!	...

Not *31 ♖xe8? ♗xe8 32 ♕xf5? ♗g6!* and Black wins!

| 31 | ... | ♗d7 |
| 32 | ♗xh6 | ... |

A difficult choice. The alternative was *32 ♗xf5 ♗xf5 33 ♕xf5* with possibilities of probing his sick Pawns.

| 32 | ... | ♖e6! |
| 33 | ♗xf8 | ... |

On *33 ♗f4 ♕e8!* looks tenable.

| 33 | ... | ♕xf8 |
| 34 | ♕h4! | ... |

On *34 ♕xf5?? ♖e1+* wins! Or *34 ♗xf5?? ♖h6* wins! The text forces Black into an ending where his weak Pawns can't be concealed by tactical tricks. On *34 ♖c7 ♕e7* holds; e.g., *35 ♗xf5? ♖e1+ 36 ♔h2* (or *36 ♔f2 ♕e3+ 37 ♔g3 ♕e5+) 36...♕e5+* wins.

	34	...	♕f6

Not *34...♕g7 35 ♖c7 ♖e2? 36 ♕d8+ ♖e8 37 ♖xd7! ♖xd8 38 ♖xd8+* wins.

	35	♕xf6+	♖xf6

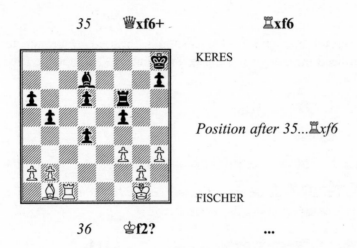

KERES

Position after 35...♖xf6

FISCHER

	36	♔f2?	...

Losing a vital tempo, which gives Black time to rush his King toward the center. At the time I rejected *36 ♖c7* because I couldn't see a winning continuation after *36...♖f7* (if *36...♗e6 37 b3!* squelches all counterplay). But I underestimated the strength of *37 ♖a7!* (*37 ♗xf5 ♖xf5 38 ♖xd7 ♖d5 39 ♔f2 d3 40 ♔e1 ♖e5+ 41 ♔d1 ♖e2* should draw) *37...♗e6 38 ♖xa6 ♖c7 39 ♔f2 ♖c1 40 ♗d3* and Black's Pawns are hopelessly weak.

	36	...	♔g7!
	37	♖c7	♖f7
	38	♔e2	...

Now *38 ♖a7* loses all of its effectiveness after the reply *38...♗c8*.

	38	...	f4!?

A risky selection in time-pressure, aimed against *39 ♔d3?? ♗f5+*. Best is simply *38...♔f6* (on *38...♗e6 39 ♖c6* is strong) *39 ♖a7* (not *39 f4 ♗e6 40 ♖c6? ♖g7 41 ♔f2 ♖xg2+!) 39...♗c8 40 ♖xf7+ ♔xf7=*.

39	♖a7	♔f6

Not *39...♗c8 40 ♖xf7+ ♔xf7 41 ♗xh7.*

40	♖xa6	♖e7+
41	♔f2	...

41 ♔d2 is refuted by ♖g7.

41	...	♗e6!

Sacrificing a second Pawn for counterplay on the open c-file. On *41...♔e5 42 ♖a7* keeps Black tied up.

42	♖xd6	♔e5
43	♖c6	...

On *43 ♖b6 ♗c4 44 b3 d3! 45 bxc4 bxc4* and Black's passed Pawns should be sufficient to draw.

43	...	♗d5

KERES

Position after 43...♗d5

FISCHER

44	♖h6	...

On *44 ♖c5 ♔d6 45 ♖xb5? ♗c4* is menacing. *44 ♖c1* is too passive to yield any real winning chances.

44	...	♖c7
45	♖h5+	♔d6
46	♖h6+	♔e5
47	♖h5+	...

Not *47 ♖b6 ♖c1 48 ♗xh7? ♗c4.*

| 47 | ... | ♚d6 |
| 48 | ♖f5? | ... |

No better is *48 ♖xh7* (if *48 ♗xh7 ♜c1* threatening *49...♗c4*) *48...♜c1 49 ♗d3 ♗c4*. The winning line is *48 b3!* (to shut him out from c4). If *48...♜c1 49 ♗e4! ♗xe4 50 fxe4*, etc.

| 48 | ... | ♜c1 |
| 49 | ♗d3 | ♜d1 |

Not *49...♗c4? 50 ♖xf4! ♗xd3 51 ♖xd4+*, etc.

50	♔e2	♜g1
51	♔f2	♜d1
52	♔e2	♜g1
53	♖g5	♗xa2?

Keres later claimed that *53...♜a1* would have drawn easily: e.g., *54 ♗xh7 ♗c4+ 55 ♔d2 ♜xa2 56 ♔c2 ♜a1*.

| 54 | ♗xb5 | ♜b1 |
| 55 | ♔d3 | h6? |

55...♜xb2 56 ♔xd4 ♗b1! should hold the draw.

56	♖h5	♜xb2
57	♔xd4	♜xg2
58	♖xh6+	...

The second adjournment. There are two technical obstacles facing White:

1) He cannot exchange Bishops; the ending where he is two Pawns ahead remains a theoretical draw with Rooks on the board.

2) He cannot exchange Rooks so long as Black's King has access to f6; the ending (even with two extra Pawns) is still a draw with Bishops on the board.

58	...	♔e7
59	♔e4	♜g5
60	♗a6?	...

Keres thought *60 ♗f1!* was the winning chance. If *60...♜g1 61 ♗a6!* and Black no longer has the defense mentioned in the next note. Wrong is the immediate *60 ♗d3* owing to *60...♗f7! 61 ♔xf4 ♜h5 62 ♖xh5 ♗xh5* followed by ...♗xf3.

KERES

Position after 60 ♗a6?

FISCHER

| 60 | ... | ♗f7? |

This slip is fatal. Keres told me he had reached this position in adjournment analysis, but had forgotten his drawing line over-the-board. Right is *60...♗b1+! 61 ♔xf4 ♖f5+ 62 ♔g4 ♖f6 63 ♖xf6 ♔xf6* with the aforementioned blockade.

| 61 | ♗c8! | ... |

Headed for g4. Not *61 ♔xf4? ♖h5* draws.

| 61 | ... | ♖g6 |

After *61...♖c5 62 ♗g4 ♖c4+ 63 ♔e5* White's penetration is decisive, even though he doesn't win a second Pawn immediately.

| 62 | ♖h7 | ♔f8 |
| 63 | ♗g4 | ♖g7 |

Not *63...♖xg4? 64 ♖xf7+!*

| 64 | ♖h6 | ... |

White still can't afford to trade.

64	...	♖g6
65	♖xg6!	♗xg6+
66	♔xf4	♔g7
67	♔g5!	...

This makes all the difference. Black's King can no longer set up a blockade on f6.

67	...	♗d3
68	f4	♗e4
69	h4	...

Of course not *69 f5? ♗xf5!* and White is left with what Hans Kmoch calls "the impotent pair."

	69	...	♗d3
	70	h5	♗e4
	71	h6+	♚h8

On *71...♚f7 72 ♗h5+ ♚g8 73 ♗g6* makes progress.

	72	♗f5	♗d5
	73	♗g6	♗e6
	74	♚f6	♗c4
	75	♚g5	♗e6
	76	♗h5	...

Back on the right track.

	76	...	♚h7
	77	♗g4!	♗c4

On *77...♗xg4 78 ♚xg4 ♚xh6 79 ♚f5* wins.

	78	f5	...

Finally the f-Pawn is free to advance.

	78	...	♗f7
	79	♗h5	♗c4
	80	♗g6+	♚g8
	81	f6	**Black resigns**

KERES

Final Position after 81 f6

FISCHER

On *81...♗b3 82 ♚f4 ♚h8 83 ♚e5 ♗c4 84 ♚d6 ♗b3 85 ♚e7 ♗c4 86 ♗f7 ♗d3 87 ♗e8! ♗c4 88 ♗d7 ♗g8 89 ♗e6 ♗h7 90 f7* and queens.

9 Walther [*Switzerland*] - Fischer

ZURICH 1959

SICILIAN DEFENSE

Betwixt the cup and the lip

Here, against a minor European master, Fischer appears to be busted after seventeen moves, and admits he was ready to resign on move 36. Nevertheless, he extracts a miraculous draw from a hopeless ending, two Pawns down. Time and again Walther fumbles, allowing Fischer to prolong the struggle until he gets his break on move 54.

What makes this game memorable is the demonstration it affords of the way in which a Grandmaster redeems himself after having started like a duffer; and how a weaker opponent, after masterfully building a winning position, often lacks the technique required to administer the coup de grâce. As Capablanca remarked, "The good player is always lucky."

1	e4	c5
2	♘f3	d6
3	d4	cxd4
4	♘xd4	♘f6
5	♘c3	a6
6	♗g5	e6
7	f4	♗e7

Sharper is *7...♕b6 8 ♕d2 ♕xb2 9 ♖b1 ♕a3* which I tried with success later in my career.

| 8 | ♕f3 | ♘bd7 |

More exact is *8...♕c7* to prevent *9 ♗c4.*

| 9 | 0-0-0 | ... |

Sharper is *9 ♗c4! 0-0 (9...♕c7? 10 ♗xe6! fxe6 11 ♘xe6 ♕b6 12 ♘xg7+ ♔f7 13 ♘f5* with a crushing attack) *10 0-0-0.* The text gives Black a chance to repair his earlier inaccuracy.

| 9 | ... | ♕c7 |
| 10 | ♗d3 | ... |

For *10* ♗e2 see game 14. For *10* g4 see games 12 and 15.

| 10 | ... | **b5** |
| 11 | **♗xf6** | ... |

Pointless. Better is *11* a3.

| 11 | ... | **♘xf6** |

Only not *11*...♗xf6? *12* ♗xb5! axb5 *13* ♘dxb5 wins.

| 12 | **♖he1** | ... |

12 a3 is necessary. Black comes out all right after *12* e5 ♗b7 *13* ♕g3 dxe5 *14* fxe5 ♘d7 *15* ♖he1 0-0-0! (Paoli-Tolush, Balatonfüred 1958.)

| 12 | ... | **♗b7** |

As I learned (see game 15), Black should avail himself of ...b4! (followed by ...♗b7 and ...d5) the instant he has the opportunity.

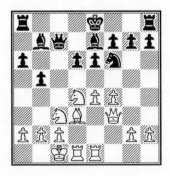

FISCHER

Position after 12...♗b7

WALTHER

| 13 | **♔b1** | ... |

At the risk of repeating myself, *13* a3 is mandatory.

| 13 | ... | **♖c8?** |

The disadvantage of this move is that Black loses his option of Q-side castling. Right is *13...b4 14* ♘ce2 g6! *15* g4 e5 *16* ♘b3 d5 *17* ♘d2 0-0 with initiative.

14	**g4**	...

14 a3 is still correct. We both suffered from the *idée fixe* that ...b4 was unplayable.

14	...	♘d7
15	**g5**	♘b6?

15...b4! 16 ♘ce2 ♘c5 still makes a fight of it.

16	**f5!**	e5

Now on *16...b4? 17* fxe6! splatters Black.
Not *16...*♗xg5? *17* ♗xb5+! ♔e7 *18* fxe6 fxe6 *19* ♘xe6!, etc. But I still thought Black was all right. Walther's next move quickly disabused me of that notion.

17	**f6!**	gxf6

I'd overlooked that on *17...exd4 18* ♘d5! is deadly.

18	**gxf6**	♗f8
19	♘d5!	...

Black's busted.

19	...	♘xd5
20	**exd5**	♔d8

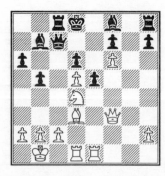

FISCHER

Position after 20...♔d8

WALTHER

21	♘c6+!	...

A wise investment. The Pawn sac is insignificant compared to the opening of the center files against Black's King.

21	...	♗xc6
22	**dxc6**	♕xc6
23	**♗e4**	♕b6
24	**♕h5**	♔c7
25	**♗f5!**	♖d8
26	**♕xf7+**	♔b8
27	**♕e6**	♕c7
28	**♖e3!**	♗h6
29	**♖c3**	♕b7
30	**f7**	...

Very business-like. Not *30* ♖xd6?? ♕h1+.

30	...	♗g7
31	**♖cd3**	♗f8
32	**♕xe5!**	...

Should be decisive. "Any resemblance to chess is purely coincidental."

32	...	dxe5
33	**♖xd8+**	♔a7
34	**♖1d7**	h5
35	**♖xb7+**	♔xb7
36	**c3**	♔c7

Ordinarily the curtain would be drawn here, but I just wanted to see what he'd do next.

| 37 | **♖a8(?)** | ... |

The wrong track. On *37* ♖e8! Black resigns.

| 37 | ... | ♔d6 |

FISCHER

Position after 37...♔d6

WALTHER

| 38 | ♖xa6+ | ... |

I was still prepared to resign after *38* ♖e8! Black has absolutely no moves. White simply strolls his King to e4, creating *zugzwang*.

| 38 | ... | ♔e7 |
| 39 | ♖e6+ | ... |

Even simpler is *39* ♖a7+ ♔f6 *40* ♗d3.

| 39 | ... | ♔xf7 |
| 40 | ♖xe5 | b4 |

The game was adjourned. Strangely enough, I began to feel the position contained some swindling prospects.

41	cxb4	♗xb4
42	h3	♔f6
43	♖b5	♗d6
44	♗e4	...

On *44* a4 ♖b8! forces the exchange of Rooks (if *45* ♖d5? ♗e5). The pure opposite-colored-Bishop ending is Black's best chance to draw.

| 44 | ... | ♖e8 |

My first threat in the entire game!

45	♖f5+	♔g7
46	♗f3	♖e1+
47	♔c2	♖f1!
48	♖d5	...

The threat was *48*...♖f2+ *49* ♔b1 (if *49* ♔b3? ♔g6 wins a piece) *49*...♖f1+ with a draw.

| 48 | ... | ♖f2+ |
| 49 | ♖d2 | ... |

49 ♔b1 ♗a3! *50* bxa3 ♖xf3 *51* ♖xh5 ♖xa3 is also hopeless for Black.

| 49 | ... | ♖xd2+ |

Or *49*...♖xf3 *50* ♖xd6 ♖xh3 *51* a4, etc.

50	♔xd2	h4
51	♔d3	♔f6
52	♔c4	♔e7

53	♔b5	♚d7

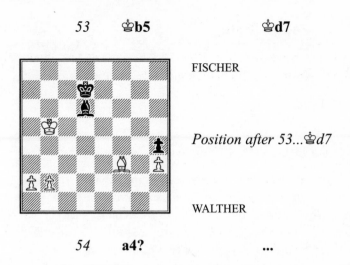

FISCHER

Position after 53...♚d7

WALTHER

| 54 | **a4?** | ... |

This natural push throws away the win! The Swiss endgame composer, Fontana, pointed out the proper method: *54* b4! ♚c7 *55* ♔a5! ♚b8 *56* b5 ♗a3 *57* b6 ♚c8 *58* ♔a6 ♚b8 *59* ♗g2! and Black is in *zugzwang*. If *59...*♚c8 (or *59...*♗c5 *60* a4) *60* ♔a7 ♗c5 *61* a4, etc.

The theme underlying Black's defense is this: once he succeeds in sacrificing his Bishop for both the Q-side Pawns, then White will be left with the "wrong Bishop" for his h-Pawn.

54	...	♚c7
55	**b4**	♚b8
56	**a5**	♚a7
57	**♔c4**	♗g3
58	**b5**	♗f2
59	**♗e2**	...

59 b6+ is met by *59...*♗xb6!

59	...	♗e3
60	**♔b3**	♗d2

60...♗f2 also draws.

61	**b6+**	♚b7
62	**♔a4**	♚c6
63	**♗b5+**	♚c5

Drawn

White's Pawns are stymied. On *64* b7 ♗f4 *65* a6 ♚b6=

10 Fischer - Unzicker *[W. Germany]*

ZURICH 1959

RUY LOPEZ

Milking the cow

The Ruy Lopez has been so extensively analyzed that often both players reel off their first twenty moves in two minutes flat. Nevertheless, it gives rise to situations that call for tact and patience. As Bronstein remarked, "When you play the Ruy, it's like milking a cow." Fischer, here, milks the cow to a fare-thee-well.

The first twenty-two moves are identical with game number 6. Unzicker then varies with the dubious ...f6, which undermines his e-Pawn and leaves him with weak squares. Retribution, though not swift, is sure. Creating simultaneous threats on both wings, Fischer finally infiltrates on the a-file. Black is so tied up that he cannot defend one of his Pawns when attacked – making defeat imminent.

1	e4	e5
2	♘f3	♞c6
3	♗b5	a6
4	♗a4	♞f6
5	0-0	♝e7
6	♖e1	b5
7	♗b3	d6
8	c3	0-0
9	h3	♞a5
10	♗c2	c5

10...c6 11 d4 ♛c7 is an interesting alternative. (ROSSOLIMO) – Black avoids weakening his d5.

11	d4	♛c7
12	♘bd2	♝d7
13	♘f1	♖fe8
14	♘e3	...

Tal and Geller recommend *14* b3 and if *14*...g6 *15* ♗g5.

14	...	g6
15	dxe5	dxe5
16	♘h2	♖ad8
17	♕f3	♗e6
18	♘hg4	♘xg4
19	hxg4	...

Against Matanovich, at Portoroz 1958, I tried the inferior *19* ♘xg4 ♗xg4 *20* hxg4 c4 *21* g3 ♘b7 *22* ♔g2 ♘c5 *23* ♖h1 f6=. Black's Knight is already prepared to parachute to d3.

UNZICKER

Position after 19 hxg4

FISCHER

| 19 | ... | ♕c6 |

White gets an edge after *19...*♘c4 *20* ♘d5 ♗xd5 *21* exd5.

20	g5!?	♘c4
21	♘g4	♗xg4
22	♕xg4	f6?

For analysis of this position see game 6. Unzicker prefers active defense. He eliminates the potential pressure along the h-file, it is true, but at the cost of weakening his e-Pawn.

23	gxf6	♗xf6
24	a4!	♘b6
25	axb5	axb5
26	♗e3	...

Because both flanks are fluid, White, with his two Bishops, is better able to penetrate and exploit the "loose" Pawns.

26	...	♖a8

26...♘c4 is met by 27 ♗b3 instituting an awkward pin.

27	♖ed1	...

If he swaps, White gains the a-file; if he doesn't, White keeps the d-file.

27	...	♔h8
28	b3	♗g7

Black should ease the pressure by 28...♖xa1 29 ♖xa1 ♖a8 30 ♖xa8+ ♘xa8, though 31 ♕d1! followed by ♕a1! forces an invasion on the Q-side.

29	♕h4	♗f6
30	♗g5!	♗xg5
31	♕xg5	...

Now White must penetrate on either the a- or d-file. Black's e-Pawn has clearly been exposed as a weakling.

31	...	♖xa1

The threat was 32 ♖xa8 ♘xa8 33 ♖d5.

32	♖xa1	♘d7

Apparently defending everything. 33 ♖a7 can be met by 33...♕d6.

UNZICKER

Position after 32...♘d7

FISCHER

33	♗d1!	...

Bringing the Bishop into the game puts additional pressure on Black's overburdened pieces.

	33	...	♘f6

Not *33...♕xe4 34 ♗f3 ♕f4* (if *34...♕c2 35 ♖a7* with a winning attack) *35 ♕xf4 exf4 36 ♗c6 ♖e7* (or *36...♖d8 37 ♖d1*) *37 ♖a8+! ♔g7 38 ♖a7* wins a piece.

	34	♖a7	...

Infiltration!

	34	...	♕d6

On *34...♘xe4? 35 ♕h6* forces mate.

	35	♗e2!	...

Simply attacking a Pawn. Curiously, Black is in too much of a straitjacket to do much about it.

UNZICKER

Position after 35 ♗e2!

FISCHER

	35	...	♖e7

How can Black defend the Pawn?

A] *35...b4? 36 ♖a6 ♘xe4 37 ♕h4 ♕d5 38 ♗f3 ♕d3 39 ♖a7* wins.

B] *35...♘xe4? 36 ♕h6 ♖e7 37 ♕f8* mate.

C] *35...♕b6 36 ♖f7 ♘g8 37 ♕h4 h6 38 ♕g4 ♖d8 39 ♗xb5!* wins.

D] *35...♖b8 36 ♖f7 ♘g8 37 ♖d7! ♕f6* (if *37...♕xd7 38 ♕xe5+ ♕g7 39 ♕xb8 ♕xc3 40 ♕xb5*) *38 ♕e3 ♕c6 39 ♖d5* when one of Black's hanging Pawns must fall.

	36	♖xe7	♕xe7
	37	♗xb5	♔g7

38	♗e2	...

The win is still far from clear. White's major technical problem is creating a passed Pawn on the Q-side while sheltering his King from a perpetual check.

38	...	♛c7

Threatening ...♘xe4.

39	♛e3	♛a5
40	g3	♛a3

Black should wait around with *40...♛c7.*

41	♔g2	...

Sharper and possibly immediately decisive is *41 b4! cxb4 42 ♛c5!*

41	...	♛a5

On *41...♛xb3 42 ♛xc5 ♘xe4 43 ♛xe5+ ♘f6 44 c4* should win.

42	♛d3	♛b6
43	♛c4	♛c6
44	♗d3	...

It's better to refrain from *44 f3* which weakens the K-field.

44	...	♛b6
45	b4	cxb4
46	cxb4	...

Step one is completed: White has a passed b-Pawn.

46	...	♘g4
47	♛c5	♛xc5

Forced. *47...♛d8?* loses a second Pawn after *48 ♗e2.*

48	bxc5	♔f7
49	f4	...

The idea is to create another passed Pawn in the center.

49	...	♔e7
50	♔f3	♘f6

On *50...h5 51 ♗c4* maintains the bind (if *51...♔d7 52 ♗f7).*

51	♗b5	...

Not *51* fxe5? ♘d7 draws.

51	...	♔e6

Striving to keep the blockade as long as possible.

52	♗c4+	♔e7
53	c6!	...

UNZICKER

Position after 53 c6!

FISCHER

53	...	♘e8

Makes it easy. The best defense was *53...exf4* (if *53...♔d6? 54* fxe5+
♔xe5 *55* c7) *54* gxf4 ♘e8 *55* e5 ♘c7 *56* ♔e4 ♘e8 (if *56...h5 57* ♔f3
wins) *57* ♗g8 ♔f8 *58* ♗xh7 ♔g7 *59* ♗xg6 ♔xg6 *60* f5+ ♔g5 *61* f6
♔g6 *62* ♔d5 ♔f7 *63* ♔c5 ♔e6 *64* ♔b6 wins.

54	fxe5	h6
55	♔e3	♘c7
56	♔d4	h5
57	♔e3!	g5
58	♗e2	h4
59	gxh4	gxh4
60	♗c4	♘e8
61	♔f4	♔d8
62	♔g4	♔c7
63	♗f7	♘g7
64	♔xh4	♔xc6
65	♔g5	**Black resigns**

After *65...♔d7 66* ♔f6 ♘e8+ *67* ♗xe8+ leads to an elementary win.

11 Fischer - Benko *[U.S.A.]*

CANDIDATES' TOURNAMENT 1959

SICILIAN DEFENSE

Unheard melodies

Paul Morphy is the idol of all the romantics who pine for the swashbuckling chess of yesteryear; but it is rarely possible to succeed with that kind of flamboyance any longer since players now are more evenly matched. A rise in the standard of defense has necessitated a corresponding adjustment in the character of attack. In modern chess most of the beauty resides in the annotations. Brilliancies often exist only as grace notes — because the opposition anticipates and thwarts them with appropriate rejoinders. To the uninitiated, some of the most hard-fought struggles seem devoid of all bravura. That is the situation in this game.

Confronted with a dozen beautiful outlandish losing variations, Benko chooses what appears to be a prosaic one. Is this "ugliness" not a by-product of skill? Though the reader may feel cheated, and the winner frustrated, does it not argue for the perspicacity of the loser who sidestepped those seductive invitations?

1	e4	c5
2	♘f3	♘c6
3	d4	cxd4
4	♘xd4	♘f6
5	♘c3	d6
6	♗c4	♛b6

For 6...♗d7 see game 13. By putting immediate pressure on the center, Black forces the Knight to a passive post.

7	♘de2	...

For 7 ♘b3 see game 58, note to Black's sixth move. No good is 7 ♘db5 a6 8 ♗e3 ♛a5 9 ♘d4 ♘xe4, etc. And 7 ♘xc6!? bxc6 only helps Black strengthen his center, but after 8 0-0 White has promising tactical chances.

7	...	e6
8	0-0	♗e7
9	♗b3	0-0
10	♔h1	...

If *10 ♗e3 ♕c7 11 f4 ♘g4!*

10	...	♘a5
11	♗g5	♕c5!

A finesse aimed at provoking *12 ♗e3 ♕c7* after which White's initiative is blunted.

	12	f4	b5

Another virtue of Black's last move was that it freed this Pawn.

	13	♘g3	b4?

Gligorich suggests simply *13...♗b7.* Also satisfactory is *13...♘xb3! 14 axb3 ♗b7* (or *14...b4*) *15 ♘h5 ♔h8=.*
The text exposes Black to a vicious attack.

	14	e5!	...

BENKO

Position after 14 e5!

FISCHER

	14	...	dxe5

A] It's too late now for *14...♘xb3 15* exf6 gxf6 (if *15...♗xf6 16 ♘ce4*) *16 ♗h6,* etc.

B] *14...bxc3 15* exf6 ♗xf6 (if *15...gxf6 16 ♗h6 f5 17 ♘h5* threatening to bring the Queen to g3) *16 ♗xf6 gxf6 17 ♘e4! ♕f5 18 ♘xd6 ♕g6*

19 ♖f3 with a decisive attack (YUDOVICH). If now *19...*♔h8 *20* ♖g3 ♕h6 *21* ♕g4 (threatening ♕g8+!) *21...*♕g6 *22* ♕h4.

	15	♗xf6	gxf6

A] On *15...*♗xf6 *16* ♘ce4 ♕e7 (if *16...*♕d4 *17* ♘xf6+ gxf6 *18* ♕g4+ ♔h8 *19* ♖ad1 ♕xb2 *20* ♘h5 ♖g8 *21* ♕xg8+! ♔xg8 *22* ♖d8 mate) *17* ♘h5! ♔h8 (if *17...*♗h4 *18* fxe5 followed by ♕g4 GLIGORICH) *18* ♘exf6 gxf6 *19* fxe5 fxe5 *20* ♘f6 threatening ♕h5 and wins.

B]   The best chance is *15...*bxc3! *16* ♘e4 ♕b4 *17* ♕g4 ♗xf6 *18* ♘xf6+ ♔h8 *19* ♕h4 h6 *20* ♘g4 threatening ♘xh6 with a strong attack.

	16	♘ce4	♕d4

Benko gave this move a lot of thought. On the alternative *16...*♕c7 *17* ♘h5! (Black holds after *17* ♕g4+ ♔h8 *18* ♕h4 ♖g8 *19* ♘xf6 ♖g7 *20* ♕h6 ♗b7!) *17...*f5 *18* ♘hf6+! ♔g7 *19* ♕h5! ♗xf6 (not *19...*h6 *20* ♖f3 ♖h8 [*20...*exf4 *21* ♖h3 ♖h8 *22* ♘e8+!] *21* ♖g3+ ♔f8 *22* ♕xh6+!) *20* ♘xf6 h6 (if *20...*♖h8 *21* ♕g5+ ♔f8 *22* ♕h6+ ♔e7 *23* ♕h4 ♔f8 *24* ♘xh7+ wins the exchange) *21* ♖f3! ♖h8 (not *21...*♔xf6 *22* ♕h4+ ♔g7 *23* ♖g3+ ♔h7 *24* ♖h3 wins) *22* ♘e8+! ♖xe8 *23* ♖g3+ ♔f8 *24* ♕xh6+ ♔e7 *25* ♕h4+ ♔d6 (if *25...*♔f8 *26* ♖h3! ♕d8 *27* ♕h6+ ♔e7 *28* ♕g5+ wins the Queen) *26* ♖d3+ ♔c6 (if *26...*♔c5 *27* ♗a4! threatens ♕f2+) *27* ♗a4+ ♔b7 *28* ♗xe8 wins material.

	17	♕h5!	...

Already Black is without a satisfactory defense.

BENKO

Position after 17 ♕h5!

FISCHER

| 17 | ... | ♘xb3 |

A] On *17*...♔h8 *18* ♕h6 ♖g8 (if *18*...exf4 *19* ♘h5 wins) *19* ♘xf6, etc.

B] *17*...exf4 *18* ♘f5! exf5 *19* ♖xf4 ♕xe4 (otherwise ♖h4) *20* ♖xe4 fxe4 *21* ♕xa5 wins. (This key line wouldn't work had Black interpolated *13*...♘xb3! earlier!)

C] *17*...♔g7 (LOMBARDY) *18* ♖ad1 ♕xb2 *19* ♕h4 ♗b7 *20* ♘xf6!

| 18 | ♕h6! | exf4 |

On *18*...f5 *19* c3! is devastating: e.g., *19*...bxc3 *20* bxc3 ♕–any *21* ♘h5 forces mate.

19	♘h5	f5
20	♖ad1!	♕e5
21	♘ef6+	♗xf6
22	♘xf6+	♕xf6
23	♕xf6	...

Now it's skin and bones.

23	...	♘c5
24	♕g5+	♔h8
25	♕e7!	♗a6
26	♕xc5	♗xf1
27	♖xf1	**Black resigns**

12 Gligorich [*Yugoslavia*] - Fischer

CANDIDATES' TOURNAMENT 1959

SICILIAN DEFENSE

Castling into it

Although not perfect, this is perhaps the most bitterly contested game in this book. Fischer chooses a difficult variation which requires Olympian judgment. He submits his King to an attack which, on the face of it, can only be described as irresistible. Why did he do it? Because, we are told, it was strategically justified.

Gligorich, too, must be given equal credit for his courage and restraint. His continuation, despite intensive post-mortem analysis, has yet to be improved upon. The complexity of each phase of this tumultuous struggle must be studied to be believed. Curiously, in the "barren" Rook and Pawn ending, Gligorich somehow missed a win — a fact which he is probably unaware of to this day.

1	e4	c5
2	♘f3	d6
3	d4	cxd4
4	♘xd4	♘f6
5	♘c3	a6
6	♗g5	e6
7	f4	♗e7
8	♕f3	♕c7
9	0-0-0	♘bd7
10	g4	b5

Gligorich and I have a standing feud with this position, which we've reached no less than three times. I've lost twice and drawn once (this one).

11	♗xf6	...

Interesting is *11* ♗g2 ♗b7 *12* ♖he1 b4 *13* ♘d5!? exd5 *14* exd5 ♔f8 *15* ♘f5 ♖e8 and Black won. (Bernstein-Fischer, US Championship 1957-8)

11	**...**	**gxf6!?**

For *11...♘xf6* see game 9.

12	**f5**	**...**

Giving up e5 in order to exert pressure on e6. Our game at Zurich 1959 continued: *12 ♗g2 ♗b7 13 ♖he1 0-0-0 14 a3 ♘b6=*.

In the US Championship 1959-60, Mednis played *12 a3* against me. The game went *12...♗b7 (12...♖b8 is sharper) 13 f5 e5 14 ♘de2 ♘b6 15 ♘d5 ♗xd5 16 exd5 ♖c8 17 ♘c3 ♘c4 18 ♗xc4 bxc4 19 ♔b1 ♖b8 20 ♔a2* with a better game for White.

12 ♗d3 ♗b7 13 ♔b1 ♘c5 14 f5 b4 15 ♘ce2 d5 16 fxe6 dxe4 17 exf7+ ♔f8 18 ♗xe4 ♗xe4 19 ♕xe4 ♘xe4 20 ♘e6+ ♔xf7 21 ♘xc7 ♖a7 is exciting but equal. (Padevsky-Evans, Havana Olympic 1966.)

12	**...**	**♘e5**

Simagin gave this a "?" and proceeded to analyze the alternative *12...b4 13 fxe6 bxc3 (if 13...♘e5 14 ♘d5!) 14 exd7+ ♗xd7 15 e5*, etc. By this logic, the whole variation is unsound for Black. We shall see.

13	**♕h3**	**0-0!**

Not *13...♗d7 14 g5! fxg5 (if 14...exf5 15 ♘d5) 15 fxe6 fxe6 16 ♘xe6* and Black's game collapses.

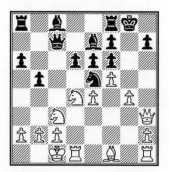

FISCHER

Position after 13...0-0!

GLIGORICH

Petrosian and Tal both happened to stroll by the board at this instant. Petrosian made a wry face which looked to me like "Can Black do this and live?"

Black's "ugly" defense is based on sound positional considerations: once he can consolidate, there is a strong potential in the two Bishops coupled with his beautifully posted Knight and compact Pawn mass. These assets, in the long run, hopefully, should outweigh the temporary weakness of his King and the immobile target on e6.

14	♘ce2!	...

The consistent strategical plan. Gligorich intends ♘f4, bringing additional pressure to bear on e6. Simagin gave the offhand *14* ♕h6 ♔h8 *15* g5! and "wins". It is incredibly naïve to imagine that a player of Gligorich's caliber could overlook such a simple refutation. In this line simply *15*...♖g8! refutes White's strategy. *16* g6 (if *16* gxf6 ♘g4 regains the Pawn with advantage) *16*...fxg6 *17* ♘xe6 (weaker is *17* fxe6 ♗b7) *17*...♗xe6 *18* fxe6 ♖ac8 *19* ♕d2 (if *19* a3 d5! *20* exd5 ♗xa3) *19*...♘c4 *20* ♗xc4 (if *20* ♕d4 ♕a5) *20*...♕xc4 *21* ♕d5 ♖ge8 threatening ...♗f8 (or ...b4).

In a sense my judgment was vindicated when Bronstein (as Black) reached the diagram against Kholmov in the 1964 USSR Championship. The continuation was *14* g5!? b4? (Kholmov gives the best defense: "*14*...fxg5! *15* fxe6 fxe6 *16* ♘xe6 ♕d7 *17* ♘d5 ♕xe6 *18* ♕xe6+ ♗xe6 *19* ♘xe7+ ♔f7 *20* ♘f5=") *15* gxf6 ♗xf6 *16* ♖g1+ ♔h8 *17* ♕h6 ♕e7 *18* ♘c6!! ♘xc6 *19* e5!! and White won brilliantly.

14	...	♔h8

14...♕b7 also comes into serious consideration.

Unsound is *14*...♗d7 *15* ♘f4 ♕c8 *16* ♕h6 ♔h8 *17* ♘h5 ♖g8 *18* ♘xf6 ♖g7 *19* ♗e2 ♕d8 *20* g5, etc.

15	♘f4	♖g8
16	♖g1	...

Gligorich gives *16* ♗e2 as correct. After *16*...♕b7 *17* fxe6 fxe6 it's anybody's game. On *16* fxe6 fxe6 *17* ♘dxe6 ♗xe6 (or ...♕a5 or ...♕b7) *18* ♘xe6 ♕c8=.

16	...	d5!

Suddenly the game opens up! But more prudent is *16*...♕b7 and if *17* ♖e1 ♕b6!

| 17 | **fxe6** | **...** |

Weak is *17* exd5? exf5! and White can't recapture because of the pin on the g-file.

| 17 | **...** | **dxe4** |
| 18 | **♘d5** | **♛c5** |

Black's game hangs by a hair. *19* exf7 ♘xf7 *20* ♘xe7 ♛xe7 is roughly even.

FISCHER

Position after 18...♛c5

GLIGORICH

| 19 | **♘xe7** | **...** |

Weird complications result from the key line *19* ♘f5!:

A) *19...*♝d8 *20* ♛h6! (not *20* ♖g3 fxe6 or *20* e7 ♝xf5 *21* exd8=♛ ♖axd8) *20...*♖g6 *21* ♘f4! ♘d3+ *22* ♖xd3! wins.

B) *19...*♛xg1 *20* ♘fxe7 ♝xe6 (if *20...*♛xg4 *21* ♛xg4 ♖xg4 *22* ♘c7 ♖b8 *23* ♖d8+ ♚g7 *24* ♘f5+ ♚g6 *25* e7 wins) *21* ♘xg8 (if *21* ♘xf6 ♖g7) *21...*♝xg4 *22* ♛h6 ♝xd1 *23* ♘gxf6 ♛g6 *24* ♛xg6 hxg6 *25* ♚xd1 with winning chances.

| 19 | **...** | **♛xe7** |
| 20 | **♘f5** | **...** |

If *20* ♛e3 ♝b7 *21* exf7 ♛xf7 Black wins a Pawn.

| 20 | **...** | **♛xe6** |
| 21 | **♛h6** | **...** |

Possibly Gligorich had originally intended *21 ♖d6? ♕xa2 22 ♕h6* overlooking that Black can win with *22...♕a1+* (if *22...♗xf5 23 ♕xf6+ ♖g7 24 ♖d8+* leads to a draw by perpetual) *23 ♔d2 ♘f3+ 24 ♔e3* (if *24 ♔e2?? ♕e1* mate; or *24 ♔c3? ♕a5+ 25 ♔b3 ♕a4+ 26 ♔c3 b4+ 27 ♔c4 ♗e6+* leads to mate) *24...♕xb2!* wins.

21	...	**♗d7!**

Defending against the powerful threat of ♖d8! Not *21...♘xg4? 22 ♖xg4! ♖xg4 23 ♖d8+ ♖g8 24 ♕g7* mate.

22	**♖d6**	...

White has no choice. Black threatened ...♖g6 followed by ...♕xa2. Or on *22 ♔b1 ♘xg4*.

22	...	**♘xg4!**
23	**♖xg4**	...

Forced. *23 ♖xe6? ♘xh6* wins a piece.

23	...	**♕xf5**
24	**♖xg8+?**	...

Handing Black the game on a silver platter. Correct is *24 ♖f4 ♕g5 25 ♕xf6+ ♕xf6 26 ♖dxf6 e3! 27 ♖xf7 ♖g1! 28 ♖xd7 e2 29 ♖d1! exd1=♕+ 30 ♔xd1 ♔g7 31 ♔e1 ♖f8 32 ♖xf8 ♔xf8 33 ♔f2* with good drawing prospects.

FISCHER

Position after 24 ♖xg8+?

GLIGORICH

Black has two ways to recapture: which one is correct?

24	...	♖xg8?

Returning the compliment! The winning line is *24...♔xg8! 25 ♖xf6 ♕e5* with an extra Pawn and a dominating position (if *26 ♖xa6? ♖xa6 27 ♕xa6 ♕f4+* wins a piece).

25	♖xf6	♕d5
26	♖d6!	♕f5

On *26...♕b7? 27 ♕f6+ ♖g7 28 ♕d8+ ♖g8 29 ♕xd7* wins.

27	♖f6	♕g5+

I should have contented myself with the draw now by *27...♕d5 28 ♖d6*, etc.

28	♕xg5	♖xg5
29	♖xf7	♗g4
30	♔d2	♗f3
31	♔e3	♖g1
32	♗h3	...

Not *32 ♔f2? ♖h1*.

32	...	♖e1+
33	♔f4	♗d1

Playing, as Dr. Tarrasch wryly put it, "for the loss." Nowadays I would know better than to try to squeeze a win out of such a simplified ending.

34	♔e5!	...

Gligorich is also playing to win – by cashing in on my inexperience. Simply *34 ♖e7 ♗xc2 35 ♗f5* holds the draw. But he is purposely inviting me to overextend myself.

34	...	e3
35	♗f5	♖g1
36	♖xh7+	♔g8
37	♖c7	♗g4?

Still chasing the chimera of the missed win. Black should simply force a draw with *37...e2 38 ♔f6 ♔h8 39 ♖h7+ ♔g8 40 ♖c7 ♔h8*, etc.

38	♗xg4	♖xg4
39	♖c3	e2
40	♖e3	♖g2

FISCHER

Position after 40...♖g2

GLIGORICH

In my excitement I had originally intended *40...♖g7?* overlooking the simple reply *41 ♔d4* (among others). Fortunately, Black can still hold the draw.

41	♔d4	e1=♕!

After *41...♖xh2? 42 ♔d3* Black is really lost!

42	♖xe1	♖xc2
43	♖b1	♔f7!

Not *43...♖xh2? 44 ♔c5* with a fatal penetration on the Q-side.

44	a3	♔e6
45	b3	...

On *45 h4 ♔d6* holds the balance. The threat now is ♖h1.

45	...	♖xh2
46	♔c5	♔d7
47	♔b6	♖a2
48	♔xa6	♖xa3+

49	♔b7	...

Trying to finagle. *49 ♔xb5 ♚c7* leads to an easy book draw.

49	...	♚d6

Crisper is *49...b4 50 ♖d1+* (on *50 ♔b6 ♚c8* the Black King gets in front of the Pawn) *50...♚e6 51 ♖d3 ♚e5 52 ♔b6 ♚e4 53 ♖h3 ♚d4 54 ♔b5 ♖a8 55 ♔xb4 ♖b8+ 56 ♔a5 ♖a8+ 57 ♔b6 ♖b8+ 58 ♔c6* (if *58 ♔a6 ♚c5=) 58...♖b4 59 ♖g3 ♖b8* with an impenetrable blockade.

50	♔b6	♚d7
51	b4	♖h3
52	♖c1	♖h8?

After the game Olafsson scolded me: "How can you play an ending like this so fast?" (I'd only been taking a few seconds a move for the last dozen moves or so.) "Because there's no danger. It's a dead draw," I replied. Had I known then what I know now, I would have selected *52...♖h5* and if *53 ♖c5 ♖xc5 54 ♔xc5 ♚c7 55 ♔xb5 ♚b7* holding the opposition, with a book draw.

FISCHER

Position after 52...♖h8?

GLIGORICH

53	♔xb5?	...

Now it's Gligorich's turn to let me out. As Olafsson showed me, White can win with *53 ♖c7+!* It's hard to believe. I stayed up all night analyzing, finally convincing myself and, incidentally, learning a lot about Rook and Pawn endings in the process. Gligorich failed to point it out in his notes to the Bled tournament book. The main point is Black cannot get his King in front of the Pawn.

A sample line is *53 ♖c7+! ♚d6 (if 53...♚d8 54 ♖c5 ♚d7 55 ♚b7!
♚d6 56 ♖xb5) 54 ♖c6+ ♚d7 (if 54...♚d5 55 ♚xb5 ♖b8+ 56 ♖b6)
55 ♚xb5 ♖b8+ (if 55...♖h4 56 ♖c1 ♖h8 57 ♚a6) 56 ♖b6 ♖h8 57 ♖b7+
♚c8 58 ♚a6 ♖h6+ 59 ♚a7* with a book win.

53	...	♖b8+
54	♚a4	♖a8+

The game was adjourned again. But the crisis has passed.

55	♚b3	♖c8
56	♖xc8	♚xc8
57	♚c4	♚b8!

Drawn

FISCHER

Final Position after 57...♚b8!

GLIGORICH

Black holds the "distant opposition." For example, *58 ♚c5*
(or *58 ♚d5 ♚b7) 58...♚c7 59 ♚b5 ♚b7*, etc.

13 Fischer - Gligorich [*Yugoslavia*]

CANDIDATES' TOURNAMENT 1959

SICILIAN DEFENSE

Something new

During the mid-fifties, Gligorich, Reshevsky, and Najdorf were considered the strongest non-Soviet Grandmasters. Within a few years Fischer managed to surpass them. However, in so doing, he succeeded in beating Gligorich only once – up to 1966 (see game 56).

On the occasion of this first win, Fischer employs a novel attacking system (13 ♕e2) against the Dragon Variation. Gligorich fails to react vigorously enough and makes the mistake of castling too soon, thereby exposing himself to the same type of sacrificial combination that demolished Larsen in game 2.

1	**e4**	**c5**
2	**♘f3**	**♘c6**
3	**d4**	**cxd4**
4	**♘xd4**	**♘f6**
5	**♘c3**	**d6**
6	**♗c4**	**♗d7**

For Benko's 6...♕b6 see game 11.

Recently in a skittles game someone tried 6...g6!? against me. The game continued: *7 ♘xc6 bxc6 8 e5 ♘h5?* (correct is *8...♘g4*. Not *8...dxe5?? 9 ♗xf7+* winning the Queen – that was another skittles game!) *9 ♕f3! e6* (if *9...d5 10 ♘xd5!*) *10 g4 ♘g7 11 ♘e4 ♕a5+* (if *11...d5 12 ♘f6+ ♔e7 13 ♕a3+*) *12 ♗d2 ♕xe5 13 ♗c3* Black resigns.

| 7 | **♗b3** | **...** |

7 ♗e3 is met by *7...♘g4!* On *7 ♗g5 e6 8 ♗xf6? ♕xf6 9 ♘db5 0-0-0 10 ♘xd6+ ♔b8* with a winning attack (GLIGORICH). Also strong is *7 0-0 g6 8 ♘xc6! ♗xc6* (or *8...bxc6 9 f4*) *9 ♗g5 ♗g7 10 ♘d5!*

| 7 | **...** | **g6** |

8	f3	...

The only other try for any advantage is *8 ♗e3 ♘g4 9 ♘xc6 bxc6 (9...♘xe3? 10 ♗xf7+!) 10 ♕f3* (not *10 ♗xa7? c5*) *10...♘e5 11 ♕g3.*

8	...	♘a5

Releasing the central tension this way is wrong. Correct is *8...♘xd4 9 ♕xd4 ♗g7* but after *10 ♗g5!* White still keeps control.

9	♗g5	♗g7
10	♕d2	h6

A concession. But on *10...0-0 11 ♗h6* followed by h4-h5 produces a strong and almost mechanical attack.

11	♗e3	♖c8
12	0-0-0	♘c4
13	♕e2!?	...

A totally new idea at the time. *13 ♗xc4 ♖xc4 14 g4* was the usual, and good, procedure. The text permits Black to capture what was considered, then, to be the more important of the White Bishops.

GLIGORICH

Position after 13 ♕e2!?

FISCHER

Bronstein was so impressed with this concept that he enthusiastically gave my thirteenth move "!!" claiming it was virtually the winning line. Alexander Kotov, the commissar of chess criticism in the Soviet Union, wrote, with more sober restraint: "It is difficult to agree with this."

13	...	♘xe3

Not *13...♕c7? 14 ♘db5.*

14	♕xe3	0-0

Reminiscent of game 12, it is now Gligorich who castles into it! At Mar del Plata 1960, Marini played against me the stronger *14...♕b6* (threatening ...e5) *15 ♕d2 ♕c5 16 f4 h5?* (better is *16...b5* or ...0-0) *17 ♘f3 ♗h6 18 e5!* with a powerful attack.

Kotov recommends *14...♕a5 15 ♔b1* (he gives only *15 g4? ♕g5!*) *15...♕c5 16 ♕d3 a6* and Black's all right. So best is probably *15 f4* (after *14...♕a5*) *15...0-0 16 h3 e6* but Black's two Bishops may offset the weakness of the d-Pawn.

15	g4	...

Timing is important. On *15 h4 h5* locks it up.

15	...	♕a5
16	h4	e6

On *16...h5 17 g5 ♘e8 18 f4-f5* gives White a strong game.

17	♘de2!	...

Black holds out after *17 g5 hxg5 18 hxg5 ♘h5 19 f4 ♕c5* (threatening ...e5).

17	...	♖c6
18	g5	hxg5

On *18...♘h5 19 gxh6 ♗f6 20 f4* continues the Pawn stampede.

19	hxg5	♘h5
20	f4	♖fc8

GLIGORICH

Position after 20...♖fc8

FISCHER

| 21 | ♔b1 | ... |

An important preparatory move. On the immediate *21* f5!? exf5 *22* ♘d5 ♕xa2! gives Black good play.

21	...	♕b6
22	♕f3	♖c5
23	♕d3!	...

Several Yugoslav chess journalists scurried forward toward the analysis room, where Matanovich was explaining the game on a demonstration board. Apparently the feeling was that I had just blundered.

The more obvious *23* f5 looks good, but Black still has defensive resources with *23...*exf5 *24* ♖xh5 (if *24* ♘d5 ♕d8 *25* exf5 ♗xf5 *26* ♖xh5? ♖xc2! wins for Black) *24...*gxh5 *25* ♘f4 ♖xc3 *26* bxc3 ♖xc3 *27* ♕xh5 ♖xb3+ *28* cxb3 ♕e3, etc.

| 23 | ... | ♗xc3 |

The threat against the d-Pawn is awkward to meet. On *23...*♖5c6 *24* f5! exf5 *25* ♖xh5! gxh5 *26* exf5 is crushing. Or if *23...*♖8c6? *24* ♘a4 wins the exchange. Finally on *23...*♗f8 *24* f5! exf5 *25* ♘d5 ♕d8 (if *25...*fxe4 *26* ♕xe4 ♗f5 *27* ♕xf5 wins a piece) *26* ♖xh5! gxh5 (*26...*♖xd5 *27* ♗xd5 gxh5 *28* exf5) *27* ♘f6+ ♔g7 *28* ♕h3 releases an avalanche.

| 24 | ♘xc3 | ... |

Not *24* bxc3? ♗b5.

24	...	♘xf4

This is what the crowd thought I had overlooked.

25	♕f3	♘h5

On *25...e5 26 ♘e2!* is decisive.

GLIGORICH

Position after 25...♘h5

FISCHER

26	♖xh5!	...

I've made this sacrifice so often, I feel like applying for a patent!

26	...	gxh5
27	♕xh5	♗e8

The best defensive try On *27...♔f8 28 ♕h8+ ♔e7 29 ♕f6+ ♔e8 30 ♖h1 ♗b5 31 ♗xe6! fxe6 32 ♕xe6+ ♔d8* (or *32...♔f8 33 ♖h8+ ♔g7 34 ♕f6 mate*) *33 ♖h8+ ♔c7 34 ♖xc8 mate.*

28	♕h6!	♖xc3
29	bxc3	...

On *29 ♖h1, ♕d4* holds out for a while.

29	...	♖xc3

White still retains a winning attack after *29...♕e3 30 ♖h1 ♕xc3 31 g6 ♕g7 32 ♕h2!* (BRONSTEIN).

30	g6!	fxg6
31	♖h1	♕d4
32	♕h7+	...

Again a mistake! *32 ♗xe6+* mates more quickly.

32	...	**Black resigns**

14 Keres [U.S.S.R.] - Fischer

CANDIDATES' TOURNAMENT 1959

SICILIAN DEFENSE

Too many cooks

Professionals spend much of their spare time hunting for "cooks" with which they hope to surprise future opponents. It was rumored, for example, that Marshall waited for over ten years before springing his famous gambit on Capablanca, at New York, in 1918. But, as it happened, the wily Cuban refuted it over-the-board!

Keres, in like manner, confronts Fischer with an innovation which the latter, in all innocence, proceeds to destroy. Rather than admit that his surprise Queen sacrifice is good for only a draw at best, Keres presses for more, offering material in order to sustain his initiative. Fischer continues to accept everything, but — at the very moment when victory is within his grasp (on move 31) — stumbles. Now he must win the game all over again; and he manages to do so, with an assist from Keres, in another twenty-two moves.

1	e4	c5
2	♘f3	d6
3	d4	cxd4
4	♘xd4	♘f6
5	♘c3	a6
6	♗g5	e6
7	f4	♗e7

Sharp is 7...♕b6 which I've tried on several occasions.

8	♕f3	♕c7

8...h6 9 ♗h4 g5!? 10 fxg5 ♘fd7 11 ♘xe6!? fxe6 12 ♕h5+ ♔f8 13 ♗b5! ♖h7! (Gligorich-Fischer, Portoroz 1958) is now considered a drawish variation!

9	0-0-0	♘bd7
10	♗e2	...

An innovation whose dubious merit appears on move 13. For *10* ♗d3 see game 9. For *10* g4 see games 12 and 15.

| 10 | ... | **b5** |
| 11 | **♗xf6** | **♘xf6** |

Not *11...♗xf6?* *12* ♗xb5! Or on *11...gxf6* *12* ♕h5 ♘b6 (if *12...0-0?* *13* ♖d3) *13* a3 followed by f5 is strong.

| 12 | **e5!?** | ... |

On *12* a3 ♖b8! followed by ...b4 gives good counterplay.

| 12 | ... | **♗b7** |

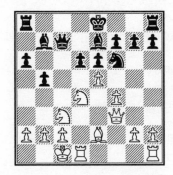

FISCHER

Position after 12...♗b7

KERES

| 13 | **exf6!?** | ... |

The crux of Keres' prepared line. After *13* ♕g3 dxe5 *14* fxe5 ♘d7 *15* ♕xg7 ♕xe5 Black stands better.

| 13 | ... | **♗xf3** |

So I chopped it off!

| 14 | **♗xf3** | **♗xf6** |

Not *14...♖c8?* *15* fxe7 ♕xe7 *16* ♘f5! (BONDAREVSKY).

| 15 | **♗xa8** | **d5** |

So far, so forced. Now ...0-0 is threatened.

| 16 | **♗xd5** | ... |

On *16* ♗c6+ ♔f8 *17* ♘ce2 ♔e7 followed by ...♖c8.

16	...	♗xd4

Not *16...*♕xf4+ *17* ♔b1 ♗xd4 *18* ♗c6+! ♔e7 *19* ♘e2, etc. Larsen suggested *16...*b4 *17* ♗c6+ ♔e7 *18* ♘ce2 ♖d8 but *19* ♖d2! (*19* g3? ♕b6!) *19...*♗xd4 *20* ♘xd4 ♕xf4 *21* ♘b3 holds for the time being.

17	♖xd4	exd5
18	♘xd5	♕c5
19	♖e1+	♔f8
20	c3	...

FISCHER

Position after 20 c3

KERES

White seems to have fair prospects. But a Queen is a Queen!

20	...	h5!

A hard move to find – even somewhat risky – over-the-board. Probably Keres had expected *20...*g6 *21* g4 ♔g7 *22* g5 h6 (if *22...*♖d8 *23* ♘f6 ♖xd4 *24* ♖e8 ♖d8! *25* ♖xd8 ♕e3+ draws) *23* h4 hxg5 *24* fxg5 ♖d8 *25* ♘f6 ♖xd4 *26* ♖e8 ♖d8! *27* ♖xd8 ♕e3+ with a draw by perpetual.

21	f5	...

To hinder ...g6.

Kotov gives *21* ♘b4 ♕c8? (simply *21...*g6 is more than sufficient; if then *22* ♘xa6 ♕c6) *22* ♘c6! and wins.

Zagoryansky also mistakenly thinks White has all the chances. He gives "*21* ♖e5! g6 (more passive is *21...*♕c8 *22* ♘e7 ♕a8 *23* ♘c6 f6

24 ♖e6 ♔f7 25 f5) 22 f5!" but *22...♔g7 23 f6+ ♔h6 (if 24 g4 b4!)* is quite satisfactory for Black.

21	...	**♖h6!**

The key to Black's defense; now the Rook sneaks into play via the side exit.

FISCHER

Position after 21...♖h6!

KERES

22	**f6?**	...

Throwing away a Pawn in an attempt to keep Black bottled up. Keres should just try to maintain the status quo with *22 ♖ed1*, although Black retains some slight winning chances. But he seems to labor under the delusion that White has the initiative.

22 ♖de4 ♔g8 23 ♖e8+ ♔h7 24 ♖d8 ♖d6 neutralizes all White's threats.

22	...	**gxf6**
23	**♘f4**	**h4**
24	**♖d8+?**	...

Continuing the "attack". The defensive *24 ♖e2* was in order.

24	...	**♔g7**
25	**♖ee8**	**♕g1+**
26	**♔d2**	**♕f2+**
27	**♘e2**	**♖g6**
28	**g3**	...

28 ♖g8+ ♔h6 29 ♖h8+ ♔g5 gets White nowhere.

28	...	**f5**
29	**♖g8+**	**♔f6**
30	**♖xg6+**	...

Or *30 ♖d6+ ♔e7 31 ♖dxg6 fxg6 32 ♖xg6 h3* wins (ZAGORYANSKY).

30	...	**fxg6**
31	**gxh4**	...

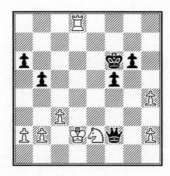

FISCHER

Position after 31 gxh4

KERES

31	...	**♛xh2?**

The winning method is *31...♛xh4! 32 ♖d6+ ♔f7 33 h3 ♛h6+!* (if *33...♛xh3 34 ♖xg6! ♔xg6?? 35 ♘f4+*) *34 ♔d1* (if *34 ♔e1 ♛xh3 35 ♖xg6 ♛h4+! 36 ♖g3 f4* wins; or on *34 ♔c2 ♛xh3 35 ♖xg6 ♛h2* wins) *34...♛xh3 35 ♖xg6 ♛f1+* and *...♔xg6.*

32	**♖d4!**	...

Now Black has to win the game over again.

32	...	**♛h1**
33	**♔c2**	...

33 ♘f4? allows penetration with *...♛b1.*

33	...	**♔e5**
34	**a4**	...

An even tighter defense is *34 ♘c1!* followed by *♘d3+* with a probable draw. But not *34 ♘f4? ♛h2+! 35 ♔d1 ♛xf4! 36 ♖xf4 ♔xf4* with a won King and Pawn ending: e.g., *37 ♔e2* (if *37 b3 ♔e3!*)

37...♔g3 38 b3 ♔xh4 39 c4 bxc4 40 bxc4 ♔g5 and the King is "in the square".

| 34 | ... | ♕f1 |

Trying to capitalize on the disjointed state of White's minor pieces.

| 35 | ♘c1 | ... |

Forced. Not 35 ♔d2? ♕a1! 36 ♔c2 bxa4, etc.

| 35 | ... | ♕g2+ |

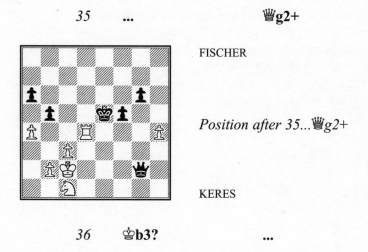

FISCHER

Position after 35...♕g2+

KERES

| 36 | ♔b3? | ... |

In time pressure, Keres creates new losing chances for himself. Also bad is 36 ♔b1 bxa4 37 ♖xa4 ♕f1 38 ♔c2 ♔f6! followed by ...f4 (if 39 ♘d3? ♕e2+).

The right defense is 36 ♔d1! bxa4 (not 36...♕xb2?? 37 ♘d3+) 37 ♘d3+ ♔f6 38 ♖xa4 a5 39 ♖d4 (not 39 ♖xa5? ♕g4+ and ...♕xh4) and Black can't make any headway.

| 36 | ... | bxa4+ |
| 37 | ♔a3 | ... |

On 37 ♖xa4 (if 37 ♔xa4 ♕c2+ 38 ♘b3 ♕xb2) 37...♕d2! 38 ♘a2 f4 is deadly.

| 37 | ... | ♕c2 |
| 38 | ♘d3+ | ♔f6 |

39	♘c5	♛c1!

Threatening ...♛a1+.

40	♖xa4	...

40 ♘xa4 f4 41 ♘c5 f3 42 ♘d3 ♛e3 transposes into the note after White's 41st move.

40	...	♛e3

The game was adjourned and Keres sealed his move.

FISCHER

Position after 40...♛e3

KERES

41	♘xa6?	...

This makes it easy.

I had expected *41 ♖d4 f4 42 ♘d3 f3*. The win is hard, but eventually Black breaks through on a3. For example, *43 ♔b3 (43 b4? f2 wins) 43...♔g7 44 ♔a3 ♛e2 45 ♔b3 ♛d1+ 46 ♔c4* (if *46 ♔a3 a5 47 ♔a2 a4 48 ♘f2 ♛b3+ 49 ♔a1 a3*, etc.) *46...a5 47 ♔b5 a4 48 ♔a5 ♛b3 49 ♔a6 a3 50 bxa3 ♛xa3+ 51 ♔b5 ♛xc3*, etc. Maybe White can improve, but Black should win because the blockade is not airtight.

41	...	f4
42	♖d4	♔f5!

The move Keres missed when he sealed his forty-first. He had probably anticipated *42...f3 43 ♘c5 f2 44 ♘e4+ ♛xe4 45 ♖xe4 f1=♛* with a dead draw since Black can't create another passed Pawn.

| 43 | ♘b4 | ... |

More resistance could have been offered by *43* ♘c5 but it's still lost after *43...*♕e7! *44* b4 ♕xh4 *45* b5 ♕f6, etc.

| 43 | ... | ♕e7! |

This temporary pin is decisive. Now Black wins the h-Pawn and his two passed Pawns become irresistible.

44	♔b3	♕xh4
45	♘d3	g5
46	c4	♕g3
47	c5	f3
48	♔c4	f2
49	♘xf2	♕xf2
50	c6	♕xb2
51	♔c5	♕c3+

FISCHER

Position after 51...♕c3+

KERES

| 52 | ♔d5 | ... |

On *52* ♖c4 ♕a5+ *53* ♔d4 ♕c7 wins.

| 52 | ... | g4 |
| 53 | ♖c4 | ♕e5 mate |

15 Smyslov *[U.S.S.R.]* - Fischer

CANDIDATES' TOURNAMENT 1959

SICILIAN DEFENSE

A whopper

Here is Fischer's first win against Vassily Smyslov; and it is hard to recall when the former world champion, conducting White, has been so badly outplayed.

On move 13 of a crucial opening variation, Smyslov makes what appears to be a "lapsus manus." Rather than fight a prolonged uphill positional battle, he sacrifices a Pawn to try to regain the initiative. This proves to be a piece of bad judgment, since, basically, the loss of this Pawn alone brings about his demise. Defending with deadly precision, Fischer gradually consolidates — the shadow of his Pawn looming larger with each approach to the endgame. Smyslov thrashes about, striving desperately for complications, avoiding exchanges like the plague. But he is unable to get off the hook.

1	e4	c5
2	♘f3	d6
3	d4	cxd4
4	♘xd4	♘f6
5	♘c3	a6
6	♗g5	...

For *6 ♗e2* see games 4 and 42. For *6 ♗c4* see games 17, 55, 58.

6	...	e6
7	f4	♗e7
8	♕f3	♕c7
9	0-0-0	♘bd7

Weak is *9...h6 10 ♗h4 ♘bd7 11 ♗d3 b5 12 e5! ♗b7 13 ♘xe6! fxe6 14 ♗g6+ ♔f8 15 exf6 ♗xf3 (better is 15...♘xf6) 16 fxe7+ ♔g8 17 gxf3 ♘f6 18 ♗xf6 gxf6 19 e8=♕+ ♖xe8 20 ♗xe8 d5* (Gligorich-Bobotsov, Hastings 1959-60); *21 f5! (MCO)* wins.

| 10 | g4 | b5 |
| 11 | ♗xf6 | ♘xf6 |

For *11*...gxf6 see game 12.

| 12 | g5 | ♘d7 |

FISCHER

Position after 12...♘d7

SMYSLOV

| 13 | ♗h3? | ... |

Innovation or omission? In either case, after this move White throws away his theoretical advantage and even loses the initiative. Necessary is *13* a3 ♗b7 (*13*...♖b8! is in vogue) and now there are two main lines:

A] *14* h4 d5 *15* exd5 ♘b6 *16* f5 ♘xd5 *17* fxe6 0-0-0 *18* ♗g2 ♘xc3 *19* ♕xb7+ ♕xb7 *20* ♗xb7+ ♔xb7 *21* bxc3 ♗xa3+ *22* ♔b1 fxe6 *23* ♘xe6 ♖c8 *24* ♖h3 g6 *25* c4 ♖he8 and shortly drawn. (Sherwin-Fischer, US Championship 1959-60.)

B] *14* ♗h3 0-0-0 *15* f5!? (interesting is *15* ♗xe6!? fxe6 *16* ♘xe6 ♕c4 [Keres recommends *16*...♕b6] *17* ♘d5 with unclear complications, though White won, Tal-Gligorich, Moscow 1963) *15*...♗xg5+ *16* ♔b1 e5 *17* ♘dxb5 axb5 *18* ♘xb5 ♕b6! (better than *18*...♕c5 which I played against Gligorich at the Candidates' 1959) *19* ♘xd6+ ♔c7 *20* ♘xf7 ♗f6 is roughly equal.

| 13 | ... | b4! |

My game with Walther (game 9) had taught me this lesson well.

| 14 | ♘ce2 | ♗b7 |
| 15 | ♔b1? | ... |

In this sharp variation, White has no time for such amenities. *15 ♘g3* avoids incurring any severe disadvantage, while the speculative *15 ♗xe6!? fxe6 16 ♘xe6 ♛c4 17 ♘xg7+* (better is *17 ♘2d4*) *17...♚f8!* favors Black.

| | 15 | ... | ♘c5 |
| | 16 | ♘g3 | d5! |

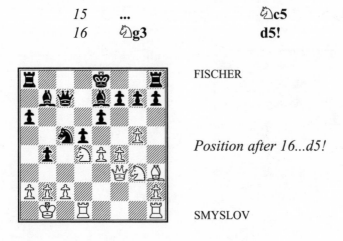

FISCHER

Position after 16...d5!

SMYSLOV

I could see from the expression on Smyslov's face that he already thought he was busted.

| | 17 | f5!? | ... |

On *17 e5 g6! 18 ♖c1 ♛b6!* and if *19 c3 a5* followed by ...0-0 with a powerful attack in the works. Smyslov's keen positional judgment tells him that such a course for White is lifeless. So he sacs a Pawn instead.

	17	...	dxe4
	18	♛g4	exf5
	19	♘dxf5	g6!

Perhaps this simple retort escaped him. Was he hoping for *19...0-0? 20 ♘h5! g6 21 ♛g3!* winning material (if *21...♗d8 22 ♖xd8! ♛xd8 23 ♘f6+,* etc.)? The rest of the game is, if one may use that hackneyed phrase, "a matter of technique." Black's a Pawn ahead with the better game to boot.

| | 20 | ♘xe7 | ... |

Not *20 ♘h6? ♗c8 21 ♛h4 ♗xh3 22 ♛xh3 ♗xg5.*

20	...	♛xe7
21	♕f4	0-0
22	♖d6	♖ad8
23	♖f6	...

Naturally Smyslov avoids swapping.

23	...	♖d5
24	♗g4	♘d7
25	♖f1	...

A desperate attempt to complicate. On *25 ♘xe4? ♖d4 26 ♗xd7 ♕xd7* wins a piece. Or *25 ♕xe4 ♖d1+! 26 ♖xd1 ♗xe4 27 ♖xd7 ♛e5.*

| 25 | ... | e3 |

Not *25...♘xf6? 26* gxf6 ♕e5 *27* ♕h6 wins.

| 26 | b3 | ♖d2 |

Threatening *27...♘xf6 28* gxf6 ♕c5! *29* ♖c1 ♕d4. To avert further material loss, Smyslov is forced to indulge in the simplifications he has been trying so hard to forestall.

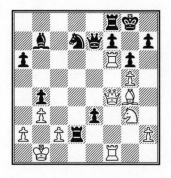

FISCHER

Position after 26...♖d2

SMYSLOV

| 27 | ♗xd7 | ... |

Forced, but now White's game rapidly deteriorates and the extra Pawn makes its presence felt.

| 27 | ... | ♖xd7 |

28	♖e1	♖e8
29	h4	♕c5!
30	♕c4	...

Horrible, but necessary, to meet the main threat of ...♕c3.

| 30 | ... | ♕xc4 |
| 31 | bxc4 | ♖d4 |

Now Black hacks away unmercifully.

32	c5	♖xh4
33	c6	♗c8
34	♖d6	♖c4
35	♔b2	♔g7
36	♔b3	♖g4
37	♘e2	♖e6!
38	♖ed1	...

Or *38* ♖xe6 ♗xe6+ *39* ♔b2 ♖c4, etc.

38	...	♖g2
39	♘f4	♖xd6
40	♖xd6	♖d2
41	♖d3	...

The only move. Smyslov might have resigned had we adjourned here. But we were both playing fast and, as a consequence, were still well in the first session, carried by sheer momentum.

| 41 | ... | ♖f2 |
| 42 | ♖d4 | ... |

Again forced. On *42* ♘d5 e2 *43* ♖e3 ♖f3 wins.

42	...	e2
43	♘d3	♗f5
44	c7	♖f3

Quicker is *44*...♗xd3 *45* c8=♕ e1=♕ *46* ♖xd3 ♕b1+ *47* ♔a4 ♖xc2, etc.

45	c8=♕	♗xc8

Again *45*...e1=♕ was quicker, but I wanted to avoid "complications."

46	♖e4	♗f5
47	♖xe2	♗xd3
48	cxd3	♖xd3+
49	♔xb4	♖d5
50	♖g2	h6
51	gxh6+	♔xh6
52	a4	g5
53	♖c2	♖d6
54	♔c5	♖e6
	White resigns	

FISCHER

Final Position after 54...♖e6

SMYSLOV

16 Fischer - Petrosian [U.S.S.R.]

CANDIDATES' TOURNAMENT 1959

CARO-KANN DEFENSE

Four Queens

Fischer extracted a slight minus score from the seven games in which he was called upon to face the Caro-Kann, prompting Botvinnik to note: "Fischer's both strong and weak point lies in that he is always true to himself and plays the same way regardless of his partners or any external factor."

This variation is not only complex and critical – but perilous. After a single slip the edge passes to Black. But Petrosian overestimates his position and, somewhat recklessly, dissipates his advantage. In time-pressure he misses a forced draw and Fischer regains the upper hand. From this point on, with four marauding Queens roaming the board, the play becomes "rich and strange" – resulting in a tortuous draw.

1	e4	c6
2	♘c3	d5
3	♘f3	...

The purpose of this line is to exclude the possibility of ...♗f5. For example, 3...dxe4 4 ♘xe4 ♗f5? 5 ♘g3 ♗g6 (if 5...♗g4 6 h3) 6 h4 h6 7 ♘e5 ♗h7 8 ♕h5 g6 9 ♗c4! e6 10 ♕e2 (threatening ♘xf7) and Black has a terrible game.

| 3 | ... | ♗g4 |

3...♘f6 4 e5 ♘e4 5 ♘e2! ♕b6 6 d4 c5 7 dxc5 ♕xc5 8 ♘ed4 ♘c6 9 ♗b5 a6 10 ♗xc6+ bxc6 11 0-0 ♕b6 12 e6! fxe6 13 ♗f4 is good for White. (Fischer-Olafsson, Candidates' 1959.)

| 4 | h3 | ♗xf3 |

In our first round game here, Smyslov played 4...♗h5 5 exd5 cxd5 6 ♗b5+ ♘c6 7 g4 ♗g6 8 ♘e5 ♖c8 9 d4 e6 10 h4 (correct is 10 ♕e2!

to prevent ...f6) *10*...f6 *11* ♘xg6 hxg6 *12* ♕d3 ♔f7 *13* h5 gxh5 *14* gxh5 ♘ge7=.

5	♕xf3	♘f6

The old *5*...e6 *6* d4 dxe4 *7* ♘xe4 ♕xd4 *8* ♗d3 gives White a good attack for the Pawn. And on *5*...dxe4 *6* ♘xe4 ♘d7 *7* ♘g5!? (better is simply *7* d4) *7*...♘gf6 *8* ♕b3 e6 *9* ♕xb7 ♘d5! Black gets good play. (Fischer-Cardoso, Portoroz 1958.)

PETROSIAN

Position after 5...♘f6

FISCHER

Inferior is *6* d4 dxe4 *7* ♘xe4!? (*7* ♕e3 ♘bd7 *8* ♘xe4 ♘xe4 *9* ♕xe4 ♘f6 *10* ♕d3 ♕d5! is equal, Fischer-Keres, Bled 1961) *7*...♕xd4 *8* ♗d3 ♘bd7 threatening ...♘e5.

On *6* e5 ♘fd7 *7* e6? (playable is *7* ♕g3 e6 *8* ♗e2 Spassky-Reshko, Leningrad 1961) *7*...fxe6 *8* d4 e5!

Finally on *6* g3 dxe4 *7* ♘xe4 ♘xe4 *8* ♕xe4 ♕d5! *9* ♕xd5 cxd5 *10* ♗g2 e6 (if *11* c4 ♘c6 *12* cxd5 ♘b4!) gives Black an even ending (SUETIN).

6	d3	e6
7	g3	...

A recent try is *7* ♗d2 followed by 0-0-0. Against Larsen, at Zurich 1959, I tried *7* a3 ♗c5 *8* ♗e2 0-0 *9* 0-0 ♘bd7 and Black got a satisfactory game.

7	...	♗b4
8	♗d2	...

Not *8* ♗g2? d4 *9* a3 ♕a5.

| 8 | ... | **d4** |

Inferior is *8...*♕b6 *9* 0-0-0 d4 *10* ♘e2.

| 9 | **♘b1** | **♗xd2+** |

In this tournament Keres and Benko both tried *9...*♕b6 forcing White to weaken the Q-side with *10* b3. But Black's Queen is slightly misplaced after *10...*♘bd7 *11* ♗g2 a5 *12* a3 ♗xd2+ (the retreat *12...*♗e7 seems illogical – even though Keres beat me with it) *13* ♘xd2 ♕c5 *14* ♕d1 h5 *15* h4! with an edge. (Fischer-Benko.) Petrosian apparently didn't want to get involved with this line despite the fact that his countryman, Tal, accused me of "bad judgment" for preferring White here.

10	**♘xd2**	**e5**
11	**♗g2**	**c5**
12	**0-0**	**♘c6**
13	**♕e2**	**...**

PETROSIAN

Position after 13 ♕e2

FISCHER

The critical juncture. In our earlier game (round two) Petrosian continued with *13...*g5 *14* ♘f3? (Simagin gives *14* f4 gxf4 *15* gxf4 ♕e7 *16* ♘c4 ♘d7 *17* ♕g4 "with advantage" but after *17...*0-0-0 *18* fxe5 ♔b8 Black succeeds in planting his Knight on e5 where it cannot be dislodged) *14...*h6 *15* h4 ♖g8 *16* a3 ♕e7 *17* hxg5 hxg5 *18* ♕d2 ♘d7 *19* c3 0-0-0 *20* cxd4 exd4 with advantage for Black.

| 13 | ... | **♕e7** |

Fearing a prepared line, Petrosian deviates.

On *13...g5* I had intended *14* c3! ♛e7 *15* ♘f3 h6 *16* cxd4! exd4 (if *16...*♘xd4 *17* ♘xd4 cxd4 *18* ♖ac1. Or *16...*cxd4 *17* h4 ♖g8 *18* hxg5 hxg5 *19* ♖fc1 0-0-0 *20* b4! ♚b8 *21* b5 ♘a5 *22* ♛d2 wins a Pawn) *17* e5! 0-0-0 *18* ♖fe1. Now the Bishop diagonal is unblocked and Black can't set up a blockade on his e5, as in our first game.

After *13...*0-0 *14* f4 ♚h8 *15* f5 ♘g8 *16* g4 f6 White has a tough nut to crack, but his initiative is permanent. The text indicates Petrosian's intention to castle long without trying to prevent f4.

14	**f4**	**0-0-0**
15	**a3**	**♘e8**

Also playable is *15...*♘d7 *16* b4 f6 and if *17* ♘c4 b5.

16	**b4**	**cxb4**

Wide open! Safer is *16...*f6 *17* b5 (if *17* bxc5 ♛xc5 *18* fxe5 ♘xe5) *17...*♘a5 *18* ♘b3 ♘xb3 *19* cxb3 ♚b8 *20* a4=.

PETROSIAN

Position after 16...cxb4

FISCHER

17	**♘c4?**	...

Now Black has time to consolidate. Correct is *17* fxe5! with advantage in all variations:

A] *17...*♛xe5 *18* ♖xf7 ♛xg3 *19* e5! ♛e3+ *20* ♛xe3 dxe3 *21* ♘c4.

B] *17...*bxa3 *18* ♘c4 ♖f8 *19* ♖xa3 (if *19...*b5 *20* ♛g4+!).

C] *17...*♘xe5 *18* axb4 ♚b8 *19* ♘f3 f6 *20* ♛f2! ♘xf3+ (if *20...*♛xb4 *21* ♘xe5 fxe5 *22* ♛f7 penetrates) *21* ♛xf3 ♘d6 (if *21...*♛xb4 *22* e5!) *22* ♖a5 a6 *23* ♛f4 ♖he8 *24* ♖d5.

D] *17...♔b8 18* axb4 ♘xb4 (*18...♘xe5 19* ♘f3 transposes to "C")
19 ♘c4 ♘c6 (if *19...♘c7 20* ♘d6! ♖hf8 *21* ♖fb1 ♘ca6 *22* ♕d2 ♕xe5
23 ♘xb7! ♔xb7 *24* ♖xa6! wins) *20* ♕f3 ♖f8 *21* e6! ♕xe6 *22* e5!
followed by ♖fb1 and White has a winning attack.

17   ...   **f6!**

I had expected *17...bxa3 18* fxe5 transposing to "B" above.

18	**fxe5**	**fxe5**
19	**axb4**	**♘c7**

Black wants to secure a Q-side blockade. The b-Pawn won't run
away.

20   **♘a5**   **♘b5!**

I already knew I'd been outplayed. Petrosian didn't even consider
20...♘xb4, opening up the lines.

21	**♘xc6**	**bxc6**
22	**♖f2**	**g6**

On *22...♕xb4? 23* ♕g4+ ♖d7 *24* ♖f7 ♖hd8 *25* ♕xg7 regains the
Pawn.

23   **h4**   **♔b7**

Ordinarily one would expect Petrosian to simplify and simplify in
order to reach a winning ending. *23...♖hf8!* is strong.

24   **h5**   **♕xb4**

Really risky! I was amazed he was allowing so much counterplay.
24...♖hf8 is still right. On *24...gxh5 25* ♕xh5 ♖hf8 *26* ♖f5!

25   **♖f7+**   **♔b6**

On *25...♔b8 26* ♕f2 ♖hf8 *27* c4! ♘c7 (if *27...dxc3 e.p.? 28* ♖axa7!
♖xf7 *29* ♕b6+) *28* ♕f6 with good play.

26	♛f2!	a5

Not *26...♖hf8? 27 c4! ♞c3 28 ♖axa7* wins.

27	c4	♞c3?

Continuing to underestimate the danger. Safer is *27...♞d6*.

PETROSIAN

Position after 27...♞c3?

FISCHER

28	♖f1?	...

Why didn't I play *28 ♛f6!* immediately? If then *28...♖df8 (28...♖hf8 29 ♖f1! ♖xf7 30 ♛xd8+! ♖c7 31 ♖f7* wins) *29 ♛xe5 ♖xf7 30 ♛xh8 ♛c5 31 e5* – it's difficult for Black in view of his exposed King and White's passed e-Pawn.

Finally, after *28 ♛f6! ♛c5 29 ♛g7! ♔a6* (if *29...a4 30 ♖a7!* or *29...♖a8 30 ♖b7+ ♔a6 31 ♛c7! ♖hc8 32 ♖b5!* wins. Or *29...♖dg8 30 ♖b7+ ♔a6 31 ♛c7 ♖c8 32 ♖xa5+!) 30 ♖a7+! ♛xa7 31 ♖xa5+ ♔xa5 32 ♛xa7+ ♔b4 33 ♛b6+ ♔a3 34 c5!* and White's c-Pawn is dangerous.

28	...	a4

Still playing with reckless abandon! Safer is *28...♛d6* to prevent ♛f6.

29	♛f6	♛c5
30	♖xh7!	...

Now I decided to start playing for the win. On *30 ♛g7 ♖dg8! 31 ♖b7+ ♔a6 32 ♛c7 ♖c8! 33 ♛g7 ♖cg8!* draws by a "perpetual check" on the Queen.

| 30 | ... | ♖df8! |

Forcing what looks like a favorable ending.

31	♕xg6	♖xf1+
32	♗xf1	♖xh7
33	♕xh7	a3

Petrosian had been banking on the speed of this Pawn.

34	h6	a2
35	♕g8	a1=♕
36	h7	...

PETROSIAN

Position after 36 h7

FISCHER

| 36 | ... | ♕d6? |

In time-pressure, Petrosian overlooks *36...♘e2+ 37 ♔f2 ♘xg3!* and White has nothing better than to take a perpetual with *38 ♕b8+*.

| 37 | h8=♕ | ♕a7 |
| 38 | g4 | ♔c5! |

A good last-ditch try. Curiously, the King will be safer in White's territory where it obtains shelter from the cluster of Pawns.

| 39 | ♕f8? | ... |

Right is *39 ♕h2!* immediately, preventing Black's King from reaching safety behind the lines. If then *39...♕f6 40 g5*. Or *39...♕a1 (39...♕a2? 40 ♕xa2 ♘xa2 41 ♕a8! wins a piece) 40 ♕g7* wins the e-Pawn. Finally on *39...♕ae7 40 ♕a8* renews the attack.

| 39 | ... | ♕ae7 |

Forced, to defend against the threat of ♕xe5+.

Not *39*...♕xf8 *40* ♕xf8+ ♔b6 *41* ♕b4+ ♔a6 (if *41*...♔c7 *42* ♕e7+) *42* ♕a3+ ♔b7 *43* ♕xa7+ ♔xa7 *44* g5 and queens.

| 40 | ♕a8 | ... |

I thought this was it! The two Queens are closing in for the kill.

| 40 | ... | ♔b4! |
| 41 | ♕h2 | ♔b3! |

Slippery as an eel!

PETROSIAN

Position after 41...♔b3!

FISCHER

Now White sealed. It's fantastically complicated!

The tournament bulletins suggest *42* c5 ♕xc5 (if *42*...♕g6 *43* ♗e2! ♕gg5 *44* ♗d1+!) *43* ♕g8+ ♔a3 *44* ♕c2 ♕b4 *45* ♕a8+ ♕a4 (not *45*...♘a4? *46* ♕c1+ ♔a2 *47* ♕g8+ ♕b3 *48* ♕c2+! wins) *46* ♕cxa4+ ♘xa4 *47* ♕xc6 "with good winning chances," but after *47*...♘c3 it's likely Black can draw.

| 42 | ♕a1 | ... |

After the game a kibitzer asked Petrosian if he thought *42* c5 would have won for White. Petrosian, who must have analyzed it for many hours (not knowing, of course, what my sealed move was), simply replied: "I don't know."

| 42 | ... | ♕a3 |

The only move to stop mate on b2.

43	♕xa3+	♚xa3
44	♕h6	...

Now White has to try to make do with the g-Pawn.

44	...	♕f7!
45	♔g2	...

On *45* ♕xc6 ♘d1!

45	...	♚b3

Not *45...*♘d1 *46* ♕c1+ ♘b2 and the Knight is stranded out-of-play. The text renews the threat of ...♘d1.

46	♕d2	♕h7!
47	♔g3	...

A gross oversight, but probably best anyway! White can't win anymore. If *47* g5 ♕h4, etc.

47	...	♕xe4!

PETROSIAN

Position after 47...♕xe4!

FISCHER

48	♕f2?	...

Having overlooked Petrosian's last move, I was somewhat shaken! Not *48* dxe4? ♘xe4+ *49* ♔h4 ♘xd2 *50* g5 ♘xf1 *51* g6 d3 wins. Also on *48* ♕d1+? (*48* ♕xc3+? dxc3 *49* dxe4 c2 wins) *48...*♘xd1 *49* dxe4 ♘e3 *50* ♗e2 ♘xc4 *51* g5 ♘d6 *52* g6 ♘e8 and Black again wins.

The right retort, however, is *48* g5! and it's still a hard fight.

48   ...   ♕h1!

I offered a draw, afraid that he wouldn't accept. Black certainly has the edge now. If *49* g5 e4! Or if *49* ♗g2 ♕h6.

After having fought so hard for the draw, however, Petrosian was obviously unprepared to readjust his frame of mind and start playing for a win. So...

Drawn

17 Fischer - Tal [U.S.S.R.]

CANDIDATES' TOURNAMENT 1959

SICILIAN DEFENSE

A very near miss

This is one of the four games that Fischer lost to Tal who, in winning this tournament, earned the right to meet and trounce Botvinnik for the world championship.

In jest the whimsical Tal signed Fischer's name, in addition to his own, when asked for an autograph. "Why not?" he quipped; "I've beaten Bobby so often ... that gives me the right to sign for him!"

A careful reading of Fischer's notes will reveal a clear echo of the strong emotions that engulfed him during this tense encounter. He misses a win in the opening and several draws along the way, demonstrating dramatically how a continuously advantageous position can abruptly be turned into defeat by seemingly insignificant miscalculations.

1	e4	c5
2	♘f3	d6
3	d4	cxd4
4	♘xd4	♘f6
5	♘c3	a6
6	♗c4	...

We had some excellent results with this. See also games 55 and 58.

6	...	e6
7	♗b3	...

I had no better luck against Blackstone, in an exhibition game at Davis, California, 1964, with *7* 0-0 ♗e7 *8* ♗b3 ♕c7 *9* f4 b5 *10* f5 b4 *11* fxe6!? (*11* ♘ce2 e5 *12* ♘f3 ♗b7 is bad for White) *11*...bxc3 *12* exf7+ ♔f8 *13* ♗g5 ♘g4! and Black should win.

| 7 | ... | b5! |

This reaction must be prompt!

In our first lap game here Tal played the weaker 7...♗e7? *8* f4 0-0 (for *8*...b5 see the note to Black's 8th move) *9* ♕f3 ♕c7 and now *10* f5! (instead of *10* 0-0? b5 *11* f5 b4! *12* ♘a4 e5 *13* ♘e2 ♗b7 and Black stands better) *10*...e5 (not *10*...♘c6 *11* ♗e3 with a bind) *11* ♘de2 b5 *12* a3 ♗b7 *13* g4 with a strong attack.

8	**f4!?**	...

Against Olafsson, at Buenos Aires 1960, I continued *8* 0-0 ♗e7 (if *8*...b4 *9* ♘a4 ♘xe4 *10* ♖e1 ♘f6 *11* ♗g5 with attack) *9* ♕f3!? ♕c7 (not *9*...♗b7? *10* ♗xe6!) *10* ♕g3 b4 *11* ♘ce2 g6 *12* c3? (*12* ♗h6! is very strong) *12*...♘xe4 *13* ♕e3 ♘f6 *14* cxb4 0-0= with a double-edged position.

R.Byrne-Evans, US Championship 1967 went *8* ♕f3, but White got nothing after *8*...♗b7 *9* ♗g5 b4 *10* ♘a4 ♘bd7 *11* 0-0 ♕a5 *12* ♗xf6 ♘xf6 *13* ♖fe1 ♗e7.

8	...	**b4!**

Indirectly undermining White's center.

9	**♘a4**	**♘xe4**

9...♗b7 is also playable.

10	**0-0**	**g6?**

Correct is *10*...♗b7.

11	**f5!**	...

This riposte caught Tal completely unaware. Black's King, trapped in the center, will soon be subject to mayhem.

11	...	**gxf5**

Not *11*...exf5 *12* ♗d5 ♖a7 *13* ♘xf5! gxf5 *14* ♕d4.

12	**♘xf5!**	...

Panov, with typical iron curtain "objectivity" commented in the Soviet tournament bulletins: "Almost all game Fischer played in Tal style. But all his trouble was in vain because Tal did not defend in Fischer style – instead he found the one and only saving counterchance!"

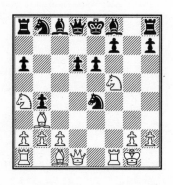

TAL

Position after 12 ♘xf5!

FISCHER

| 12 | ... | ♖g8 |

Woozy, Tal stumbles into a dubious defense. Better is *12...d5* (not *12...exf5?* *13* ♕d5 ♖a7 *14* ♕d4 spearing a Rook) *13* ♘h6 ♗xh6 *14* ♗xh6.

| 13 | ♗d5! | ... |

A shot!

| 13 | ... | ♖a7 |

"*13...exd5 14* ♕xd5 ♗xf5 *15* ♖xf5 ♖a7 *16* ♕xe4+ ♖e7 *17* ♕xb4 ♖e2 *18* ♗g5! ♖xg5 *19* ♖xg5 ♕xg5 *20* ♕xb8+ wins." (PANOV.)

| 14 | ♗xe4? | ... |

Correct is *14* ♗e3! ♘c5 *15* ♕h5! ♖g6 (if *15...*♘xa4 *16* ♗xa7 exd5 *17* ♖ae1+) *16* ♖ae1! and White's every piece is bearing down on Black's King (KEVITZ).

| 14 | ... | exf5 |
| 15 | ♗xf5 | ... |

Probably it's better to avoid exchanges with *15* ♗d5 or *15* ♗f3.

| 15 | ... | ♖e7! |

A unique way of shielding the e-file.

16	♗xc8	♛xc8
17	♗f4?	...

The right move is simply *17* c3! (not *17* ♛xd6? ♖xg2+ *18* ♔xg2 ♖e2+ *19* ♔f3 ♗xd6 *20* ♔xe2 ♛xc2+ wins) and if *17*...♛c6 *18* ♖f2.

17	...	♛c6!
18	♛f3	♛xa4!

Such a surprise that I didn't dare believe my eyes! I had expected *18*...♛xf3 *19* ♖xf3 ♖e2 *20* ♖f2 ♖xf2 *21* ♔xf2 and White has a slight edge after a3 because of Black's disconnected Pawns.

19	♗xd6	♛c6!

Tal finds an inspired defense.

20	♗xb8	♛b6+

White remains a clear Pawn ahead after *20*...♛xf3 *21* ♖xf3 ♗g7 *22* c3.

21	♔h1	♛xb8

TAL

Position after 21...♛xb8

FISCHER

The crowd was shouting and whistling with each move. Later I was informed that many sport fans were in the audience. Maybe some soccer match had been canceled. As a consequence chess was the main attraction that day in Belgrade.

22	♛c6+	...

Many annotators believed that *22* ♖ae1 was the winning move. Tal himself confessed he thought Black was lost after that. But *22*...♔d8! holds in all lines (not *22*...♖g6? *23* ♛xf7+ ♔d7 *24* ♖d1+! ♖d6 *25* ♖xd6+ ♔xd6 *26* ♖f6+! wins). I've studied this position for ages, it seems, and the best I can find is *23* ♖d1+ ♔c7! *(23...♔c8?* *24* ♕c6+ wins) *24* ♕f4+ (if *24* ♖d4 ♕b7!) *24...♔b7* *25* ♖d6 ♕c7 *26* ♕xb4+ ♔c8 *27* ♖xa6 ♕b7! *28* ♕xb7+ ♔xb7 *29* ♖af6 ♖g7=.

| 22 | ... | ♖d7 |
| 23 | ♖ae1+ | ... |

Black holds after *23* ♖ad1 ♗d6 *24* ♖xf7 (if *24* ♖f6 ♖g6 *25* ♖dxd6? ♕xd6!) *24...♕c7*, etc. And on *23* ♖xf7 ♕d6.

| 23 | ... | ♗e7 |

Finally Tal "develops" his Bishop. Not *23...♔d8* *24* ♖xf7! ♗e7 *25* ♖fxe7 ♖xe7 *26* ♖d1+ wins.

| 24 | ♖xf7 | ♔xf7 |
| 25 | ♕e6+ | ♔f8! |

I thought he had to go to g7, whereupon *26* ♕xd7 wins easily.

TAL

Position after 25...♔f8!

FISCHER

| 26 | ♕xd7 | ... |

Not *26* ♖f1+ ♔g7 *27* ♖f7+ ♔h8 and if *28* ♕xd7 ♖d8 *29* ♕g4 ♕e5 wins.

| 26 | ... | ♕d6 |
| 27 | ♕b7 | ♖g6 |

Within a handful of moves the game has changed its complexion. Now it is White who must fight for the draw!

| 28 | c3! | ... |

Black's extra piece means less with each Pawn that's exchanged.

28   **...**   **a5**

On *28...bxc3 29* ♕c8+ ♗d8 *30* ♕xc3=.

29   ♕**c8+**   **...**

On the wrong track. Right is *29* cxb4! ♕xb4 (if *29...axb4 30* a3! bxa3
31 bxa3 ♕xa3 draws) *30* ♕f3+ ♔g7 *31* ♕e2 draws, since Black can't
possibly build up a winning K-side attack and his own King is too
exposed.

29	**...**	♔**g7**
30	♕**c4**	♗**d8**
31	**cxb4**	**axb4**

On *31...*♕xb4 *32* ♕e2 White should draw with best play.

32   **g3?**   **...**

Creating losing chances. I don't see how Black can make any
progress after *32* ♕e4. If *32...*♗c7 *33* ♕e7+ ♔g8 *34* ♕e8+ ♕f8
35 ♕e4, etc.

32	**...**	♕**c6+**
33	♖**e4**	♕**xc4**
34	♖**xc4**	♖**b6!**

I overlooked this. Now Black has winning chances. I had planned on
a draw after *34...*♗e7? *35* a3! dissolving Black's b-Pawn (*35...*b3 is
answered by *36* ♖c7 followed by ♖b7).

35	♔**g2**	♔**f6**
36	♔**f3**	♔**e5**
37	♔**e3**	**...**

37 a3 is met, as always, by ...b3. Once White can eliminate Black's
b-Pawn it's a theoretical draw.

37	**...**	♗**g5+**
38	♔**e2**	♔**d5**
39	♔**d3**	♗**f6**

White might be able to draw this ending, but it's an ugly defensive
chore.

40   ♖**c2?**   **...**

Too passive. I wanted to avoid immobilizing my Q-side Pawns with *40* b3, but it's the best hope now. On *40...♗e7 41 ♖d4+* preserves drawing chances.

TAL

Position after 40 ♖c2?

FISCHER

40	...	♗e5
41	♖e2	♖f6
42	♖c2	♖f3+
43	♔e2	♖f7
44	♔d3	♗d4!

Little by little Tal inches his way in.

45	a3	...

On *45* b3 ♖f3+ *46* ♔e2 ♖f2+ *47* ♔d3 ♖xc2 *48* ♔xc2 ♔e4 wins.

45	...	b3
46	♖c8	...

Equally hopeless is *46* ♖e2 (or *46* ♖d2 ♖f3+ *47* ♔e2 ♖f2+) *46...*♖f3+ *47* ♔d2 ♗xb2, etc.

46	...	♗xb2
47	♖d8+	♔c6
48	♖b8	♖f3+
49	♔c4	♖c3+
50	♔b4	♔c7
51	♖b5	♗a1
52	a4	b2!
	White resigns	

If *53* ♔xc3 b1=♕+!

The discovered-check theme is strangely reminiscent of the finale of game 31.

18 Spassky *[U.S.S.R.]* - Fischer

KING'S GAMBIT

Old wine in a new bottle

*Here is the second of the three losses contained in this volume.
As in the previous example, Fischer misses a win by inches.
Deviating from his cherished Sicilian, he enables Spassky to employ
the King's Gambit – not quite believing he would. Spassky is one
of the few Grandmasters who still does so in competition.
Fischer promptly wins a Pawn and hangs on to it, but neglects to steer
for a highly favorable ending (23...♕g3). Just four moves later,
27 ♖e5! effects his undoing.*

*Undaunted by this early setback, Fischer scored 12½ out of his
last 13, pulling neck and neck with Spassky for first.*

1	e4	e5
2	f4	exf4
3	♘f3	g5

This loss spurred me to look for a "refutation" of the King's Gambit,
which I published in the *American Chess Quarterly*, Vol. 1 (1961),
No. 1. The right move is *3...d6!*

4	h4	...

The only realistic try for any advantage. There is no longer anything
"romantic" about the Muzio Gambit, which has been analyzed to a
draw after *4 ♗c4 g4 5 0-0 (if 5 ♘e5 ♕h4+ 6 ♔f1 ♘c6!) 5...gxf3
6 ♕xf3 ♕f6*, etc.

4	...	g4
5	♘e5	♘f6

On *5...h5 6 ♗c4 ♖h7 7 d4 d6 8 ♘d3 f3 9 gxf3 ♗e7 10 ♗e3 ♗xh4+
11 ♔d2 ♗g5 12 f4 ♗h6 13 ♘c3* White has more than enough
compensation for the Pawn. This is vintage analysis.

6	**d4**	...

On *6* ♗c4 d5 *7* exd5 ♗g7 (the old *7*...♗d6 is also adequate) is the modern panacea. And on *6* ♘xg4 ♘xe4 *7* d3 ♘g3 *8* ♗xf4 ♘xh1 *9* ♕e2+ (*9* ♗g5 ♗e7 *10* ♕e2 h5 *11* ♕e5 f6! *12* ♘xf6+ ♔f7 wins – Steinitz) *9*...♕e7 *10* ♘f6+ ♔d8 *11* ♗xc7+ ♔xc7 *12* ♘d5+ ♔d8 *13* ♘xe7 ♗xe7 and Black should win. Morphy-Anderssen, Paris 1858.

6	...	**d6**
7	**♘d3**	**♘xe4**
8	**♗xf4**	**♗g7**

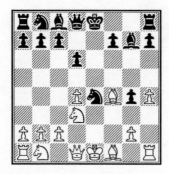

FISCHER

Position after 8...♗g7

SPASSKY

9	**♘c3?**	...

After this White has no compensation for the Pawn. Better is *9* c3 ♕e7 *10* ♕e2 ♗f5. At least White keeps a grip on his f4 – for what that's worth.

9	...	**♘xc3**
10	**bxc3**	**c5**

Immediately nibbling at White's center. Keres gives *10*...0-0 first.

11	**♗e2**	...

On *11* ♕e2+ ♗e6 (*12* d5? ♗xc3+).

11	...	**cxd4**
12	**0-0**	**♘c6**

It doesn't pay to be greedy with *12*...h5. After *13* ♗g5 f6 *14* ♗c1 followed by ♘f4 Black's K-side is all messed up.

13	♗xg4	0-0
14	♗xc8	♖xc8
15	♕g4	f5

Winning a second Pawn, but creating a K-side weakness. Simply *15*...♔h8 is stronger.

| 16 | ♕g3 | dxc3 |
| 17 | ♖ae1 | ... |

Black snatches the initiative after *17* ♗xd6 ♖f6 *18* ♗f4 ♖g6.

| 17 | ... | ♔h8 |

Also good is *17*...♕d7 *18* ♗xd6 ♖fe8 and if *19* ♘c5 ♕f7 (KMOCH).

| 18 | ♔h1? | ... |

More accurate is *18* ♗xd6 ♖f6 (if *18*...♖g8 *19* ♘e5!) *19* ♗e5 ♘xe5 *20* ♘xe5 with a little play left for White.

| 18 | ... | ♖g8 |

On *18*...d5 *19* ♘c5 creates problems.

| 19 | ♗xd6 | ♗f8! |

The key! On *19*...♗d4 *20* ♕h2 ♖g4 *21* ♗e5+! (to prevent Black from doubling Rooks on the g-file), *21*...♔g8 (if *21*...♗xe5 *22* ♘xe5 ♖xh4? *23* ♘f7+) *22* ♗g3 holds.

| 20 | ♗e5+ | ♘xe5 |
| 21 | ♕xe5+ | ♖g7! |

Now White's h-Pawn must fall.

| 22 | ♖xf5 | ... |

What else? On *22* ♕xf5 (not *22* ♖f4? ♗d6 or *22* ♕f4? ♖g4) *22*...♕xh4+ *23* ♔g1 ♕g4 forces a favorable exchange of Queens (if *24* ♕f2 ♗d6 produces a strong attack).

	22	...	♕xh4+
	23	♔g1	...

FISCHER

Position after 23 ♔g1

SPASSKY

	23	...	♕g4?

Drifting. Not realizing the danger, I thought Black could whip up an attack along the g-file. But correct is *23*...♕g3! *24* ♕xg3 (if *24* ♕e2 ♗d6) *24*...♖xg3 (threatening *25*...♖xd3 followed by ...c2) and White, a Pawn down, has a tough ending to hold – as Spassky pointed out in our post-mortem analysis.

	24	♖f2	♗e7

Threatening ...♗h4.

	25	♖e4	♕g5

I started to feel uncomfortable, but little did I imagine that Black's game would collapse in four short moves! I should have taken a draw by repetition with *25*...♕d1+ *26* ♖e1 ♕g4 *27* ♖e4 ♕d1+, etc. And if *28* ♔h2 ♖c6 *29* ♕b8+ ♖g8 *30* ♕e5+ ♖g7.

	26	♕d4!	...

This powerful centralization completely paralyzes Black.

26   ...   ♖f8?

Overlooking White's real threat. I was worried about ♘e5, not realizing it could be met successfully with ...♗c5. The right defense is 26...♗f8! 27 ♕xa7 (if 27 ♘e5 ♗c5 28 ♘f7+ ♔g8 29 ♘xg5 ♗xd4 30 ♖xd4 ♖xg5) 27...♗d6=.

27   ♖e5!   ...

I had reckoned on 27 ♘e5? ♖xf2 28 ♕xf2 ♗c5! 29 ♕xc5 ♕xg2 mate.

FISCHER

Position after 27 ♖e5!

SPASSKY

Incredibly, Black must lose a piece. While trying to figure out what was going on in Spassky's head, I blundered and lost the game!

27   ...   ♖d8

Trying to squirm out! The Queen has no shelter. On 27...♕g6 28 ♖xe7 wins. Or 27...♕h4 28 ♖xf8+. Or 27...♗f6 28 ♕d6!

28   ♕e4   ♕h4

I knew I was losing a piece, but just couldn't believe it. I had to play one more move to see if it was really true!

29   ♖f4   **Black resigns**

On 29...♕g3 30 ♖xe7 is most efficient.

19 Gudmundsson *[Iceland]* - Fischer

REYKJAVIK 1960

GRUENFELD DEFENSE

A long voyage home

Illustrating, rather subtly, how a weaker player may be lured to his own destruction, Fischer entices his opponent to abandon his passive though solid attempts to settle for a draw. Wrongly convinced that he holds an advantage, Gudmundsson, with 16 e4, gives Fischer the opportunity to launch a long, unclear sacrificial combination. Gudmundsson makes matters unexpectedly easy with 24 ♖b1, but the analysis accompanying the text shows the sacrifice to be sound in all variations. Fischer's performance from here on is typical in its clarity and forcefulness.

1	**d4**	**♘f6**
2	**♘f3**	**...**

Solid but passive.

2	**...**	**d5**
3	**e3**	**...**

Voluntarily locking in the Bishop lacks energy and reduces White's options.

3	**...**	**g6**
4	**c4**	**...**

4 c3 would lead to the Colle System.

4	**...**	**♗g7**
5	**♘c3**	**0-0**
6	**♕b3**	**...**

After *6 ♗e2 c5!* it's difficult for White to equalize:
A] *7 0-0?* cxd4 *8 ♘xd4* ♘c6 *9 cxd5* ♘xd5 *10 ♘xd5* ♕xd5 *11 ♗f3*

♕c4 *12* ♘xc6 bxc6 and Black stands better. Aaron-Gligorich, Stockholm 1962.

B] *7* cxd5 ♘xd5 *8* ♕b3 ♘xc3 *9* bxc3 ♕c7 *10* 0-0 b6 *11* a4 ♘c6 again Black's better. Goglidze-Botvinnik, Moscow 1935.

C] *7* dxc5 ♕a5 *8* cxd5 (if *8* 0-0 dxc4 *9* ♗xc4 ♕xc5) *8*...♘xd5 *9* ♕xd5 ♗xc3+ *10* ♗d2 (after *10* ♔f1 ♗g7 *11* ♗d2 ♕c7 Black regains his Pawn at will, with a strong attack) *10*...♖d8! *11* ♗xc3 ♕xc3+ *12* bxc3 ♖xd5 with the superior ending (if *13* ♖d1 ♖xc5 *14* ♖d8+ ♔g7 *15* 0-0 ♘c6 *16* ♖e8 b6).

| 6 | ... | e6 |

Another good build-up is *6*...c6 followed by ...e6, ...b6, ...♗b7, ...♘bd7, ...c5, etc.

| 7 | ♗e2 | ♘c6 |
| 8 | ♕c2 | ... |

Probably best (Black threatened ...♘a5 winning the two Bishops). As Evans pointed out in *Trophy Chess* (in an analogous position): "*8* cxd5 exd5 permits Black to solve the problem of his QB. He has the semi-open e-file and good squares for his pieces. It is now White who must fight for equality!"

8	...	dxc4
9	♗xc4	e5!
10	dxe5	...

Also good is *10* ♘xe5 (if *10* d5? ♘a5) *10*...♘xe5 *11* dxe5 ♘g4 *12* e6! (not *12* f4? ♘xe5! *13* fxe5? ♕h4+ *14* g3 ♕xc4, etc.) *12*...♗xe6 *13* ♗xe6 fxe6 *14* 0-0=.

| 10 | ... | ♘g4 |

FISCHER

Position after 10...♘g4

GUDMUNDSSON

11	**0-0**	**...**

Stronger is *11* e6! ♗xe6 *12* ♗xe6 fxe6 *13* 0-0 (*13* ♕e4? ♘ce5! *14* ♘xe5? ♘xf2! *15* ♕c4 ♗xe5 *16* ♕xe6+ ♖f7 *17* ♕xe5 ♘d3+ wins), and Black seems to have nothing better than a draw by perpetual after *13*...♖xf3 *14* gxf3 ♕h4 *15* fxg4 ♕xg4+ *16* ♔h1 ♕f3+, etc.

11	**...**	**♘cxe5**
12	**♘xe5**	**♘xe5**
13	**♗e2**	**c6**

The chances are now equal.

14	**f4**	**...**

Apparently stronger is *14* e4 but after *14*...♕h4! *15* h3 (if *15* f4 ♘g4) *15*...g5! *16* f4 (or *16* ♘d1 f5 *17* f4 ♘g6 *18* fxg5 f4!) *16*...gxf4 *17* ♗xf4 (on *17* ♖xf4 ♕g3) *17*...♔h8 gives Black good prospects along the ventilated g-file.

14	**...**	**♘g4!**
15	**h3**	**♗f5!**

White was doubtlessly expecting *15*...♘f6 *16* e4 with an ideal center.

FISCHER

Position after 15...♗f5!

GUDMUNDSSON

16	**e4?**	**...**

Provoking a powerful combination.

White should abandon his hopes in the center and settle for *16* ♕b3 ♘f6 *17* ♕xb7 ♘e4! *18* ♕xc6 ♖c8 *19* ♕a6 ♘xc3 *20* bxc3 ♗xc3

21 ♗a3 ♗xa1 22 ♗xf8 ♗d4! 23 exd4 ♛xd4+ 24 ♔h1 ♔xf8. Black is better, but White has excellent drawing chances.

16	...	♛d4+
17	♔h1	♘f2+
18	♖xf2	...

All forced. Not *18 ♔h2 ♘xe4.*

18	...	♛xf2
19	exf5	♗xc3!

This clean-cut line reduces White's options. Inexact would be *19...♖fe8 20 ♘e4! ♛e1+ 21 ♔h2 gxf5 (if 21...♗d4 22 ♗e3! ♛xa1 23 ♗xd4) 22 ♘g3 and if 22...♗d4? 23 ♗e3!*

20	bxc3	♖ae8
21	♗d3	♖e1+
22	♔h2	♛g1+
23	♔g3	♖fe8

Just as complicated is *23...gxf5 24 ♗xf5 ♖fe8 25 ♗xh7+ ♔g7 26 ♛f5,* etc.

FISCHER

Position after 23...♖fe8

GUDMUNSSON

24	♖b1?	...

Also bad is *24 ♛f2 ♖8e3+! 25 ♗xe3 ♖xe3+ 26 ♛xe3 ♛xe3+.*

The toughest defense is *24 fxg6! hxg6* and now:

A] *25 ♗xg6? ♖1e2!* (not *25...♖8e2 26 ♗xf7+ ♔h8 27 ♛f5 ♖xg2+ 28 ♔h4 ♛f2+ 29 ♔h5 ♛f3+ 30 ♔h6! and White wins!) 26 ♗xf7+ ♔h8*

27 ♕f5 ♖xg2+ 28 ♔h4 ♕e1+ 29 ♔h5 ♔g7! (threatening 30...♖h8+) 30 ♗xe8 ♕xe8+ 31 ♔h4 ♕d8+ 32 ♕g5+ ♖xg5 33 fxg5 ♕d1 with an easy win.

B] 25 ♖b1 ♖8e3+! 26 ♗xe3 (if 26 ♔g4 ♕h2 27 ♗xe3 leads to the same) 26...♖xe3+ 27 ♔g4 (not 27 ♔h4? ♕h2 28 ♕f2 ♖xh3+!) 27...♕h2 28 ♕f2 (if 28 ♗xg6 ♕g3+ 29 ♔h5 ♕xf4! 30 ♗f5 ♖g3! 31 ♗g4 ♔g7 32 ♕c1 [if 32 ♔h4 ♖xg4+ 33 hxg4 ♕h2+ mates] 32...♖e3 wins), 28...♖xd3 (if 28...♖xh3!? 29 ♗xg6! fxg6 30 ♖h1! holds) 29 ♖b2! (29 ♖xb7 loses to 29...♖xh3! 30 ♖b8+ ♔h7 31 f5 ♖h6!) 29...♖xc3 30 ♖d2 and White has drawing chances even though a Pawn behind.

24	...	**gxf5**

Threatening either .... ♔h8 or .... ♖8e6 with a devastating check to follow on the g-file.

25	**♗d2**	...

No better is 25 ♗xf5 ♖1e2 26 ♗xh7+ ♔h8 27 ♕f5 ♖xg2+ 28 ♔h4 ♖g7 (among others) wins.

25	...	**♖xb1**
26	**♕xb1**	**♕xb1**
27	**♗xb1**	**♖e2**

This is what Gudmundsson overlooked. If now 28 ♗c1 ♖e1 picks off one of the Bishops. So...

White resigns

FISCHER

Final Position after 27...♖e2

GUDMUNDSSON

20   Fischer - Euwe *[Holland]*

LEIPZIG OLYMPIC 1960

CARO-KANN DEFENSE

Theoretical scuffle

Former world champion, Dr. Max Euwe had for decades been considered one of the world's leading authorities on opening theory. His Chess Archives *ranks with* Modern Chess Openings *as an indispensable source of reference. It is no small wonder, then, when he selects a risky but playable variation. Fischer, however, just a little better versed in its intricacies, introduces a nuance on move 15 which ruffles his opponent no end.*

   Fischer's method of dispatching his veteran adversary – on home grounds, as it were – is deceptively simple. After a mere eighteen moves the opening has become an ending and the duel is over. Euwe fights on, but to no avail.

1	e4	c6
2	d4	d5
3	exd5	cxd5
4	c4	...

At that time I was convinced the Panov-Botvinnik attack was the sharpest.

4	...	♘f6
5	♘c3	♘c6

In our game at Buenos Aires 1960, Ivkov played 5...e6 6 ♘f3 ♗e7 7 c5 0-0 8 ♗d3 b6 9 b4 bxc5 (better is 9...a5 10 ♘a4 ♘fd7!) 10 bxc5 ♘c6 11 0-0 ♗d7 12 h3 ♘e8 13 ♗f4 with a bind.

6	♘f3	...

On Botvinnik's old 6 ♗g5 e6! (6...dxc4? 7 d5 ♘e5 8 ♕d4 is strong) 7 cxd5 exd5 8 ♗xf6 ♕xf6 9 ♘xd5 ♕d8 10 ♘c3 (if 10 ♗c4 ♗e6 11 ♕e2? b5!) 10...♕xd4 11 ♕xd4 ♘xd4 12 0-0-0 ♗c5 13 ♘a4 ♘e6=.

| 6 | ... | &g4!? |

Risky but playable. Safer is 6...e6.

7	**cxd5**	♘xd5
8	**♕b3**	&xf3
9	**gxf3**	**e6**

On *9...♘db4!? 10* &e3 *♘xd4 11* &xd4 ♕xd4 *12* &b5+ *♘c6 13* 0-0 White gets a strong attack. (Evans-Henin, Las Vegas Open 1965.)

10	**♕xb7**	♘xd4
11	**&b5+**	♘xb5
12	**♕c6+**	♔e7
13	**♕xb5**	♘xc3

An alternative is *13...*♕d7 *14* ♘xd5+ exd5 (*14...*♕xd5 *15* ♕xd5 exd5 *16* 0-0 gives White good play against Black's isolated d-Pawn and a-Pawn) *15* ♕b4+ (*15* ♕e2+ ♔f6 *16* h4 wins, according to Evans) *15...*♔e8 *16* ♕d4 with a clear advantage.

| 14 | **bxc3** | ♕d7 |

After *14...*♕d5 *15* ♕xd5 exd5 *16* ♖b1 gives White a slight edge.

EUWE

Position after 14...♕d7

FISCHER

| 15 | **♖b1!** | ... |

The innovation. Months before the game I had shown this line to Benko and he suggested this innocent-looking move. Upon looking deeper I found that, horrible as White's Pawn structure may be, Black can't exploit it because he'll be unable to develop his K-side normally.

It's the little quirks like this that could make life difficult for a chess machine.

| 15 | ... | ♖d8? |

Also difficult is *15...♕xb5 16 ♖xb5 ♔d6! 17 ♖b7 f6 18 ♔e2 ♔c6 19 ♖f7 a5 20 ♗e3* with an enduring pull.

16	♗e3	♕xb5
17	♖xb5	♖d7
18	♔e2	...

18 ♖a5 is unnecessary. White can win the a-Pawn at his leisure.

| 18 | ... | f6 |
| 19 | ♖d1! | ... |

To swap Black's only active piece.

19	...	♖xd1
20	♔xd1	♔d7
21	♖b8!	...

21 ♗xa7 ♗d6 22 ♖b7+ ♔c6 23 ♖xg7 ♗xh2 would be hard to win. Now the threat is *22 ♗c5*.

EUWE

Position after 21 ♖b8!

FISCHER

| 21 | ... | ♔c6 |
| 22 | ♗xa7 | g5 |

Striving to untangle the K-side.

23	a4	♗g7
24	♖b6+	♔d5
25	♖b7	♗f8
26	♖b8	...

Still trying to decide how to squeeze the most out of it.

26	...	♗g7
27	♖b5+	♔c6
28	♖b6+	♔d5
29	a5	f5
30	♗b8!	♖c8
31	a6	♖xc3
32	♖b5+	...

EUWE

Position after 32 ♖b5+

FISCHER

| 32 | ... | ♔c4 |

After the game Euwe showed me a cute trap he might have played for – and almost fainted when I fell into it! The line arises after *32...♔c6 33 ♖a5 ♗d4* and he asked, "What do you do now?" I looked a few seconds and played *34 ♗e5?* whereupon he uncorked *34...♖c5!* which leads to a draw. Upon reconsideration, however, simply *34 ♔e2* wins. It's these tidbits that you remember best.

33	♖b7	♗d4
34	♖c7+	♔d3
35	♖xc3+	♔xc3
36	♗e5	**Black resigns**

He can't stop the a-Pawn.

21 Letelier [*Chile*] - Fischer

LEIPZIG OLYMPIC 1960

KING'S INDIAN DEFENSE

A Queen for the King

Letelier transgresses opening principles by neglecting his development in order to win material. Pugnaciously, he mixes it up with the unorthodox 5 e5 and proceeds to snatch Pawns. But his judgment proves to be unwise.

Striking from behind the lines, Fischer causes the overextended White center to crumble. Letelier, busily engaged on a material hunt, neglects to safeguard his rear, leaving his King marooned in the center. Fischer rapidly encircles the hapless monarch and, with a startling Queen sacrifice, induces abdication.

1	**d4**	♘**f6**
2	**c4**	**g6**
3	♘**c3**	♗**g7**
4	**e4**	**0-0**
5	**e5**	...

Weak. Letelier snapped at the chance to take me "out of the book," but this premature advance leaves White with all the responsibility of holding his overextended center Pawns.

5	...	♘**e8**
6	**f4**	**d6**

Weaker is 6...c5 7 dxc5 ♕a5 8 ♗e3 f6? 9 ♘f3 fxe5 10 fxe5 ♘c6 11 ♗e2 ♘c7 12 0-0 ♘e6 13 ♘d5 ♕d8 14 ♕d2 etc. (Koralev-Roshal, USSR 1962.)

7	♗**e3**	...

7 ♘f3 is safer, though White can no longer lay claim to any kind of initiative. My game with Schoene in the US Junior Championship 1957 continued: 7...dxe5 8 fxe5 (better is 8 dxe5) 8...♗g4 9 ♗e2 c5 10 ♗f4 cxd4 11 ♕xd4 ♘c6 12 ♕xd8 ♖xd8 soon winning a Pawn.

7   ...   **c5!**

"Now the artificially constructed White center begins to crumble."
(LOMBARDY.)

8   **dxc5**   ♘**c6**

"Black rapidly develops his pieces while White nurtures his own
dreams with ill-gotten gains." (LOMBARDY.)

9   **cxd6**   ...

White tries to compensate for his lack of development by continuing
to snatch material. Instead he should be seeking to return the Pawn in
the least damaging way (by keeping the lines closed). Better is *9* ♘*f3*
♗*g4 10* ♗*e2.*

9   ...   **exd6**
10   ♘**e4**   ...

"More realistic would have been *10* ♘*f3.*" (LOMBARDY.) I intended
10...♗g4. After the text White no longer has time to castle.

10   ...   ♗**f5!**

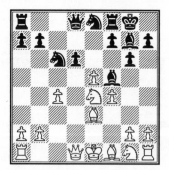

FISCHER

Position after 10...♗f5!

LETELIER

11   ♘**g3?**   ...

A better chance is *11* ♘*xd6* ♘*xd6 12* ♕*xd6* ♕*xd6 13 exd6* ♗*xb2*
14 ♖*d1* ♘*b4!* (threatening ...♗c2) *15* ♔*f2* (if *15* ♘*e2* ♗*c2 16* ♖*d2*
♘*d3+) 15...*♘*xa2 16* ♘*e2* (if *16* ♖*d2?* ♘*c3!) 16...a5.* Black is better but
White may have drawing resources.

| 11 | ... | ♗e6 |

I also considered *11...♕c7 12 ♘xf5 gxf5*. White's center must collapse.

| 12 | ♘f3 | ... |

By now White is more than willing to return the Pawn in order to catch up in development.

| 12 | ... | ♕c7 |

Also playable is *12...dxe5 13 ♕xd8 ♖xd8 14 ♗c5 exf4*. But I wanted to fracture him in the middle game.

| 13 | ♕b1 | ... |

Continuing his "attack". On *13 ♗e2 dxe5 14 ♗c5 ♕a5+ 15 b4 ♘xb4 16 ♗xf8 ♔xf8! 17 0-0 exf4 18 ♘e4 ♗f5* is overwhelming. And on *13 ♕c2* (in order to prepare 0-0-0) *13...dxe5 14 f5 gxf5 15 ♘xf5 ♘b4 16 ♕b3* (if *16 ♕b1 ♗xf5 17 ♕xf5 ♘d6 18 ♕b1 ♘xc4 19 ♘g5 f5 20 ♘e6 ♕c6 21 ♗xc4 ♕xc4 22 ♘xf8 ♖xf8* with a winning attack) *16...♗xf5 17 ♕xb4 ♘f6!* is strong. If *18 ♕c5 ♕b8* (threatening *...♘g4*).

| 13 | ... | dxe5 |
| 14 | f5 | e4! |

"An unexpected shot that sends White spinning." (LOMBARDY.)

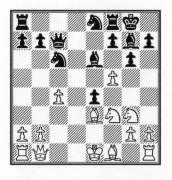

FISCHER

Position after 14...e4!

LETELIER

| 15 | fxe6 | ... |

On *15* ♕xe4 gxf5! *16* ♘xf5? (if *16* ♕h4 ♗xb2) *16*...♕a5+ wins a piece.

15	...	exf3
16	gxf3	f5!

"The Pawn on e6 can be ignored in favor of the attack." (LOMBARDY.) The threat is ...f4.

17	f4	♘f6
18	♗e2	♖fe8
19	♔f2	♖xe6

Finally Black regains the Pawn with interest.

20	♖e1	♖ae8
21	♗f3	...

"Anyone interested in sui-mate (helpmate) problems?" (LOMBARDY.)

21	...	♖xe3!
22	♖xe3	♖xe3
23	♔xe3	♕xf4+!

White resigns

FISCHER

Final Position after 23...♕xf4+!

LETELIER

On *24* ♔xf4 ♗h6 mate! Or *24* ♔f2 ♘g4+ *25* ♔g2 ♘e3+ *26* ♔f2 ♘d4 *27* ♕h1 ♘g4+ *28* ♔f1 ♘xf3 with a winning attack.

22 Szabo [*Hungary*] - Fischer

KING'S INDIAN DEFENSE

Bad judgment

Once a contender for the title, Szabo's performances nowadays are spotty and unpredictable. Here, with breathtaking bluntness, he attempts to wipe Fischer from the board. In the process he leaves himself wide open on the dark squares. Fischer promptly invades on the Q-side, by means of a curious Queen maneuver, while Szabo, preoccupied with his own K-side attack, fails to realize the danger in time. 21...♖e3! is the blow that ends all effective resistance. Rather than fight on against hopeless odds, Szabo resigns three moves later.

1	**d4**	♘**f6**
2	**c4**	**g6**
3	♘**c3**	♗**g7**
4	**e4**	**0-0**
5	♗**g5**	**...**

For *5* e5 see game 21. For *5* ♘f3 see games 7, 28 and 30.

5	**...**	**d6**

After 5...h6 6 ♗e3! allows White to set up a Saemisch formation (*6*...d6 7 f3) where the inevitable ♕d2 will be more effective than usual.

6	♕**d2**	**...**

Better is simply 6 ♗e2 c5 7 d5 e6 8 ♘f3 h6 9 ♗h4 exd5 10 cxd5 g5 11 ♗g3 ♘h5 (not *11*...b5? *12* ♘d2!) with a double-edged struggle. Larsen-Fischer, Santa Monica 1966.

6	**...**	**c5!**
7	**d5**	**...**

On 7 ♘f3 (7 dxc5 dxc5 8 ♕xd8 ♖xd8 9 e5 ♘g4 10 f4 f6 is better for Black) 7...cxd4 8 ♘xd4 ♘c6=.

| 7 | ... | e6 |
| 8 | ♗d3 | ... |

8 dxe6 ♗xe6 9 ♘f3 ♘c6 10 ♗e2 ♗g4! 11 0-0 ♖e8 12 ♕f4 ♗xf3 13 ♗xf3 ♘d4 14 ♖ad1 ♖e5 leads to equality. (Evans-Gligorich, Dallas 1957.)

| 8 | ... | exd5 |

FISCHER

Position after 8...exd5

SZABO

White has no advantageous way to recapture.

| 9 | ♘xd5 | ... |

A] 9 exd5 ♘bd7 10 f4 (to stop ...♘e5) 10...h6 11 ♗h4 ♖e8+ 12 ♘ge2 ♘e4! 13 ♗xd8 ♘xd2 14 ♗c7 ♗xc3 15 bxc3 ♘e4 16 ♗xe4 ♖xe4 17 ♗xd6 ♘b6 18 ♔f2 ♗g4! with a promising ending.

B] 9 cxd5 a6! 10 f4 (if 10 a4 ♕a5 threatening ...b5) 10...h6 11 ♗h4 ♘xe4! 12 ♗xd8 ♘xd2 13 ♗c7 ♗xc3 14 bxc3 ♘e4! 15 ♗xe4 ♖e8 etc.

In this opening variation Black must play sharply. White has a space advantage, but he temporarily lags in development.

| 9 | ... | ♗e6 |
| 10 | ♘e2 | ♗xd5 |

Releasing the tension and, by forcing White to recapture with a Pawn, eliminating the backward d-Pawn on an open file.

11	**exd5**	**...**

On *11* cxd5 c4! *12* ♗c2 ♘bd7 *13* 0-0 ♘c5 *14* ♘c3 b5!

11	**...**	**♘bd7**
12	**0-0**	**...**

Not *12* f4 ♕e8! *13* ♕c2? (to stop ...♘e4) *13*...♘g4! invading on the weak dark squares (notably e3).

12	**...**	**♘e5**

FISCHER

Position after 12...♘e5

SZABO

13	**f4?**	**...**

After *13* ♘c3 the game is even.

This lemon, weakening White's e3 and e4, came as a pleasant surprise. Szabo misjudges White's attacking prospects.

13	**...**	**♘xd3**
14	**♕xd3**	**h6**
15	**♗h4**	**♖e8**
16	**♖ae1**	**...**

16 ♘c3 is the best of a bad choice, though *16*...♕b6! (threatening ...♘g4) creates problems. If *17* h3 ♘h5! increases the pressure on White's game.

16	**...**	**♕b6!**
17	**♗xf6**	**...**

On *17* b3 ♘e4! gives Black a nice bind.

17	...	♗xf6
18	f5	g5
19	b3	♕a5!

A nettlesome maneuver!

FISCHER

Position after 19...♕a5!

SZABO

20	♖c1?	...

20 a4 loses to *20*...♗d4+ *21* ♔h1 (not *21* ♘xd4? ♖xe1) *21*...♖e3 *22* ♕d1 ♖ae8 and the pin on the e-file is decisive.

The best defense is *20* ♕b1!

20	...	♕xa2
21	♖c2	♖e3!
22	♕xe3	♕xc2
23	♔h1	a5
24	h4	a4
	White resigns	

White's Pawns fall like ripe apples. I'll never forget the disgusted look on Szabo's face as he took his King and just sort of shoved it gently to the center of the board, indicating his intention to resign.

23 Fischer - Tal [U.S.S.R.]

LEIPZIG OLYMPIC 1960

FRENCH DEFENSE

No holds barred

Their first encounter after Tal became world champion proves to be an old-fashioned slugfest. Typically aggressive, Fischer rapidly achieves a winning bind, but unwisely permits Tal to touch off "a dazzling array of fireworks" with 14...♘xe5! The struggle seesaws for seven moves before settling in a perpetual check.

The quality of this confrontation left little doubt that, in time, Fischer would yet take Tal's measure. He did just that less than a year later, after Tal had lost his return match with Botvinnik (Game 32). Reading Tal's palm, Fischer predicted: "The next world champion will be ... Bobby Fischer!"

1	e4	e6
2	d4	d5
3	♘c3	♗b4
4	e5	c5
5	a3	♗a5

A dubious alternative to 5...♗xc3+ (see game 24).

6	b4!	...

Alekhine's recommendation.

6	...	cxd4

6...cxb4 7 ♘b5 yields a potent attack.

7	♕g4	♘e7

Or 7...♔f8 8 bxa5 dxc3 9 a4! followed by 10 ♗a3+ is strong.
(LILIENTHAL and ZAGORYANSKY)

8	**bxa5**	...

Also good is *8* ♘b5.

8	...	**dxc3**
9	♕**xg7**	♖**g8**
10	♕**xh7**	♘**bc6**

On *10*...♘d7 *11* ♘f3 ♕c7 *12* ♗b5 a6 *13* ♗xd7+ ♗xd7 *14* 0-0 d4!?
(*Archives*) *15* ♘xd4 ♕xe5 *16* ♕d3 is better for White.

11	♘**f3**	...

11 f4 bolsters the center but shuts in the QB and weakens the dark
squares.

11	...	♕**c7**

On *11*...♕xa5 *12* ♘g5! ♖f8 *13* f4 (followed by the advance of the
h-Pawn) ties Black up.

12	♗**b5!**	...

Harmoniously pursuing development without losing time. Also
playable is *12* ♗f4 ♗d7 *13* ♗e2 0-0-0 *14* ♕d3 ♕xa5 *15* 0-0 ♖g4
16 ♗g3. (Unzicker-Duckstein, Zurich 1959.)

12	...	♗**d7**

Not *12*...♖xg2 *13* ♔f1! ♖g8 *14* ♖g1! ♖xg1+ *15* ♔xg1 and Black's
King remains hemmed in the center while White merely marches his
h-Pawn to victory.

13	**0-0**	...

Unsound is *13* ♗xc6? ♗xc6 *14* 0-0 d4! *15* ♘g5 ♕xe5 *16* ♕xf7+ ♔d7
with advantage.

13	...	**0-0-0**

After the game Petrosian suggested *13*...♘xe5 but *14* ♘xe5 ♕xe5
15 ♗xd7+ ♔xd7 *16* ♕d3! keeps White on top (if *16*...♕e4? *17* ♕xe4
dxe4 *18* f3! wins a Pawn).

TAL

Position after 13...0-0-0

FISCHER

14   &g5?   ...

I simply underestimated the force of Tal's reply.

Correct is *14* &xc6! &xc6 (if *14*...♛xc6 *15* &g5 d4 *16* h4! or
14...♘xc6 *15* ♖e1 followed by &g5 and h4 with a decisive bind)
15 ♛xf7 d4 (unsound is *15*...♖xg2+!? *16* ♔xg2 d4 *17* ♔g1 ♖g8+
18 ♘g5) *16* ♛xe6+ &d7 (*16*...♔b8 *17* ♘g5 is hopeless) *17* ♛xe7
♖xg2+ *18* ♔xg2 &h3+ *19* ♔xh3 ♛xe7 *20* &g5 and White soon
consolidates to victory.

14   ...   ♘xe5!

Setting off a dazzling array of fireworks! I thought Tal was merely
trying to confuse the issue.

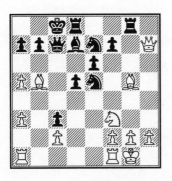

TAL

Position after 14 ... ♘xe5!

FISCHER

15   ♘xe5   ...

Originally I'd intended *15* &xd7+ but saw that after *15*...♖xd7
16 ♘xe5 (if *16* &xe7 ♘xf3+ *17* ♔h1 ♛xh2+!) *16*...♛xe5 *17* &xe7

♖h8! Black regains his piece with greater activity: e.g., *18* ♖ae1 ♖xh7
19 ♖xe5 ♖xe7 and the compact center Pawns far outweigh White's
passed h-Pawn.

Not playable is *15* ♗xe7? ♘xf3+ *16* ♔h1 ♖h8!

	15	...	♗xb5

Playing for the win. After *15...*♕xe5 *16* ♗xe7 ♖h8 *17* ♖fe1
(*17* ♖ae1? loses to *17...*♕b8!) *17...*♕xe1+ *18* ♖xe1 ♖xh7 *19* ♗xd8
♔xd8 (weak is *19...*♗xb5 *20* ♗f6!) *20* ♗xd7 ♔xd7 *21* ♖e3! bails
White out.

	16	♘xf7	...

White could still have kept some tension with *16* ♗xe7 ♕xe7
(if *16...*♕xe5? *17* ♖fe1) *17* ♖fe1, etc.

	16	...	♗xf1!

16...♖df8 *17* ♖fb1 ♗c6 *18* ♘d6+! ♕xd6 *19* ♕xe7 is about equal.

	17	♘xd8	♖xg5
	18	♘xe6	♖xg2+!

TAL

Position after 18...♖xg2+!

FISCHER

	19	♔h1!	...

The saving move. Not *19* ♔xf1? ♖xh2! *20* ♕f7 (if *20* ♘xc7 ♖xh7
wins a piece) *20...*♖h1+! produces a winning attack from nowhere!

19	...	♛e5

On *19...♛c4 20 ♛xe7 ♖g8 21 ♘f4!* holds nicely (if *21...♛xf4? 22 ♛e6+ ♚c7 23 ♛xg8*).

20	♖xf1	♛xe6

On *20...♖g6 21 ♛xe7 ♖xe6 22 ♛f8+ ♖e8 23 ♛f3* is in White's favor.

21	♚xg2	♛g4+

Drawn

Black has a perpetual check.

TAL

Final Position after 21...♛g4+

FISCHER

24 Fischer - Darga *[W.Germany]*

WEST BERLIN 1960

FRENCH DEFENSE

Asking for trouble

The Winawer Variation has given Fischer consistent trouble. He has had the utmost difficulty cracking Black's tortoise-like shell; even his successes are unconvincing. Maintaining the same line of attack year after year has provided his opponents with ample opportunity to sharpen their defenses.

Darga's 12...f6 obliges Fischer, in order to get something out of the opening, to speculate on a Pawn sacrifice (13 ♗a3!?). Though Darga's reaction may not be ideal, he proceeds sensibly and equalizes. Underestimating Fischer's chances, however, he falls prey to a scintillating mid-game attack. And so, once again, by virtue of his native ability, Fischer avoids the retribution that is the usual price for failing to secure an advantage in the opening.

1	e4	e6
2	d4	d5
3	♘c3	♗b4
4	e5	c5
5	a3	♗xc3+

For 5...♗a5 see game 23.

6	bxc3	♘e7
7	a4	...

Smyslov's favorite, largely responsible for Botvinnik's giving up the Winawer Variation. Sharper is 7 ♕g4. I felt that Black's carapace could be cracked only by positional means, but my results have been somewhat disheartening.

DARGA

Position after 7 a4

FISCHER

7 ... ♛c7

More usual is 7...♘bc6 8 ♘f3 ♛a5 9 ♛d2 (on 9 ♗d2 ♗d7 10 ♗e2 c4 11 h4!? f6 12 h5 fxe5 13 h6 gxh6 14 ♘xe5 ♘xe5 15 dxe5 0-0-0 16 ♖xh6 ♘g6 Black's better, Fischer-Padevsky, Varna 1962) 9...♗d7 10 ♗d3 and now Black has two main continuations:

A] 10...c4 11 ♗e2 f6 12 ♗a3 0-0-0 (if 12...♘g6 13 0-0 0-0-0 14 ♗d6 White keeps the edge. Fischer-Uhlmann, Buenos Aires 1960) 13 0-0 ♘f5 14 ♖fe1 ♗e8 15 g4!? ♘fe7 16 ♗f1 ♗d7= (Fischer-Weinstein, US Championship 1960-1.)

B] 10...f6! 11 0-0 fxe5 12 ♘xe5 (no better is 12 dxe5 as Smyslov tried against Uhlmann at Havana 1964) 12...♘xe5 13 dxe5 0-0 14 c4 ♛xd2 15 ♗xd2 ♗c6= (Fischer-Uhlmann, Stockholm 1962.)

I may yet be forced to admit that the Winawer is sound. But I doubt it! The defense is anti-positional and weakens the K-side.

8 ♘f3 b6

The idea is to eliminate the bad Bishop with ...♗a6. An alternative is 8...♗d7 9 ♗d3 ♘bc6.

9 ♗b5+! ♗d7

More radical is 9...♔f8!? 10 ♗d3 ♗a6.
On 9...♘ec6 (after 9...♘bc6 Black can no longer enforce ...♗a6) 10 0-0 ♗a6 11 ♘g5 h6 12 ♘h3 is in White's favor.

10 ♗d3 ...

After *10* 0-0 ♗xb5 *11* axb5 a5 *12* ♘g5 h6 *13* ♘h3 ♘d7 *14* ♘f4 0-0! (Ivkov-R.Byrne, Sousse 1967) Black has no problems.

10	**...**	♘bc6

Black has gained a tempo, but whether his Pawn belongs on b6 is moot.

11	**0-0**	c4

Not *11*...0-0? *12* ♗xh7+! ♔xh7 *13* ♘g5+, etc.

12	♗e2	f6
13	♗a3!?	...

Keeping tension in the center at the cost of a Pawn. *13* ♖e1 is solid but less aggressive. I tried this same Pawn sac against Mednis in the 1962-3 US Championship with the slight but significant difference that Black's b-pawn was still on b7. The sac may well have been unsound in that game.

13	**...**	fxe5

Mednis declined and castled, but after *14* ♖e1! got a cramped game (*14*...fxe5 is answered by *15* ♘xe5! keeping the e-file open).

14	**dxe5**	...

White doesn't have anything to show after *14* ♘xe5 ♘xe5 *15* dxe5 ♕xe5 *16* ♖e1 ♕xc3 *17* ♗h5+ g6 *18* ♗g4 (if *18* ♗xe7 ♔xe7 *19* ♕xd5? ♕xa1! wins) *18*...♕f6, etc.

14	**...**	♘xe5

After *14*...0-0 *15* ♘d4! is followed by f4 and White has not been inveigled into misplacing his Rook on e1.

15	**♖e1**	...

The threat is *16* ♘xe5 ♕xe5 *17* ♗h5+.

DARGA

Position after 15 ♖e1

FISCHER

| 15 | ... | ♘7c6 |

Black has a seeming multiplicity of defenses:

A] *15...♘5c6 16 ♘g5! 0-0!* (if *16...h6 17 ♗h5+ g6 18 ♘xe6 ♗xe6 19 ♖xe6 gxh5 20 ♕xd5! ♖d8 21 ♕xh5+ ♔d7 22 ♖ae1* regains the piece) *17 ♗g4 ♕f4!* (if *17...e5 18 ♗e6+ ♔h8 19 ♗xd5!*) *18 ♗xe6+!* (if *18 ♘xe6 ♕xf2+ 19 ♔h1 ♖f7!*) *18...♗xe6 19 ♘xe6 ♕xf2+ 20 ♔h1 ♖f5! 21 ♖e2! ♕h4 22 ♘d4! ♖h5* (not *22...♘xd4? 23 ♗xe7*) *23 ♘f3 ♕f6 24 ♕e1 ♖e8 25 ♖e6 ♕f7 26 ♕e2! ♖h6 27 ♖e3* followed by ♖e1 and Black's crushed.

B] *15...♘5g6 16 h4!* (on *16 ♘g5 0-0! 17 ♗g4 ♕f4* holds) *16...♘c6 17 ♘g5* and it's difficult for Black's King to escape the crisscross; if *17...0-0-0? 18 ♘f7.* Or *17...h6? 18 ♘xe6! ♗xe6 19 ♗g4.* Or on *17...♘f4 18 ♗g4* continues the pressure.

C] *15...♘7g6 16 ♘xe5 ♘xe5* transposes to the game.

| 16 | ♘xe5 | ♘xe5 |
| 17 | f4 | ♘c6 |

On *17...♘f7* (*17...♘g6? 18 f5*) *18 ♗h5 g6 19 f5! 0-0-0 20 fxe6 ♗xe6 21 ♖xe6 gxh5 22 ♕xh5* White stands much better.

| 18 | ♗g4 | ... |

Better is the finesse *18 ♗h5+! g6* (*18...♔d8 19 f5* is unhealthy) *19 ♗g4 0-0-0 20 ♗xe6 ♗xe6 21 ♖xe6 ♖d7 22 ♕f3 ♘d8 23 ♖f6! ♖e8 24 ♖d1* etc.

| 18 | ... | 0-0-0 |
| 19 | ♗xe6 | ♗xe6 |

20	♖xe6	♖d7
21	f5	...

To continue with f6 which gets a grip on the f-file. On *21* ♕f3 ♘d8 *22* ♖e5 ♕c6=.

21	...	♘d8!

Driving the Rook from its command outpost on the sixth rank.

22	♖e3	♕f4

Darga is defending with vigor!

23	♖f3	♕e4
24	a5!	...

Commencing operations against the castled King while Black's Queen is temporarily cut off from the Q-flank.

24	...	♘c6?

Correct was *24*...b5 with an even game.

25	axb6	axb6
26	♕b1!	♔c7

The opening of the a-file is already decisive. On *26*...♔b7 *27* ♗c5 wins. Or *26*...♖b7 *27* f6 gxf6 *28* ♖xf6 d4 *29* ♕b5, etc

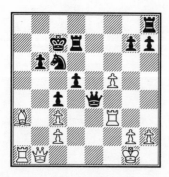

DARGA

Position after 26...♔c7

FISCHER

Problem: White to play and win.

27	♗c1!		♛e1+

There's no satisfactory defense to the threat of ♗f4+. On *27...*♘e5 *28* ♗f4 ♖e8 *29* ♛b5 penetrates decisively.

28	♖f1		♛xc3
29	♗f4+		♚b7
30	♛b5!		**Black resigns**

25 Lombardy *[U.S.A.]* - Fischer

USA CHAMPIONSHIP 1960-1

SICILIAN DEFENSE

When the Maroczy didn't bind

Geza Maroczy left a strange legacy: the discovery that a certain type of Pawn formation imposes a near-decisive cramp on the opponent. In this game, after Lombardy's sixth move, he obtains, with Fischer's consent, the dread "Maroczy bind." From here on, given a few developing moves, White's game almost plays itself – unless Black takes early and energetic counter-measures. This is easier said than done.

The method that Fischer chooses to free himself (9...d5) involves the sacrifice of a Pawn. Lombardy reacts sluggishly, overlooking a neat tactical point (17...♗h4+) at the tail-end of a combination. Even so, he still has excellent drawing chances. But somewhat discouraged by the rapid turn of events, he indulges in a unique form of self-immolation. In short, Lombardy, not Maroczy, lost.

1	e4	c5
2	♘f3	d6
3	d4	cxd4
4	♘xd4	♘f6
5	f3	...

A passive, non-developing move which leads to nothing. White wants to gain control of d5, establishing a Maroczy bind with c4, ♘c3 etc. But after going to all that trouble he can't prevent ...d5 after all. Correct is that tired old move – 5 ♘c3.

5	...	♘c6

Sharper is 5...e5! 6 ♗b5+ (6 ♘b5 a6 7 ♘5c3 ♗e6 8 ♘d5 ♘xd5 9 exd5 ♗f5=) 6 .... ♘bd7 7 ♘f5 d5! 8 exd5 a6 9 ♗xd7+ ♕xd7 10 ♘e3 ♗c5 11 c4 b5=. (Cardoso-Fischer, 5th match game 1957.)

6	c4	e6

6...♘xd4 7 ♕xd4 g6 is a sound alternative.

7	♘c3	♗e7

Premature is 7...d5? 8 cxd5 exd5 9 ♗b5 winning a Pawn.

8	♗e3	...

8 ♘c2 0-0 9 ♘e3 d5!? 10 cxd5 exd5 11 exd5? (better is 11 ♘exd5) 11...♘e5 12 ♕b3 ♗c5 13 ♗d2 ♖e8 14 ♗e2 ♘g6 15 ♘c2 ♘h4 16 0-0-0 ♘xg2 with advantage (Foguelman-Fischer, Mar del Plata 1960.)

8	...	0-0
9	♘c2	d5!?

Reckoning that the loss of a Pawn is compensated for by superior development. 9...♖e8 is sound but passive.

FISCHER

Position after 9...d5!?

LOMBARDY

10	cxd5	exd5
11	♘xd5	...

Better is 11 exd5 ♘b4 (11...♘e5 doesn't work well now because of 12 ♕d4 followed by 0-0-0) 12 ♗c4 ♗f5 13 ♘xb4 ♗xb4 14 0-0 ♖c8. Black regains the Pawn, but with an inferior position.

11	...	♘xd5
12	♕xd5	...

On 12 exd5 ♘b4 13 ♗c4 ♗f5 14 ♘xb4 ♗xb4+ 15 ♔f2 ♖e8 with good play for the Pawn. (If 16 ♕b3 ♗a5 threatening ...♖xe3.)

12	...	♕c7!
13	♕b5?	...

Too intent on holding on to the Pawn. Correct is *13* ♗e2 ♗h4+!
14 g3 ♗f6 *15* 0-0 ♗xb2 *16* ♖ab1 =.

13	...	♗d7
14	♖c1	...

Again too optimistic. After *14* ♕e2 ♗f6 *15* 0-0-0 White can survive
– temporarily anyway (if *15*...♘b4 *16* ♖xd7!).

FISCHER

Position after 14 ♖c1

LOMBARDY

14	...	♘b4!

This unexpected "discovery" jolts White back to reality.

15	♘xb4	...

Loses the exchange, but avoids the worst. On *15* ♕e2 ♘xa2 regains
the Pawn with continuing pressure. And on *15* ♕c4 ♕a5 *16* ♘xb4
♗xb4+ *17* ♔f2 ♖ac8 *18* ♕d5 ♖xc1 *19* ♗xc1 ♗e1+! White meets a
devastating attack wherever he turns: i.e., *20* ♔e3 (if *20* ♔g1? ♕b6+)
20...♕b6+ *21* ♔f4 (not *21* ♕d4? ♗f2+ or *21* ♔e2 ♕f2+ *22* ♔d1 ♗e6)
21...♕c7+ *22* e5 ♕xc1+, etc.

15	...	♕xc1+
16	♗xc1	♗xb5
17	♘d5	...

FISCHER

Position after 17 ♘d5

LOMBARDY

| 17 | ... | ♗h4+! |

The scorpion's sting at the tail-end of the combination.

| 18 | g3 | ♗xf1 |
| 19 | ♖xf1 | ♗d8 |

The smoke clears. Black is an exchange ahead for a Pawn. But there are still great technical difficulties. White's Knight is on a dominating outpost and his Pawn structure is solid.

| 20 | ♗d2 | ♖c8 |
| 21 | ♗c3 | f5! |

Weaker would be *21...♖e8* because of *22 g4* blocking the K-side.

| 22 | e5 | ... |

This advance is necessary, but it undermines the support of the Knight (which can now be driven away).

| 22 | ... | ♖c5 |
| 23 | ♘b4 | ... |

23 ♘f4 (or *23 ♘e3*) would cost a pawn after *23...♗a5*.

23	...	♗a5
24	a3	♗xb4
25	axb4	♖d5
26	♔e2	♔f7
27	h4	♔e6

| 28 | ♔e3 | ♖c8 |
| 29 | ♖g1 | ♖c4 |

Black has steadily improved his grip, but his winning chances are still problematic, hinging mainly on sacrificing on b4 or e5 at the right moment.

| 30 | ♖e1? | ... |

A gross blunder. Correct is *30* ♖a1 a6 *31* ♖g1.

FISCHER

Position after 30 ♖e1?

LOMBARDY

| 30 | ... | ♖xc3+! |

Swapping everything leads to a won King and Pawn ending.

31	bxc3	♖xe5+
32	♔d2	♖xe1
33	♔xe1	♔d5
34	♔d2	♔c4
35	h5	b6
36	♔c2	g5
37	h6	f4
38	g4	a5
39	bxa5	bxa5
40	♔b2	a4
41	♔a3	♔xc3
42	♔xa4	♔d4
43	♔b4	♔e3
	White resigns	

26 Fischer - Reshevsky *[U.S.A.]*

NEW YORK 1961: 2nd Match Game

SICILIAN DEFENSE

Time will tell

> The opening has always been regarded as the old warrior's weak point, and were it not for this handicap who knows how far Reshevsky might have gone toward the summit?
>
> Whatever the case, being familiar with the latest wrinkles does have the merit of saving time on the clock and, hopefully, of catching an opponent off guard. Although Reshevsky is bested in the theoretical duel (after 13 ♗f3) his practical cunning enables him to extricate himself – at a great cost of time. In the end it is the clock, as much as Fischer's persistence, that causes his downfall.

1	e4	c5
2	♘f3	♘c6
3	d4	cxd4
4	♘xd4	g6

Allowing White the chance to get a Maroczy bind (with 5 c4). Apparently Reshevsky had booked up on this for the match. Black's idea is to dispense with an early ...d6 and possibly strive for a later ...d5 (thereby saving a tempo).

5	♘c3	...

In match game 8 I got an edge with the more traditional 5 c4 ♘f6 6 ♘c3 ♘xd4 7 ♕xd4 d6 8 ♗e2 ♗g7 9 ♗e3 0-0 10 ♕d2, etc.

5	...	♗g7
6	♗e3	♘f6
7	♗e2	...

In the 4th and 6th games of the match I continued with 7 ♗c4 0-0 8 ♗b3 ♘g4 (8...♘a5? brought Reshevsky to grief against me in the US Championship 1958-9 after 9 e5 ♘e8 10 ♗xf7+! ♔xf7 11 ♘e6!! winning Black's Queen) 9 ♕xg4 ♘xd4 and White got a clear advantage both with 10 ♕h4 and 10 ♕d1 respectively.

7	...	0-0

On *7...d5? 8* ♗b5 wins a Pawn.

8	f4	...

Despite his familiarity with the Dragon Variation, I felt Reshevsky really didn't know the latest wrinkles in Alekhine's Attack. The point of Black's "accelerated fianchetto" becomes apparent after the indifferent *8* 0-0? d5! *9* exd5 ♘b4=.

8	...	d6

Now on *8...d5? 9* e5 ♘e4 *10* ♘xe4 dxe4 *11* ♘xc6 bxc6 *12* ♕xd8 ♖xd8 *13* ♗c4 gives White a winning ending. (Olafsson-Larsen, Wageningen 1957.)

9	♘b3	...

RESHEVSKY

Position after 9 ♘b3

FISCHER

9	...	♗e6

I was right. This is the old (and second-rate) move. Correct is *9...a5!* *10* a4 ♗e6 *11* ♘d4? (after *11* g4 ♘b4! Black's Knight can no longer be dislodged by a3; the best White has is *11* 0-0 ♖c8=) *11...*♕b6! *12* ♘xe6 ♕xe3 *13* ♘xf8 ♘g4 with a strong attack. (Makievsky-Veresov, USSR 1954.)

10	g4	d5
11	f5	♗c8

Lipnitzky recommends *11...gxf5!?* It's interesting.

12	**exd5**	♘**b4**

RESHEVSKY

Position after 12...♘b4

FISCHER

13	♗**f3!**	...

The modern way – White maintains his center Pawn and sacs two Pawns on the K-side where Black must expose his King to get them.

13 d6 has been known to be only a draw since the famous Alekhine-Botvinnik encounter, Nottingham 1936, which continued: *13*...♕xd6! (if *13*...exd6? *14* g5) *14* ♗c5 ♕f4 *15* ♖f1 ♕xh2 *16* ♗xb4 ♘xg4! *17* ♗xg4 ♕g3+ *18* ♖f2 ♕g1+ with a perpetual.

Another weak line is *13* fxg6 hxg6 *14* ♗f3 ♗xg4! *15* ♗xg4 ♘xg4 *16* ♕xg4 ♘xc2+ *17* ♔f2 ♘xa1 *18* ♖xa1 ♖c8! with a good game. If *19* ♗d4? ♖c4. (PANOV)

13	...	**gxf5**
14	**a3**	**fxg4**
15	♗**g2!**	...

On *15* axb4 gxf3 *16* ♕xf3 ♗g4 followed by ...♗h5-g6. White's whole idea is to keep Black's QB restricted to the Q-side.

15	...	♘**a6**
16	♕**d3!**	...

Ney's improvement over *16* ♕e2 ♗f5! and the Bishop retreats to g6, when necessary, defending the K-side.

16	...	**e6**

The best choice in a difficult position. Up to here we had both played briskly, but now Reshevsky began to consume time on the clock. After

16...♘d7 *17* 0-0-0 ♘e5 *18* ♕e2 Black's game is lifeless. White has h3 and ♗d4 in the offing.

17	**0-0-0**	...

Black gets the initiative after *17* d6? ♘d5! *18* ♗xd5 exd5 *19* ♕xd5 ♖e8, etc.

17	...	♘xd5

The lesser evil. On *17*...exd5 *18* h3 g3 *19* ♗d4 is strong.

18	**h3!**	**g3**
19	**♖hg1**	**♕d6!**

Reshevsky is putting up a first-rate defense.

20	**♗xd5**	**exd5**

RESHEVSKY

Position after 20...exd5

FISCHER

Despite his material deficit, it is obvious White has a strong attack. His problem is how to land a haymaker.

21	♘xd5?	...

This gives Black a little breathing space.

Nowadays I would have played *21* ♗d4! without giving it a second thought. After *21*...♗xd4 *22* ♖xg3+ ♗g7 (*22*...♔h8 *23* ♕xd4+ f6 *24* ♖f3 leads to a bind) *23* ♖dg1 ♕h6+ *24* ♔b1 ♗e6 *25* ♖xg7+ ♕xg7 *26* ♖xg7+ ♔xg7 *27* ♕g3+ ♔h8 (if *27*...♔f6 *28* ♕d6 ♗g7 *29* ♘xd5 wins) *28* ♕e5+ ♔g8 *29* ♕g5+ ♔h8 *30* ♕f6+ ♔g8 *31* ♘e2 with a winning bind.

21	...	♔h8
22	♗f4	...

22 ♗d4 is less convincing now after 22...♗xd4 (if 22...f6? 23 ♖xg3 ♕xd5 24 ♗xf6!) 23 ♕xd4+ f6 and White has no forced win.

22	...	♕g6
23	♕d2	...

Overlooking his reply. Vukovich suggests 23 ♕f3 but 23...♗f5! 24 ♖xg3 ♕c6 holds.

23	...	♗xh3!

Reshevsky chopped it off fast – he doesn't wait to be asked twice.

24	♖xg3	♗g4

Black has succeeded in transferring the Bishop to the K-side and in sealing the g-file.

25	♖h1	...

So White begins operations on the h-file!

25	...	♖fe8
26	♘e3	...

RESHEVSKY

Position after 26 ♘e3

FISCHER

26	...	♕e4?

Anxious to simplify and ease the tension (in time-pressure), Reshevsky finally goes astray.

The tempting *26...*♕f6 is refuted by *27* ♘xg4 ♕xb2+ *28* ♔d1 ♖ad8 *29* ♖d3, etc.

But simply *26...*f5! holds (if *27* ♕h2 ♔g8).

| 27 | ♕h2! | ... |

Now the roof caves in.

| 27 | ... | ♗e6 |

The late Abe Turner suggested *27...*♗f5 but after *28* ♖xg7! ♔xg7 *29* ♘xf5+ ♕xf5 *30* ♘d4 wins.

| 28 | ♖xg7! | ... |

That does it. Once this Bishop is gone, White has a field day.

"Why didn't White play *28* ♘d2...? So far as I can see Black can then resign. Or am I missing something?" (A.R.B.Thomas in a letter to *Chess*) Right, Mr. Thomas!

| 28 | ... | ♔xg7 |
| 29 | ♕h6+ | ♔g8 |

Or *29...*♔h8 *30* ♗e5+ mates in two.

30	♖g1+	♕g6
31	♖xg6+	fxg6
32	♘d4	♖ad8
33	♗e5	♖d7
34	♘xe6	♖xe6
35	♘g4	♖f7
36	♕g5	♖f1+
37	♔d2	h5
38	♕d8+	**Black resigns**

After *38...*♖f8 *39* ♘h6+ taxes even Reshevsky's defensive ability.

27 Reshevsky *[U.S.A.]* - Fischer

LOS ANGELES 1961: 5th Match Game

SEMI-TARRASCH DEFENSE

Sheer pyrotechnics

Here, in probably the most exciting game of the match, Fischer, trying to win a Pawn, unwittingly triggers a series of "desperado" combinations which are brilliant and unorthodox. Pure tactics predominate for a period of ten moves (19 to 29). It is almost impossible to determine who is winning until Reshevsky emerges a clear exchange ahead. In the tricky ending that ensues Fischer obviously is fighting for a draw. But, once again, he has the clock as an ally.

In time-pressure, trying to preserve his slim advantage, Reshevsky plays an aggressive line in which Fischer finds a hole — enabling him to reverse their roles. Conscious of his newly acquired advantage, Fischer storms down the board with his K-side Pawns and overwhelms his opponent.

1	d4	♘f6
2	c4	e6
3	♘c3	d5
4	cxd5	...

This exchange variation, though insipid, has always been to Reshevsky's taste.

4	...	♘xd5

4...exd5 leads to the kind of wood pushing that always bored me.

5	♘f3	...

Prematurely forceful is *5 e4 ♘xc3 6 bxc3 c5 7 ♘f3 cxd4 8 cxd4 ♗b4+ =.*

5	...	c5

6	e3	♘c6
7	♗d3	...

Botvinnik and Robert Byrne prefer *7* ♗c4. A possible continuation might be *7*...cxd4 *8* exd4 ♗e7 *9* 0-0 0-0 *10* ♖e1 a6= (weaker is *10*...b6 *11* ♘xd5 exd5 *12* ♗b5 Botvinnik-Alekhine, AVRO 1938).

7	...	♗e7

An alternative is *7*...cxd4 *8* exd4 g6 *9* h4!? (*9* 0-0 ♗g7 *10* ♗e4 is the positional approach) *9*...♗g7 (better is *9*...h6) *10* h5 ♘db4 *11* ♗g5 ♘xd3+ *12* ♕xd3 ♕a5 *13* ♔f1 h6? *14* hxg6! hxg5 *15* ♖xh8+ ♗xh8 *16* gxf7+ ♔xf7 *17* ♕h7+ ♗g7 *18* d5! White won shortly. (Balcerovsky-Dunkelblum, Varna 1962.)

8	0-0	0-0
9	a3	cxd4
10	exd4	...

FISCHER

Position after 10 exd4

RESHEVSKY

Fairly typical of the semi-Tarrasch formation: White has the freer game and attacking prospects, but the drawback of his isolated d-Pawn should not be minimized. Chances are even.

10	...	♘f6

Also playable is *10*...♗d7 *11* ♕c2 g6 *12* ♗h6 ♖e8 *13* ♘e4 ♖c8 *14* ♕e2 f5 *15* ♘c3 ♗f6 (R.Byrne-Bisguier, US Championship 1963-4). Another possibility is *10*...b6!? *11* ♘xd5 ♕xd5 *12* ♕c2 ♗b7! *13* ♗xh7+ ♔h8 *14* ♗e4 ♘xd4 *15* ♗xd5 ♘xc2 *16* ♗xb7 ♘xa1 *17* ♗xa8 ♖xa8 *18* ♗g5 f6=.

11	♗c2	...

A more flexible plan is *11* ♗e3 followed by ♕e2 and ♖ad1.

11	...	b6
12	♕d3	♗b7
13	♗g5	g6
14	♖fe1	♖e8
15	h4	...

Evans criticized this "aggressive pass" and Barden extolled it. I don't see how else White can make headway. He has to create some K-side threats before Black consolidates and piles up on his d-Pawn.

15	...	♖c8
16	♖ac1	♘d5
17	♘e4	f5!?

I knew this was an "ugly positional blunder." But I actually thought Black would get the better of it after *18 ♘c3 ♗xg5 19 hxg5 ♘xc3 20 bxc3* (not *20 ♕xc3? ♘e5*) *20...♘a5!* (threatening ...♗xf3 and ...♕xg5).

18	♘c3	♗xg5
19	♘xg5!	...

Crossing me up!

19	...	♘f4
20	♕e3	...

Not *20 ♕g3? ♘h5 21 ♕e3 ♘xd4.*

20	...	♕xd4
21	♘b5!	...

FISCHER

Position after 21 ♘b5!

RESHEVSKY

Marvelously alert! After the practically forced trade of Queens, White wins the exchange because of the imminent fork on d6.

| 21 | ... | ♕xe3 |

Best. After the game we analysed *21...♕d5 22 ♕xf4 ♕xb5* (if *22...♘d4? 23 ♗e4! ♖xc1 24 ♕xc1! fxe4 25 ♕c7*) *23 ♘xe6 ♕xb2* (if *23...♕d5 24 ♘c7 ♖xe1+ 25 ♖xe1 ♕f7 26 ♘e6* keeps the advantage); *24 ♕h6!* (RESHEVSKY) with an irresistible attack. On *24...♘a5* (to stop ♗b3; if *24...♖xe6 25 ♖xe6 ♘d4 26 ♖e7* wins) *25 ♗xf5! gxf5* (if *25...♕f6 26 ♘g5!* or *25...♖xc1 26 ♖xc1 gxf5 27 ♖c7* wins) *26 ♖b1 ♕h8* (if *26...♕c3 27 ♖e3*) *27 ♕g5+ ♔f7 28 ♕xf5+ ♔g8* (not *28...♕f6? 29 ♕xh7+*) *29 ♖e3 ♖c3 30 ♘g5! ♖f8 31 ♖e8!* forces mate.

22	fxe3	♘xg2!
23	♔xg2	♘d4 dis.+
24	♗e4!	...

FISCHER

Position after 24 ♗e4!

RESHEVSKY

This game was played at the Beverly Hilton Hotel in Los Angeles, and I can still hear the audience gasping with each blow, thinking each of us had overlooked it in turn. "Fischer is winning!" "Reshevsky is winning!" The true state of affairs will crystallize in a matter of moves.

24	...	♗xe4+
25	♘xe4	♘xb5
26	♘f6+	...

So the fork, after all, takes place here instead of d6!

26	...	♔f7
27	♘xe8	♖xe8
28	a4!	...

Inaccurate is *28 ♖ed1 ♖e7!* and the Knight can climb back into the game via c7-d5.

| 28 | ... | ♘d6 |

29	♖c7+	♔f6!

Black can't afford *29...♖e7 30 ♖ec1*. The Rook is needed to mobilize the K-side Pawns.

30	♖ec1!	...

Keeping control of the open file. On either *30 ♖xa7* or *♖xh7, ...♖c8*.

30	...	h6
31	♖xa7	♘e4
32	♖a6	♖d8!

32...♖b8 33 ♖c6 is hopeless.

FISCHER

Position after 32...♖d8!

RESHEVSKY

Now it's clear that Black's fighting for a draw.

33	♖c2	...

The only way to preserve winning chances. After *33 ♖xb6 ♖d2+ 34 ♔g1 g5 35 hxg5+* (on *35 ♖cc6 gxh4 36 ♖xe6+ ♔g5 37 ♖g6+ ♔h5 38 ♖xh6+ ♔g4* Black has enough play on the K-side to hold the draw; but not *35 a5? gxh4 36 a6 h3 37 a7 h2+ 38 ♔h1 ♘g3* mate) *35...hxg5 36 ♖cc6* (not *36 a5? g4 37 a6 ♘g5 38 a7 ♘f3+ 39 ♔f1 g3 40 a8=♕ g2* mate!) *36...g4 37 ♖xe6+ ♔g5 38 ♖h6 f4* keeps the balance.

33	...	♖d3
34	♖xb6	...

After *34 ♔f3 ♖b3* Black is in great shape.

34	...	♖xe3

	35	**a5**		**f4**

FISCHER

Position after 35...f4

RESHEVSKY

	36	**♖f2?**		**...**

Short of time, Reshevsky probably didn't see how Black's Rook could get back in time to stop the a-Pawn. But now it is doubtful that White can even draw!

White should settle for *36* a6 f3+ *37* ♔f1 (not *37* ♔h2? ♖e2+) *37...*♖d3 *38* ♔e1 ♖e3+ *39* ♔f1 ♖d3 with a draw. If *40* ♔g1 ♖d1+ *41* ♔h2 f2 *42* ♖xf2+ ♘xf2 *43* ♖b3 (*43* a7 ♖a1 wins) *43...*♖d7 *44* ♖f3+ ♔g7 *45* ♖xf2 ♖a7=.

	36	**...**		**♘xf2**
	37	**♔xf2**		**♖e5!**
	38	**b4**		**♖e3!**

This maneuver permits the Rook to get behind the passed Pawn.

	39	**a6**		**♖a3**

Now White is stymied. In order to mobilize his Q-side Pawns, he must inch forward with b5, ♖b7, a7, b6, etc. But a half-dozen moves, in chess, can be a lifetime.

	40	**♖c6**		**...**

The last move of the time-control, and it definitely loses. The best chance is *40* b5 with the possibility of ♖b8 and b6 (giving up the a-Pawn) followed by b7, in some key variations.

	40	**...**		**g5**
	41	**hxg5+**		**hxg5**
	42	**b5**		**g4**

The sealed move. Black's Pawns suddenly proliferate from nowhere!

FISCHER

Position after 42...g4

RESHEVSKY

43	♖c8	...

The line I had expected was *43* ♖c1 (intending to bolster the Pawns from behind with ♖b1) *43...g3+ 44* ♔g1 (on *44* ♔g2 ♖a2+ *45* ♔f3 ♔f5 wins) *44...*♖a2! *45* ♖b1 f3 *46* b6 ♖g2+ *47* ♔f1 ♖h2! *48* ♔e1 ♖h1+ *49* ♔d2 ♖xb1 *50* a7 f2 *51* a8=♕ f1=♕ and Black wins, since White has no perpetual check.

43	...	♔f5
44	b6	g3+
45	♔e1	...

He decides to let the Pawns through rather than get mated after *45* ♔g2 ♖a2+ *46* ♔g1 f3, etc.

45	...	♖a1+
46	♔e2	g2
47	♖f8+	...

On *47* ♖g8 ♖xa6 *48* b7 (if *48* ♖xg2 ♖xb6 wins) *48...*♖b6 is decisive.

47	...	♔e4
48	♖xf4+	♔xf4
49	b7	g1=♕

A hasty slip which, fortunately, still wins. As Isaac Kashdan pointed out after the game *49...*♔e4! wins outright: e.g., *50* b8=♕ ♖a2+ *51* ♔–any g1=♕ mate. "What will the Russians say when they see this match?" he inquired, with gentle irony.

FISCHER

Position after 49...g1=♕

RESHEVSKY

50	b8=♕+	♔f5
51	♕f8+	♔e4
52	♕a8+	...

No better is *52* ♕f3+ ♔e5 *53* ♕c3+ (if *53* ♕h5+ ♔d6) *53*...♕d4 *54* ♕g3+ ♔d5 *55* ♕f3+ ♕e4+, etc.

52	...	♔d4

Delicate footwork is required to escape the perpetual.

53	♕d8+	...

Better than *53* ♕h8+ ♔c4 *54* ♕c8+ ♕c5 *55* ♕xe6+ ♔b4 *56* ♕e4+ ♕c4+.

53	...	♔c4
54	♕d3+	♔c5
55	♕c3+	♔d6
56	♕d2+	♔e5
57	♕b2+	♔f5
	White resigns	

He runs out of checks after *58* ♕b5+ ♔f6 *59* ♕b2+ e5.

28 Reshevsky *[U.S.A.]* - Fischer

LOS ANGELES 1961: 11th Match Game

KING'S INDIAN DEFENSE

A peccable draw

What proved to be the last game of this ill-starred match is a good example of how Reshevsky, by virtue of pluck, stamina, and alertness, salvages a draw from a lost position. It exemplifies, too, the demoralizing effect that continuously strong resistance can have on even the most robust opponent.

Fischer rapidly wrests the initiative and wins the exchange as the result of a pretty combination (28...♕xe4). However, he has difficulty gaining the offensive because Reshevsky throws obstacle after obstacle in his path. Nevertheless, Fischer's material advantage begins to make itself felt. He misses clear wins (on moves 38 and 42), whereupon his game deteriorates sufficiently to permit his stubborn opponent to set up an adequate defense. Still, there are several surprises in store just at the very end.

1	c4	♘f6
2	d4	g6
3	♘c3	♗g7
4	e4	0-0
5	♗e2	...

Inferior is *5 e5*. See game 21.

5	...	d6
6	♘f3	e5
7	0-0	...

For *7 d5* see game 7.

7	...	♘c6
8	d5	...

Match game 9 (Reshevsky as White) had continued: *8 ♗e3 ♖e8 9 dxe5 (9 d5 ♘d4! equalizes fully) 9...dxe5 10 ♕xd8 ♘xd8 11 ♘b5 ♘e6 12 ♘g5* ("full of sound and fury, signifying nothing" – Evans) *12...♖e7=.* See game 57 note to Black's move *13*.

8	...	♘e7
9	♘e1	♘d7
10	♘d3	f5
11	exf5	...

11 f3 f4 followed by ...g5 etc gives Black a strong K-side attack.

| 11 | ... | ♘xf5 |

11...gxf5 keeping Black's Pawn front mobile is very strong.

| 12 | f3 | ♘d4 |

For *12*...♘f6 see game 30.

| 13 | ♘e4 | b6 |

Hindering White's thematic break with c5.

FISCHER

Position after 13...b6

RESHEVSKY

| 14 | ♗g5? | ... |

Apparently gaining a tempo, but only driving the Queen to a better square. *14* ♗d2 or ♖e1 appear to be more accurate.

| 14 | ... | ♕e8 |
| 15 | ♗d2 | ... |

This Bishop must retreat eventually after ...h6. The idea is to prepare b4 without having to fear the reply ...a5.

15	...	**a5**

Gaining more time. White must now stop for b3 (to enforce b4). On the immediate *16* a3 a4! fixes the Q-side.

16	♖**e1**	♘**xe2+**

Otherwise the Bishop retreats to f1.

17	♕**xe2**	**h6**
18	**b3**	**g5**
19	**a3**	♕**g6**

Now it's obvious that it was a mistake to force Black's Queen to e8 – its presence on g6 lends momentum to the K-side initiative.

20	**b4**	♘**f6**
21	**bxa5?**	...

Correct is *21* ♘df2, but after ...♘h5 Black stands better.

FISCHER

Position after 21 bxa5?

RESHEVSKY

Now Reshevsky is hoping to get some counterplay after *21...*bxa5 *22* ♘df2 ♘h5 *23* c5, etc. But –

21	...	**g4!**

– doesn't give him time to get it in.

22	♘**df2**	...

Not *22* axb6? gxf3 *23* ♕xf3 ♘xe4 *24* ♕xe4 ♗f5 wins a piece. On *22* ♘xf6+ ♗xf6 *23* f4 ♗f5 White's in trouble.

22	...	**gxf3**
23	♕**xf3**	♘**h5**

Increasing the pressure. On *23...*♘xd5 *24* ♕g3 holds.

24	♕e3	bxa5

Finally!

25	♖ac1	...

Typically, Reshevsky wants to mobilize his Q-side without making any concessions or creating any K-side weaknesses. After *25* g3 ♘f4 *26* ♔h1 ♘h3! it's just a matter of time before Black invades on the light squares.

25	...	♗f5
26	c5	...

Loses material, but probably the best chance. On *26* g3 ♖f7 followed by ...♖af8, White is not long for this world.

26	...	♘f4
27	♕g3	...

Blunders the exchange. But no longer possible is *27* g3 ♘xd5, etc.

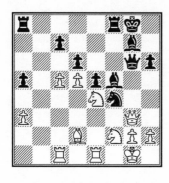

FISCHER

Position after 27 ♕g3

RESHEVSKY

27	...	♗xe4!
28	♖xe4?	...

Flustered, White makes the task somewhat easier. Better is *28* ♘xe4 (not *28* ♗xf4? exf4) *28*...♕xg3 *29* hxg3 ♘d3 *30* cxd6 cxd6 *31* ♖c6 ♘xe1 *32* ♗xe1 with many more chances of holding the ending than in the actual game.

28	...	♕xe4!
29	♘xe4	♘e2+
30	♔h1	♘xg3+
31	hxg3	♖a6!
32	cxd6	cxd6
33	a4	...

"Black has won the exchange, but the technical difficulties confronting him are enormous. His Pawns are discombobulated, his Bishop is hemmed in and his Rooks are virtually immobilized. Still, one has the feeling Fischer should win this game." (EVANS.)

33	...	♖f7
34	g4	♗f8
35	♔h2	♔h7
36	♖c8	♖b6
37	♖a8	♖b3
38	♗xa5	...

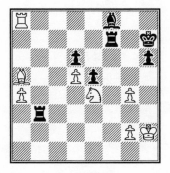

FISCHER

Position after 38 ♗xa5

RESHEVSKY

38	...	♖f4?

The right concept is to destroy the blockade on e4 with *38...♖e3!* *39 ♘c3* (if *39 ♘g3 ♖d3*) *39...e4 40 ♖e8 ♗g7 41 ♘xe4 ♗e5+*, etc.

39	♗c7!	...

With his usual tenacity, Reshevsky finds the only move to keep the game alive. White is still quite lost, however.

39	...	♖xe4
40	♖xf8	♖d3
41	♖f6	♖xg4
42	♖xd6	♖g7?

Now the "technical difficulties" become more real than apparent. Correct is *42...♖d2!* *43 ♖d7+ ♔g6 44 ♗xe5 ♖gxg2+ 45 ♔h3 ♖g5* wins easily.

43	♖c6!	...

Forced. *43 ♗b6* loses to *43...♖d2*. And *43 ♗a5* loses to *43...♖dg3*.

43 ... ♖xd5

If *43...♖d2 44 ♗xe5 ♖gxg2+ 45 ♔h3 ♖g5 46 ♗f4 ♖d3+ 47 ♔h2* (if *47 ♔h4? ♖d4 48 ♖f6 ♔g7*) *47...♖h5+ 48 ♔g2 ♖dxd5 49 ♖c7+! ♔g6 50 ♖c6+* draws.

44 ♖c2! ...

Again I had overlooked White's reply.

44 ... e4

Discouraged, I gave it one last try.

45 a5 ♖d3

On *45...e3 46 ♗f4 ♖e7 47 ♖e2* draws.

46 ♗f4 ♖f7
47 g3 e3
48 ♖c1 ...

Reshevsky, once more in severe time-pressure, overlooked that *48 ♔g2* draws easily. For on *48...♖xf4 49 ♖c7+!* is the saving clause.

48 ... ♖e7
49 ♖e1 ♖a3
50 ♖e2 ♔g6
51 ♔g2 ...

Not *51 ♗d6? ♖d7! 52 ♗xa3 ♖d2* wins.

51 ... ♖xa5
52 ♖xe3 ...

52 ♗xe3 draws easily. Black can't make anything out of the pin on the e-file.

52 ... ♖a2+
53 ♔f3? ...

A comedy of errors. Correct is *53 ♔h3!* in order to keep Black's King out of g4 after the exchange of Rooks: e.g., *53...♖xe3 54 ♗xe3 h5 55 ♗f4 ♖a1 56 ♗c7 ♔f5 57 ♗f4 ♖b1 58 ♗c7! ♖h1+ 59 ♔g2 ♖c1 60 ♗f4!* (gaining a vital tempo by hitting the Rook), *60...♖–any 61 ♔h3!* maintaining the blockade.

FISCHER

Position after 53 ♔f3?

RESHEVSKY

| 53 | ... | ♖b7? |

Returning the favor.

As Evans originally pointed out in *Chess Life*, "The best winning chance is *53...♖xe3+ 54 ♗xe3 h5* followed by ...♔f5."

Disgusted, I no longer thought there was a win. However, later I worked out a problem-like variation (after *54...h5*):

A] *55 g4? h4* wins.

B] *55 ♔e4 ♔f6! 56 ♗d4+ ♔e6 57 ♔f4 ♖a4 58 ♔e3 ♔f5* leads to variations similar to "D".

C] *55 ♔f4 ♖a5! 56 ♗d2 ♖f5+ 57 ♔e4 ♔f6* and Black's King will eventually penetrate to g4. For example, *58 ♗f4* (*58 ♔e3? ♔g5*) *58...♖a5* followed by ...♖a4+ and ...♔f5.

D] *55 ♗f4 ♔f5 56 ♗d6 ♖b2 57 ♗f4 ♖b3+ 58 ♔g2 ♔g4 59 ♗d6 ♖b2+ 60 ♔g1 ♔h3 61 ♗e5 ♖b4! 62 ♗c7* (not *62 ♗f4? h4*) *62...♖g4! 63 ♔f2 ♔h2 64 ♗e5 ♔h1 65 ♔f3 ♖g8 66 ♗f4 ♖f8 67 ♔f2* (if *67 ♔e3 ♔g2*) *67...h4 68 ♔f3 h3 69 ♔f2 h2 70 ♔f1 ♖a8 71 ♔f2 ♖a2+ 72 ♔f1 ♖a3! 73 ♔f2 ♖f3+!! 74 ♔xf3 ♔g1 75 ♗e3+ ♔f1* and the Pawn queens.

54	♖e6+	♔f5
55	♖e5+	♔f6
56	♖d5	♖b3+
57	♔g4	

Drawn

29 Fischer - Geller *[U.S.S.R.]*

BLED 1961

RUY LOPEZ

Hoist with his own petard

As was his wont, Geller gambles with 7...♕f6 in an attempt to assume an early offense. To thwart this maneuver, part of a patently prepared variation, Fischer sacrifices a Pawn (9 d4). Undaunted, Geller tries to continue his attack. But it backfires. With a series of rapier-like thrusts, Fischer demolishes Black in a mere twenty-two moves.

Subsequent attempts to improve on Geller's play have likewise failed. Thus, this fruitful encounter offers what has come to be accepted as the refutation of Black's ultra-aggressive system.

1	e4	e5
2	♘f3	♘c6
3	♗b5	a6
4	♗a4	d6
5	0-0	...

At that time this was considered inferior because it allows the pin which Black can initiate with his next move. 5 ♗xc6+ or 5 c3 were more standard. The text is more non-committal. White can deploy his forces to greater effect after he gets a look at Black's reply.

5	...	♗g4

This aggressive sally weakens Black's Q-side.

6	h3!	...

It's important to kick immediately, otherwise after ...♕f6 followed by ...♗xf3 White's Pawn formation could be smashed.

6	...	♗h5

As a result of this game 6...h5 became fashionable. I had intended *7 d4 b5 8 ♗b3 ♘xd4?* (*8...♕f6* is better) *9 hxg4 hxg4 10 ♘g5*. Unclear is *7 c4!? b5* (if *7...♕f6 8 ♕b3! 0-0-0 9 ♗xc6 bxc6 10 hxg4 hxg4 11 ♘h2 ♕h6 12 ♕g3* – but *11...d5!* is dangerous, Zhuravlev; *7...♗d7* avoids the piece sac, but after *8 d4* White has a superior variation of the Duras Attack) *8 cxb5 ♘d4 9 bxa6+ c6 10 ♘xd4! ♗xd1 11 ♗xc6+ ♔e7 12 ♘f5+ ♔f6 13 ♗xa8 ♕xa8 14 ♖xd1 ♕xe4 15 ♘c3 ♕a8 16 ♘e3 ♕xa6 17 d4 ♔g6 18 b4* and White's passed Q-side Pawns should win. (Grabczewski-Brzuska, Warsaw 1961.)

7	**c3**	**♕f6?**

Geller looked quite happy after his novelty, but sounder is *7...♘f6 8 d4 ♘d7* bolstering the center.

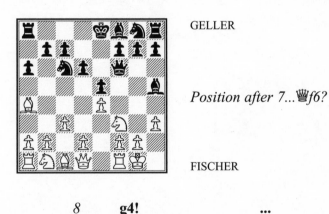

GELLER

Position after 7...♕f6?

FISCHER

8	**g4!**	**...**

I realized the danger inherent in weakening my K-side, but felt that I could capitalize on Black's lack of development (the traffic jam on his K-side) before he could get to my King.

8	**...**	**♗g6**
9	**d4!**	**...**

It's worth a Pawn to open up the game.

9	**...**	**♗xe4**

What else? The threat was *10 ♗g5* followed by *11 d5* winning a piece. He still looked happy.

10	♘bd2	♗g6

No better is *10...♗xf3 11 ♘xf3 e4 12 ♖e1 d5 13 ♗g5 ♕d6* (on
13...♕e6 14 c4! is the bone-crusher; or *13...♕g6 14 ♕b3! b5 15 ♕xd5
bxa4 16 ♘e5 ♕e6 17 ♕xe6+ fxe6 18 ♘xc6* wins) *14 c4! dxc4* (if
*14...f6 15 cxd5 ♕xd5 16 ♗b3) 15 d5! b5 16 dxc6 bxa4 17 ♖xe4+ ♘e7
18 ♗xe7 ♗xe7 19 ♕e2* wins.

An attempt to rehabilitate Geller's line was made in Smyslov-
Medina, Tel Aviv 1964, which continued *10...♗d3 11 ♗xc6+ bxc6
12 ♖e1 0-0-0* but *13 ♖e3!* proved to be very strong.

11	♗xc6+	...

Trading old advantages for new. Now Black's Q-side Pawns are a
shambles and his King can expect no shelter there.

11	...	bxc6

GELLER

Position after 11...bxc6

FISCHER

12	dxe5	...

A few weeks after the game it dawned on me that *12 ♕a4* would have
been a tremendous shot. After *12...♘e7* (apparently forced) *13 dxe5
dxe5 14 ♖e1 e4 15 ♘xe4 ♕xf3 16 ♕xc6+! ♘xc6 17 ♘f6++ ♔d8
18 ♖e8* mate. I was kicking myself for not having taken this course, but
then I found that after *12 ♕a4 ♔d7! 13 dxe5 dxe5 14 ♘c4 ♗d6* White
has no immediate way to exploit the exposed King.

12	...	dxe5

| 13 | ♘xe5! | ♝d6 |

On *13...0-0-0 14* ♕e2 ♚b7 *15* ♘b3 (intending ♘a5+) is murderous.

| 14 | ♘xg6! | ... |

A little surprise, permitting him to open his h-file. Of course not *14* ♘xc6 h5.

| 14 | ... | ♕xg6 |

Geller took a half hour on this recapture and stopped looking happy. He rejected *14*...hxg6 *15* ♘e4 ♕h4 *16* ♘xd6+ cxd6 *17* ♕xd6 ♕xh3? *18* ♖e1+ and mates.

| 15 | ♖e1+ | ♚f8 |

Another difficult decision. On *15*...♘e7 *16* ♘c4 0-0-0 *17* ♕a4 White's attack comes first.

| 16 | ♘c4 | h5 |

Still hoping to rise from the ashes and fan his attack.

| 17 | ♘xd6 | cxd6 |

The best chance is *17*...♕xd6.

| 18 | ♝f4 | d5? |

Loses outright. In the post-mortem Tal tried to hold the game with *18*...♖d8 *19* ♕e2 hxg4 but after *20* hxg4 Black is in virtual *zugzwang*. If *20*...♕h7? *21* ♝xd6+ wins.

| 19 | ♕b3 | hxg4 |

Geller spent about forty minutes on this move. If *19*...♘e7 *20* ♖xe7! ♚xe7 *21* ♕b7+ wins. Or *19*...♘f6 *20* ♕b7 ♖e8 *21* ♖xe8+ ♘xe8 *22* ♖e1 ♕f6 *24* ♕c8, etc.

GELLER

Position after 19...hxg4

FISCHER

| 20 | ♕b7! | ... |

Stronger than *20* ♕b4+ ♘e7 *21* ♕xe7+ ♔g8 *22* h4, etc.

20	...	gxh3 dis.+
21	♗g3	♖d8
22	♕b4+	**Black resigns**

He must now lose both a Knight *and* a Rook.

GELLER

Final Position after 22 ♕*b4+*

FISCHER

30 Gligorich [*Yugoslavia*] - Fischer

BLED 1961

KING'S INDIAN DEFENSE

A lyrical performance

This draw has the charm of perfection. Each move is interesting and, to this day, appears flawless.

With 17...c5 Fischer launches an intricate double-Pawn sacrifice which involves exact timing. Gligorich rises to the occasion, returning material in an attempt to wrest the advantage.
The economy and ingenuity displayed by both players produces a harmonious flow of movement, remarkable in its esthetic appeal. The effect is of a pas de deux *in which each partner contributes equally to the total symmetry.*

1	d4	♘f6
2	c4	g6
3	♘c3	♗g7
4	e4	d6
5	♘f3	0-0
6	♗e2	e5
7	0-0	♘c6
8	d5	♘e7
9	♘e1	♘d7
10	♘d3	...

The older *10* f3 f5 *11* ♗e3 f4 *12* ♗f2 g5 has been abandoned. Black's K-side attack has practically been worked out to a forced mate!

10	...	f5
11	exf5	...

Petrosian-Tal, in this same tournament, continued (with Black's N on e8): *11* f4 exf4 *12* ♗xf4 fxe4 *13* ♘xe4 ♘f5 *14* ♗g5 ♘f6 *15* g4 ♘d4 *16* ♘df2 ♕e7=.

11	...	♘xf5

In this line White gets a grip on e4, Black on d4. *11*...gxf5 is more energetic.

12	f3	♘f6

For *12...♘d4* see game number 28. Both moves give Black a nice game.

13	♘f2	♘d4
14	♘fe4	♘h5

White has the c5 lever; Black has the dynamic break with ...g5-g4. Chances are roughly even.

15	♗g5	♛d7

Keeping an eye on the d-Pawn so that ...c5 becomes possible.

16	g3	h6

In a later round Gligorich (as Black) played against Tal *16...c5?* but after *17 ♘b5! ♘xb5 18* cxb5 White obtained a bind.

17	♗e3	c5!

I was informed that Gligorich thought I had blundered a Pawn, but it is a deliberate sac. On *17...♘xe2+ 18* ♛xe2 g5 *19* c5 White has it all his own way.

18	♗xd4	...

Not *18 ♘b5 ♘f5 19 ♗d2* a6, etc.

18	...	exd4
19	♘b5	a6

Not *19...♗e5? 20* f4.

20	♘bxd6	...

Apparently Black has lost a Pawn without any visible compensation. His pieces, which are now so awkwardly placed, soon spring to life, however.

20	...	d3!
21	♛xd3	...

A double-edged game would result from *21 ♗xd3 ♗d4+ 22 ♔h1 ♘xg3+ 23 ♘xg3 ♛xd6 24 ♛c2 ♗h3*.

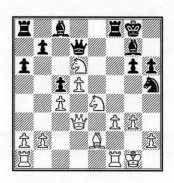

FISCHER

Position after 21 ♕xd3

GLIGORICH

21	...	♗d4+

The combination requires intricate footwork. A mistake would be *21...♗xb2 22 ♘xc8 ♗xa1 23 ♘b6* and it's all over (*23...♗d4+? 24 ♕xd4*).

22	♔g2	...

After *22 ♔h1 ♘xg3+ 23 ♘xg3 ♕xd6* White is weak on all the squares and his K-side looks like Swiss cheese. Chances would be even.

22	...	♘xg3!

This is the resource it was necessary to visualize as far back as move *17*.

FISCHER

Position after 22...♘xg3!

GLIGORICH

23	♘xc8!	...

Best. Not *23 hxg3?* (or *23 ♔xg3*) *23...♕h3* mate. On *23 ♘xg3 ♕xd6* again is good.

23	...	♘xf1
24	♘b6!	♕c7!

Blow for blow! The threat of mate on h2 keeps the exchange.

25	♖xf1	♛xb6
26	**b4!**	...

The saving clause.

26	...	♛xb4

I saw the draw coming but felt the position was too precarious to play for a win. On *26...cxb4 27 c5!* ♗xc5 *28* ♘xc5 ♛xc5 *29* ♛xg6+ ♔h8 *30* ♛xh6+ ♔g8 *31* ♔h1 wins. The only other try is *26...*♖f7 *27* bxc5 ♗xc5 *28* ♖b1 followed by d6 with tons of play.

27	♖b1	♛a5
28	♘xc5	...

On *28* ♖xb7 ♖f7.

28	...	♛xc5
29	♛xg6+	♗g7
30	♖xb7	♛d4

The only move. Gligorich was so sure I'd "find" it that he wrote it down on his scoresheet while I was taking a minute to look for something better.

31	♗d3	♖f4

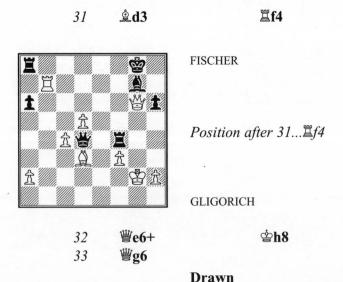

FISCHER

Position after 31...♖f4

GLIGORICH

32	♛e6+	♔h8
33	♛g6	

Drawn

31 Fischer - Petrosian *[U.S.S.R.]*

BLED 1961

CARO-KANN DEFENSE

The sincerest form of flattery

This is Fischer's only win against Petrosian and it is achieved through an unconscious mimicry of the latter's style. Right up to the endgame Fischer seems content to return the ball without trying to force the issue. Each attempt to seize the initiative is meticulously rebuffed. Move by move, they seem to be drifting toward a draw. Petrosian offers one at move 27, but Fischer declines. Perhaps out of irritation, Petrosian immediately commits his first and only error. And Fischer, reverting to his normal style of play, takes full advantage of it.

1	**e4**	**c6**
2	**d4**	...

For *2 ♘c3* see game 16.

2	...	**d5**
3	**♘c3**	...

For *3 exd5* see game 20.

3	...	**dxe4**
4	**♘xe4**	**♘d7**

For *4...♗f5* see game 49.

5	**♘f3**	...

5 ♕e2 ♘df6 (weaker is *5...♘gf6 6 ♘d6 mate*) gives White nothing. I tried *5 ♗c4* against Portisch at Stockholm 1962, which continued: *5...♘gf6 6 ♘g5 ♘d5* (the idea is to omit the usual ...e6 until after the QB has been developed) *7 ♘1f3 h6 8 ♘e4 ♘7b6 9 ♗b3* (better is *9 ♗d3 ♘b4 10 0-0 ♘xd3 11 ♕xd3 e6 12 ♘e5!* with pressure) *9...♗f5 10 ♘g3 ♗h7 11 0-0 e6=*.

5	...	**♘gf6**

| 6 | ♘xf6+ | ... |

The knight is not particularly well-placed after *6 ♘g3*.

6	...	♘xf6
7	♗c4	♗f5
8	♕e2	e6
9	♗g5	♗g4!

This super-refinement reduces all of White's attacking prospects. Petrosian has a knack of snuffing out such dreams twenty moves before they even enter his opponent's head! After *9...♗e7 10* 0-0-0 h6 *11 ♗h4 ♘e4!? 12* g4 *♗h7 13 ♗g3 ♘xg3 14* fxg3 *♕c7 15 ♘e5 ♗d6 16* h4 keeps the initiative. (Tal-Fuster, Portoroz 1958.)

| 10 | **0-0-0** | ♗e7 |
| 11 | **h3** | ... |

It might have been better to prevent further simplifications with *11 ♔b1 ♘d5 12 ♗c1!* 0-0 (not *12...♗xf3 13 ♕xf3 ♗g5 14 ♕g3!*) *13 ♗d3*, etc.

| 11 | ... | ♗xf3 |
| 12 | ♕xf3 | ♘d5! |

Forces an exchange of bishops. If *13 ♗d2 ♗g5*, etc.

| 13 | ♗xe7 | ♕xe7 |
| 14 | ♔b1 | ♖d8 |

I had expected *14...0-0-0*.

| 15 | ♕e4 | b5! |

PETROSIAN

Position after 15...b5!

FISCHER

Now it's apparent why Black didn't castle long. He wants to drum up counterplay on the Q-side, which he couldn't do if his King lived there.

16	♗d3	a5
17	c3	...

The threat was ...a4-a3. Weaker is *17* a3 b4. Already White has been thrown on a mild defensive.

17	...	♕d6

17...a4 would be met by *18* a3.

18	g3	...

I thought he wanted to exchange Queens.

18	...	b4!
19	c4	...

Practically forced – but now the d-Pawn is weak.

19	...	♘f6
20	♕e5	...

After *20* ♕e2 0-0 (*20*...♕xd4 *21* ♗xh7) *21* ♗c2 c5 White could easily end up with the bad Bishop.

20	...	c5

After *20*...♕xe5 *21* dxe5 ♘d7 *22* f4 ♘c5 produces a drawn ending. And not *20*...♕xd4 *21* ♕xa5.

21	♕g5	...

This looked like a shot –

21	...	h6!

– but instead it's a shock.

PETROSIAN

Position after 21...h6!

FISCHER

22	**♕xc5**	...

Now I saw that *22 ♕xg7 ♔e7! 23 dxc5 ♕c6!* (not *23...♕xc5 24 ♖he1 ♖dg8 25 ♖xe6+! ♔xe6 26 ♖e1+* should win) *24 ♗g6* (forced) *24...♖df8 25 ♗xf7 ♕e4+! 26 ♔a1 ♖h7!* and Black wins.

22	...	**♕xc5**
23	**dxc5**	**♔e7**

23...♖c8 immediately is also good.

24	**c6**	**♖d6**
25	**♖he1**	**♖xc6**
26	**♖e5**	**♖a8**
27	**♗e4**	...

After *27 ♖b5 ♖a7* followed by *...♘d7-c5* Black's solid as a rock. Right after I made this move, Petrosian offered a draw. I was ready to accept, but Tal happened to be standing there at that instant, hovering anxiously, since a drawn result would practically clinch first place for him. So I refused – not because I thought White has anything in the position, but because I didn't want to give Tal the satisfaction!

27	...	**♖d6?**

Serendipity. Simply *27...♘xe4* leads to a dead draw.

PETROSIAN

Position after 27...♖d6?

FISCHER

28	**♗xa8**	...

This obvious capture shattered Petrosian, who apparently had been engrossed in analyzing the intricacies of *28 ♖xd6 ♔xd6 29 ♖xe6+ fxe6 30 ♗xa8 ♔c5 31 b3 ♘d7 32 ♔c2 ♔d4* with an absolute bind on the dark squares.

28	...	♖xd1+
29	♔c2	♖f1

There's no turning back. If *29...♖d8 30 ♖xa5* wins.

30	♖xa5	♖xf2+
31	♔b3	♖h2
32	c5	♔d8

On *32...♖xh3 33 ♖a7+ ♔d8 34 ♖xf7 ♖xg3+ 35 ♔xb4* the Q-side Pawns hurtle toward a touchdown. The Bishop, since it can control both wings at once, is vastly superior to the Knight.

33	♖b5!	...

Not *33 ♖a7 ♘d7! 34 c6 ♘b6* holds.

33	...	♖xh3

Now *33...♘d7* is refuted by *34 c6.*

34	♖b8+	♔c7

Or *34...♔e7 35 ♔xb4* (not *35 c6? ♘d5*) *35...♖xg3 36 a4* wins.

35	♖b7+	♔c6

I suspect Petrosian saw White's reply, but wanted to be put out of his misery. *35...♔c8 36 ♖xf7 ♖xg3+ 37 ♔xb4* is futile.

36	♔c4!	**Black resigns**

There's no defense to the discovered checkmate.

PETROSIAN

Final Position after 36 ♔c4!

FISCHER

32 Fischer - Tal *[U.S.S.R.]*

BLED 1961

SICILIAN DEFENSE

The moral victor

After an early lapse by Tal on move 6, Fischer relentlessly presses home his advantage. He misses several opportunities to shorten Tal's resistance, but the outcome is never really in doubt.

"Finally, he has not escaped me!" exulted Fischer.

"It is difficult to play against Einstein's theory," sighed Tal, who went on to capture first prize.

But it was Fischer, finishing a strong second, who had the consolation of scoring 3½ out of 4 against the Russian contingent, and of being the only player (in a field of twenty) to emerge undefeated.

1	e4	c5
2	♘f3	♘c6
3	d4	cxd4
4	♘xd4	e6
5	♘c3	...

No doubt Tal expected 5 ♘b5 which I had played exclusively at Buenos Aires 1960. I still think that might be best (see game 54).

5	...	♕c7
6	g3	...

A perfectly legitimate treatment which Botvinnik labeled a "very cunning and well-masked idea." Actually no trap is intended. It becomes one only by virtue of Tal's reply.

6	...	♘f6?

Probably the losing move! Tal looked worried immediately after having made it, but I'm not sure he was convinced he had really been careless. Correct is 6...a6 7 ♗g2 ♘f6 8 0-0, etc.

7 ♞db5! ...

Curiously enough, Bisguier, who was present at Bled and witnessed the game, forgot this move when he reached the identical position against Benko at San Antonio 1962!

7 ... ♛b8

On 7...♛a5 *8* ♝d2 ♛d8 *9* ♝f4 e5 *10* ♝g5 is strong.

8 ♝f4 ♞e5

Tal took a long time on this risky reply. The alternative *8*...e5 *9* ♝g5 a6 *10* ♝xf6 (not *10* ♞a3 b5 *11* ♝xf6 b4!) *10*...axb5 (not *10*...gxf6 *11* ♞a3 b5 *12* ♞d5) *11* ♝g5 gives a clear advantage.

9 ♝e2! ...

Perhaps Tal underestimated this simple move. It prepares ♛d4 and keeps an eye on the b5 square.

TAL

Position after 9 ♝e2!

FISCHER

On *9*...a6 *10* ♛d4 d6 *11* ♜d1 axb5 *12* ♝xe5 wins at least a Pawn. Or *9*...d6 *10* ♛d4 ♞c6 *11* ♞xd6+ (Tal pointed out *11* ♛xd6! ♝xd6 *12* ♝xd6) *11*...♚d7 *12* ♝b5 ♝xd6 *13* 0-0-0, etc.

In the tournament book Tal suggested the rather startling *9*...♞g8 to avoid material loss. After *10* ♛d4 f6 *11* 0-0-0 (if *11* ♝xe5 fxe5 *12* ♛c4 ♚d8! holds) *11*...a6 *12* ♞d6+ ♝xd6 *13* ♛xd6 ♛xd6 *14* ♜xd6 leads to a promising endgame.

9 ... ♝c5

10	♗xe5!	♕xe5
11	f4	♕b8
12	e5	a6

Tal didn't give this a second thought. On *12...♘g8 13 ♘e4 ♗e7 14 ♕d2* followed by ♘bd6+ and 0-0-0 is crushing.

13	exf6	axb5
14	fxg7	...

Keres thought *14 ♘e4 ♗f8 15 ♕d4* was stronger. But I wanted the Pawn. With only two draws against Tal, out of six times at bat, I was in no mood to speculate!

14	...	♖g8
15	♘e4	♗e7
16	♕d4	♖a4

A desperate attempt to complicate. *16...♕c7* (BOTVINNIK) held out more chance for survival.

17	♘f6+	♗xf6

17...♔d8? loses to *18 ♕b6+*.

18	♕xf6	♕c7
19	0-0-0!	...

19 ♗h5 is answered by *19...d5*. And *19 ♗xb5? ♕a5+* wins a piece.

19	...	♖xa2
20	♔b1	...

TAL

Position after 20 ♔b1

FISCHER

20	...	♖**a6**

Not *20...*♖a5 since *21* ♗h5 d5 (if *21...*d6 *22* ♖xd6!) *22* ♖xd5! exd5
23 ♖e1+ wins outright.

Also bad is *20...*♕a5 *21* b3! and the threat of ♗h5 is decisive.

21	♗**xb5**	...

I was so intent on snatching material and not botching this one that I
missed *21* ♗h5 d6 (or *21...*d5 *22* ♖xd5!) *22* ♖he1 ♕e7 *23* ♕h6 ♔d7
24 ♕xh7 with a quick win in view.

21	...	♖**b6**
22	♗**d3**	e5

The best chance. On *22...*♕d8 *23* ♕h6 f5 *24* ♕h5+ ♔e7 *25* g4 cracks
Black open.

23	**fxe5!**	...

Black was hoping for *23* ♕xe5+ ♕xe5 *24* fxe5 ♖xg7 with some
drawing prospects, even though a Pawn behind. In top-flight chess, you
have to drive your advantage home unmercifully.

23	...	♖**xf6**
24	**exf6**	...

TAL

Position after 24 exf6

FISCHER

The threat is simply ♗xh7.

24	...	♕**c5**

The only move. *24...*♕b6 *25* ♖hf1 wins easily.

25	♗**xh7**	♕**g5**
26	♗**xg8**	♕**xf6**
27	♖**hf1**	♕**xg7**

| 28 | ♗xf7+ | ♚d8 |

Black has succeeded in staving off immediate defeat, but the endgame is hopeless.

| 29 | ♗e6 | ♕h6 |

On 29...♚c7 30 ♗f5 maintains the pressure.

30	♗xd7	♗xd7
31	♖f7	♕xh2
32	♖dxd7+	♚e8
33	♖de7+	♚d8
34	♖d7+	♚c8
35	♖c7+	♚d8
36	♖fd7+	♚e8
37	♖d1	...

White has been gaining time on the clock.

| 37 | ... | b5 |
| 38 | ♖b7 | ♕h5 |

38...♕xg3 39 ♖xb5 is equally convincing.

| 39 | g4 | ♕h3 |

Or 39...♕xg4 40 ♖h1 ♕d4 41 ♖h8+! ♕xh8 42 ♖b8+ wins.

40	g5	♕f3
41	♖e1+	♚f8
42	♖xb5	♚g7
43	♖b6	♕g3
44	♖d1	♕c7
45	♖dd6	...

Threatening 46 ♖g6+ ♚h7 47 ♖h6+ ♚g7 48 ♖bg6+ ♚f8 49 ♖h8+ ♚f7 50 ♖h7+ winning the Queen.

| 45 | ... | ♕c8 |

45...♕c5 46 ♖b7+ ♚–any 47 ♖d8 mate.

| 46 | b3 | ♚h7 |
| 47 | ♖a6 | **Black resigns** |

Black must submit to the loss of his Queen or get mated. There is no defense against 48 ♖a7+ ♚g8 49 ♖dd7, etc.

33 Fischer - Trifunovich [*Yugoslavia*]

BLED 1961

RUY LOPEZ

The drawing master

Trifunovich has earned the reputation of being a very hard man to beat, and the other Grandmasters have acquired a healthy respect for his technical skill. At Bled, for example, he lost only this one game.

Trifunovich's experiment with a dubious line in the opening meets with an abrupt and effective antidote (13 ♘xd4), saddling him with an isolated e-Pawn for the duration of the mid-game. He decides, perhaps unwisely, to sacrifice it at an appropriate moment to gain some counterplay. Although he succeeds in outplaying Fischer in the endgame, he cannot overcome his material deficit. What ultimately defeats him is force majeure.

1	e4	e5
2	♘f3	♘c6
3	♗b5	a6
4	♗a4	♘f6
5	0-0	♘xe4
6	d4	b5
7	♗b3	exd4?

Considered to be weak – and it is. But Trifunovich must have had some equalizing idea in mind, since he rarely chooses a genuinely risky line. The tried and tested 7...d5 must be played.

8	♖e1	...

A reader of Tal's Latvian chess magazine (*Shakhmaty*) suggested 8 ♘xd4 but 8...♘e7! seems to hold: e.g., 9 ♖e1 (if 9 ♗xf7+ ♔xf7 10 ♕f3+ ♔g8 11 ♕xe4 d5 is adequate) 9...d5 10 ♘c6! ♘xc6 11 ♗xd5 ♗b7! 12 ♗xe4 ♗e7 13 ♗xc6+ ♗xc6 14 ♕e2 ♔f8, etc.

8	...	d5
9	♘c3!	...

9 ♘xd4? ♘xd4 10 ♕xd4 ♗e6 (threatening ...c5) is better for Black.

| 9 | ... | ♗e6 |

On *9...dxc3 10* ♗xd5 ♗b7 *11* ♗xe4 (not *11* ♖xe4+? ♘e7!) *11...*♗e7 (*11...*♕xd1? loses to *12* ♗xc6++) *12* ♕e2 prevents Black from castling.

10	♘xe4	dxe4
11	♖xe4	♗e7
12	♗xe6	fxe6

TRIFUNOVICH

Position after 12...fxe6

FISCHER

| 13 | ♘xd4! | ... |

An improvement over the "book" line. Trifunovich probably expected the usual *13* ♖xe6 but after *13...*♕d5! *14* ♕e2 0-0 *15* ♖xe7 ♘xe7 *16* ♕xe7 ♖ae8 *17* ♕xc7 ♖f7 *18* ♕g3 ♖xf3! *19* gxf3 ♖e1+ *20* ♔g2 ♕c4 *21* ♔h3 ♕e6+ *22* ♕g4 ♕c6 and shortly drawn. (Dolodonov-Kicin, corres., USSR 1965.)

| 13 | ... | 0-0 |

He thought quite a while on this. Weak is *13...*e5? *14* ♕h5+ g6 *15* ♘xc6, etc. On *13...*♕d5 *14* ♕g4 0-0-0 *15* ♗e3 Black's e-Pawn is untenable. Finally the "simplifying combination" *13...*♘xd4 *14* ♖xd4 ♕xd4? *15* ♕xd4 ♖d8 falls short after *16* ♕g4.

14	♕g4	♘xd4
15	♖xd4	♕c8
16	♖e4	♖f6

White has a strategically won game, but the technical problems are considerable. Moreover a tempting trap now stared me in the face.

TRIFUNOVICH

Position after 16...♖f6

FISCHER

| 17 | ♗e3 | ... |

Keres suggests *17 ♗f4* in the tournament book, but *17...♗d6* is an adequate reply.

I was considering the blunder *17 ♗g5? ♖g6 18 h4 h6 19 ♕h5* but Trifunovich seemed too quiet all of a sudden, and I suspected he had tuned in on my brain waves. At the last minute I saw *19...♕e8!* wins; for if *20 ♗xe7 ♖xg2+! 21 ♔xg2 ♕xh5.*

17	...	♕d7
18	♖d1	♕c6
19	♗d4	♖g6
20	♕e2	♖d8
21	g3	♕d5

Threatening ...c5.

| 22 | ♖e1! | c5 |

Black's welcome to *22...♕xa2 23 b3 ♕a5* (otherwise *♖a1*) *24 ♖xe6* with a crushing attack.

23	♗c3	♖d6
24	♗e5	♖d8
25	♗f4!	...

Preventing ...♕d2.

| 25 | ... | c4 |

Again *25...♕xa2* is met by *26 b3* followed by *♖xe6*. Black decides to sacrifice his e-Pawn in order to get some activity. After *25...♔f7 26 b3* (threatening a4 at the right moment) leaves Black with little to do but sit back and wonder where White will penetrate next.

26	♖xe6	♖xe6
27	♕xe6+	♕xe6
28	♖xe6	♗f6
29	♖xa6	♖d1+
30	♔g2	...

TRIFUNOVICH

Position after 30 ♔g2

FISCHER

| 30 | ... | ♗xb2 |

After the game Gligorich suggested that *30...♖b1!* offered drawing chances. It makes things harder, but White should win after *31 a4!* (not *31 b3 ♖b2*) *31...♖xb2* (if *31...b4 32 ♖c6 ♖xb2 33 ♖xc4 ♗c3 34 ♗d6!*) *32 axb5 ♖xb5 33 ♖c6 c3 34 ♖e6 ♔f7 35 ♖e2* and eventually White's King marches to d3 and, after trading Bishops, captures the weak c-Pawn.

31	♖b6	♖a1
32	♖xb5	♖xa2
33	♖c5	♖a4

On *33...c3 34 ♗e5 ♗a1 35 ♖c7 ♖xc2 36 ♖xg7+ ♔f8 37 ♖c7* leads to an easy win. Black's c-Pawn isn't going anywhere.

| 34 | ♗e5 | ♗xe5 |
| 35 | ♖xe5 | ♖a2 |

On *35...♖a3 36 ♖e3! ♖a2 37 ♖c3* wins.

36	♖e2	♔f7
37	♔f3	♔f6
38	♔e4	g5
39	♔d4	♔f5
40	f3	...

While not bad in itself, the text indicates a wrong frame of mind. White should be looking for the quickest win, not ways to prolong Black's agony.

Simply *40 ♔xc4 ♔g4 41 ♔b3* is easy.

40	...	c3!
41	♖f2?	...

The simplest path is *41 ♔xc3 ♖a3+ 42 ♔d4 ♖xf3 43 c4*, etc. (KERES) Curiously now, I never do win his c-Pawn!

41	...	♖a3
42	♔c4	h5
43	♔b4	♖a8
44	f4	...

On *44 ♔xc3 h4* offers a few little problems.

44	...	♔e4!

I hadn't seen this defense. Now Black saves his c-Pawn and the win takes twenty moves longer than it should have.

45	fxg5	♔e3
46	♖g2	...

If the Rook leaves the second rank, then ...♔d2.

46	...	♔d4

On *46...♖c8 47 h4 ♔f3 48 ♖g1 ♔f2 49 ♖d1 ♔xg3 50 ♖d4* followed by *♖c4* does the trick.

TRIFUNOVICH

Position after 46...♔d4

FISCHER

47	♖e2	♖b8+

48	♔a4	♖g8
49	h4	♖f8
50	♖e7	♖f3
51	♖d7+	♔c4
52	♖c7+	♔d4
53	♖d7+	...

Repeating moves to gain time on the clock.

53	...	♔c4
54	♖c7+	♔d4
55	♔b3	♖xg3
56	♖d7+	♔e4
57	♖h7	♔d4
58	♖xh5	♖g1
59	♖h8	♖b1+
60	♔a4	♖a1+

There is no time for *60...♖b2* because of *61* g6.

61	♔b5	♖b1+
62	♔c6	♖g1
63	♖d8+	♔c4
64	♖e8	...

Threatening ♖e4 mate!

| 64 | ... | ♔b4 |
| 65 | ♔d5 | ♖d1+ |

On *65...♔a3 66 ♖b8* wins.

66	♔e6	♖e1+
67	♔f7	♖f1+
68	♔g6	♖f2
69	h5	...

Now the h-Pawn becomes the dangerous candidate.

69	...	♖xc2
70	h6	♖h2
71	h7	c2
72	♖c8	♔b3
73	♔g7	**Black resigns**

34 Bertok [*Yugoslavia*] - Fischer

STOCKHOLM 1962

QUEEN'S GAMBIT DECLINED

Hanging pawns unhung

Classical theory expounds the danger of "hanging Pawns," but Fischer demonstrates here, in a revolutionary manner, that they are just as often an asset as a liability.

Bertok's errors seem insignificant, yet he drifts into a passive position. On the verge of exploiting Black's loose center, he always lacks just the one tempo needed to do so. Meanwhile, using the open b-file as a base of operations, Fischer manages to force White into a defensive posture. In the midst of this Q-side tension, the winning move (21...g5) comes unexpectedly on the opposite wing.

1	d4	d5
2	c4	e6
3	♘c3	♗e7

A refinement attributed to Petrosian, but actually played by Charousek in the 'nineties – and probably dating back even farther.

4	♘f3	...

White, having no other good waiting move, is obliged to develop, thus restricting his option of playing this Knight to e2.

4 cxd5 exd5 5 ♗f4 c6 6 e3 ♗f5 7 g4 (R.Byrne's 7 ♘ge2! is best) 7...♗e6 (7...♗g6! is better) 8 h3 was played frequently in the 1963 title match between Botvinnik and Petrosian. White is slightly better.

4	...	♘f6
5	♗g5	...

Back to the main line. The shadow boxing is over.

5	...	0-0

6	e3	h6

Petrosian usually omits this move (see note to Black's 8th).

7	♗h4	b6

Tartakover's Defense.

8	cxd5	...

The best procedure, opening the c-file and preparing ♖c1 with pressure on Black's c-pawn. An alternative is *8* ♗d3 ♗b7 *9* 0-0 ♘bd7 *10* ♖c1 c5 *11* ♕e2 dxc4 *12* ♗xc4 ♘e4=. (Petrosian-Fischer, Candidates' 1959.)

8	...	♘xd5

Inferior here is *8...exd5 9* ♗d3 and *10* ♘e5! followed by f4 with a Pillsbury attacking formation: White has g4-g5 in the air – this line is playable for Black only with his pawn on h7 (instead of h6).

9	♗xe7	♕xe7
10	♘xd5	exd5

The text is drawish, but I had already clinched first prize.

FISCHER

Position after 10...exd5

BERTOK

11	♗e2	...

Sharper is *11* ♖c1 ♗e6! *12* ♕a4 c5 *13* ♕a3 ♖c8 *14* ♗e2 and now *14...♔f8* levels while *14...♕b7!* is the prescription for maintaining tension. If *15* dxc5 bxc5 *16* 0-0 (*16* ♖xc5? ♖xc5 *17* ♕xc5 ♕xb2 is bad for White) *16*...♕b6 is double-edged.

11	...	**♗e6!**

The right post. At b7 this Bishop would block the b-file and obstruct later operations there.

12	**0-0**	**c5**
13	**dxc5?**	...

Producing hanging center Pawns which, in this case, exert a tremendously cramping influence on White's future development. Better is *13* ♘e5 ♘d7 (not *13*...c4? *14* b3 b5 *15* a4) with equality.

13	...	**bxc5**
14	**♕a4**	**♕b7!**
15	**♕a3**	**♘d7**
16	**♘e1**	...

What else is there? Black's center is well-protected, and he is ready to assume the Q-side initiative with ...a5 and ...♕b4.

16	...	**a5**
17	**♘d3**	**c4**
18	**♘f4**	**♖fb8**

FISCHER

Position after 18...♖fb8

BERTOK

19	**♖ab1?**	...

White's game is already difficult, e.g., *19* ♗f3 ♘f6 *20* ♖fd1 ♕xb2 *21* ♕xb2 ♖xb2 *22* ♘xd5 ♘xd5 *23* ♗xd5 ♗xd5 *24* ♖xd5 c3! *25* ♖dd1 (if *25* ♖c5 c2 *26* ♖c1 ♖d8 wins) *25*...c2 *26* ♖dc1 ♖ab8 *27* ♔f1 ♖b1 *28* ♔e2 ♖xa1 *29* ♖xa1 ♖b1 wins.

Best is *19* ♘xe6 fxe6 *20* ♗g4 ♖a6! *21* b3! (if *21* ♕e7? ♘f8 or *21* ♖ab1 ♕b4 *22* ♕c3 ♕xc3 *23* bxc3 ♖ab6) *21*...cxb3 *22* axb3 ♕xb3 *23* ♕e7 ♘f8 *24* ♖a3 with good drawing chances (if *24*...♕b4 *25* ♕xb4 ♖xb4 *26* ♗e2 ♖a7 *27* ♖fa1 a4 *28* ♗d1, etc.).

19	...	♗f5!
20	♖bd1	♘f6
21	♖d2	...

The following variation gives some insight into the nature of White's problem: *21* ♗f3 ♕xb2 *22* ♕xb2 ♖xb2 *23* ♘xd5 ♘xd5 *24* ♗xd5 (if *24* ♖xd5 ♗e6 *25* ♖c5 ♖c8! *26* ♖xa5 c3 *27* ♖c1 c2 *28* ♗e4 ♖b1! *29* ♖xb1 cxb1=♕+ *30* ♗xb1 ♖c1 mate) *24*...♖c8 *25* e4 ♗e6! *26* ♗xe6 fxe6 *27* a4 c3 *28* ♖c1 c2 and White, completely tied up, must lose material.

| 21 | ... | g5! |

FISHER

Position after 21...g5!

BERTOK

Practically forcing the win of a piece.

| 22 | ♘xd5 | ... |

To break the hammer-lock. On *22* ♘h5 ♘e4 *23* ♖c2 ♕b4 is crushing.

| 22 | ... | ♘xd5 |
| 23 | ♗xc4 | ... |

Not *23* ♗f3? ♗d3.

23	...	♗e6

Black has some temporary discomfort but it's only a matter of time before he consolidates and wins with his extra piece.

24	♖fd1	...

Blundering a Pawn. The lesser evil is *24* ♗xd5 ♗xd5 *25* f3 but White is still lost if Black exercises a modicum of caution.

24	...	♘xe3!

Threatening mate.

25	♕xe3	♗xc4
26	h4	♖e8
27	♕g3	♕e7
28	b3	♗e6
29	f4	g4

Sealing the g-file and neutralizing all threats.

30	h5	♕c5+
31	♖f2	♗f5
	White resigns	

FISCHER

Final Position after 31...♗f5

BERTOK

35 Fischer - Julio Bolbochan *[Argentina]*

STOCKHOLM 1962

SICILIAN DEFENSE

A brilliant cadenza

Called upon to face his favorite defense, Fischer quickly obtains the advantage against Black's rather passive opening strategy. Bolbochan, burdened with a bad Bishop against a good Knight, defends with extreme care but is gradually forced to retreat behind his lines. Disdaining several opportunities to enter a favorable ending, Fischer presses for a quick decision in the mid-game. His judgment is rewarded when the pressure which he painstakingly has accumulated erupts in a violent attack, beginning with 34 hxg6. Fischer's invasion on the weakened squares is a model of accuracy. It culminates in a keen combination which, appropriately, earned a tie for the first brilliancy prize.

1	e4	c5
2	♘f3	d6
3	d4	cxd4
4	♘xd4	♘f6
5	♘c3	a6
6	h3	...

Black's loss of time with ...a6 may possibly justify this loss of time. The variation is specifically directed against the characteristic ...e5 of the Najdorf System. Thus if *6*...e5 *7* ♘de2 ♗e7 (or *7*...♗e6 *8* g4 d5 *9* exd5 ♘xd5 *10* ♗g2 with a comfortable edge) *8* g4 0-0 *9* ♘g3! g6 *10* g5 ♘e8 *11* h4 with a powerful attack: e.g., *11*...f6? *12* ♗c4+ ♔g7 *13* h5 fxg5 *14* hxg6 hxg6 *15* ♘h5+!.

6	...	♘c6

For *6*...g6 see game 43. For *6*...b5 see game 41.

7	g4	♘xd4
8	♕xd4	e5
9	♕d3	♗e7

More accurate is *9*...♗e6 immediately.

| 10 | g5! | ... |

Weak is *10* b3 as played in Gereben-Geller, Budapest 1952.

| 10 | ... | ♘d7 |

Now the Knight interferes with the normal development of the QB. But on *10...*♘h5 *11* h4 followed by an eventual ♗e2 will cause trouble.

| 11 | ♗e3 | ... |

Sharper is *11* h4 ♘c5 *12* ♕f3.

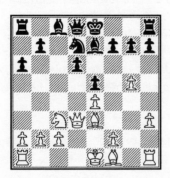

BOLBOCHAN

Position after 11 ♗e3

FISCHER

| 11 | ... | ♘c5? |

The best chance is *11...*♗xg5 *12* ♗xg5 ♕xg5 *13* ♕xd6 ♕e7 *14* ♕xe7+ ♔xe7 *15* ♘d5+ ♔f8 *16* 0-0-0 g6 (котоv) holding White to a minimal endgame edge.

12	♕d2	♗e6
13	0-0-0	0-0
14	f3	♖c8
15	♔b1	...

Amateurs are often puzzled by this apparent loss of time. Actually it is a handy defensive move, getting out of the pin on the c-file which could become annoying after ...b5-b4. One never knows when lightning will strike!

| 15 | ... | ♘d7 |

The knight has no future on c5, so Bolbochan tries to bring it into play via b6.

16	h4	b5
17	♗h3	♗xh3

After *17...♘b6 18* ♗xb6 ♕xb6 *19* ♘d5 ♕d8 (not *19...♗xd5? 20* ♗xc8) *20* ♘xe7+ ♕xe7 *21* ♕xd6, etc.

On *17...♖e8 18* ♘d5 ♗f8 *19* h5 with a tremendous bind. Black has to reckon with the possible breakthrough on g6.

18	♖xh3	♘b6
19	♗xb6	♕xb6
20	♘d5	...

White has a strategically won game; his Knight cannot be dislodged.

20	...	♕d8
21	f4	...

Threatening f5. An example of some of the nonsense that has been written about my games, both by admirers and detractors, is the following (by Lublinsky) in the 1962 Russian *Yearbook:* "Brilliant intuition! Fischer refuses to enter into the Rook and Pawn endgame and plays to continue his attack." But White can't! Not *21* ♘xe7+? ♕xe7 *22* ♕xd6?? ♖fd8 and Black wins.

21	...	exf4
22	♕xf4	♕d7
23	♕f5	♖cd8

Insufficient is *23...♖fd8?* (or *23...♕xf5? 24* ♘xe7+) *24* ♕xd7 ♖xd7 *25* ♘b6.

24	♖a3!	...

Shows how ideal the position is – White can afford the luxury of probing weaknesses on both wings.

24	...	♕a7

BOLBOCHAN

Position after 24...♛a7

FISCHER

| 25 | ♖c3 | ... |

Tempting is *25 ♘f6+!? ♗xf6* (if *25...gxf6? 26 gxf6 ♚h8 27 ♕g5 ♖g8 28 fxe7!*) *26 gxf6 g6 27 ♕g5 ♚h8* and White has no forced win in sight.

Objectively best is *25 ♘xe7+ ♕xe7 26 ♖xa6 ♖fe8 27 a4!* But I was hoping to win in the middle game. Ironically, I wouldn't have been awarded the brilliancy prize had I chosen the best line here. They don't give medals for endgame technique!

| 25 | ... | g6! |

On *25...♕d7? 26 ♖c7* wins. On *25...♖d7? 26 ♘f6+! ♗xf6* (*26...gxf6 27 gxf6 ♚h8 28 fxe7* wins) *27 gxf6 g6 28 ♕g5 ♚h8 29 ♕h6 ♖g8 30 ♖c8!* forces mate.

| 26 | ♕g4 | ♕d7 |
| 27 | ♕f3 | ♕e6 |

Not *27...♖c8? 28 ♖xc8 ♖xc8 29 ♘b6.*

| 28 | ♖c7 | ♖de8 |

On *28...♖d7 29 ♘f4* wins. And after *28...♖fe8 29 ♖f1* Black has hardly any moves. *29...♖c8* is answered by *30 ♖a7 ♖a8 31 ♖xa8 ♖xa8 32 ♘c7.*

29	♘f4	♕e5
30	♖d5	♕h8
31	a3	...

BOLBOCHAN

Position after 31 a3

FISCHER

| 31 | ... | h6 |

A bid for freedom – otherwise ♖a7 mops up the Q-side Pawns. On *31...f6 32* ♕b3! ♖f7 *33* ♖xd6 fxg5 *34* hxg5 ♕e5 *35* ♖f6! ♖ef8 *36* ♖xf7 ♖xf7 *37* ♖c8+ ♗f8 *38* ♘e6 wins.

| 32 | gxh6 | ♕xh6 |

On *32...*♗xh4? *33* ♘xg6! fxg6 *34* ♕b3 is decisive (*34...*♖f7 *35* ♖f5).

| 33 | h5 | ♗g5 |

After *33...g5 34* ♘e2 followed by ♘d4(or g3)-f5 maintains a winning bind. Black also has to contend with the threat of ♖a7.

| 34 | hxg6! | fxg6 |

On *34...*♗xf4 *35* gxf7+ ♖xf7 *36* ♖xf7 ♔xf7 *37* ♖h5! wins.

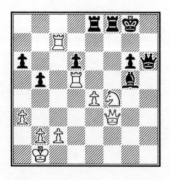

BOLBOCHAN

Position after 34...fxg6

FISCHER

| 35 | ♕b3! | ... |

The *coup de grâce*.

| 35 | ... | ♖xf4 |

On *35...*♔h8 (or *35...*♗xf4 *36* ♖h5+) *36* ♘xg6+ ♕xg6 *37* ♖xg5 ♖f1+ (*37...*♕xg5 *38* ♕h3+ forces mate) *38* ♔a2 ♕xg5 *39* ♕h3+ ♔g8 *40* ♕xf1 leads to a win.

| 36 | ♖e5+ | ♔f8 |
| 37 | ♖xe8+ | **Black resigns** |

After *37...*♔xe8 *38* ♕e6+ ♔f8 *39* ♕c8+ mates.

36 Fischer - Korchnoi *[U.S.S.R.]*

STOCKHOLM 1962

RUY LOPEZ

Gaston and Alphonse

"I like to coax my opponents into attacking, to let them taste the joy of the initiative, so that they may get carried away, become careless, and sacrifice material," wrote Korchnoi, whose comments are interwoven in the notes.

Fischer needs no coaxing. He improves on a well-known Capablanca line (with 15 d5). Still, the advantage he derives, if any, is microscopic. Korchnoi seems to labor under the delusion that he has the worst of it, though Fischer keeps asserting that White has nothing. Nevertheless, he overreaches himself, giving Korchnoi a chance to assume the initiative. But Black falters and then cracks under the pressure of the clock.

1	e4	e5
2	♘f3	♘c6
3	♗b5	a6
4	♗a4	♘f6
5	0-0	♗e7
6	♖e1	b5
7	♗b3	0-0
8	c3	d6
9	d4	...

An old try, championed by Yates and Alekhine, but discarded in the course of progress. It is still theoretically crucial – on its success (or failure) hinges the necessity of White's losing a tempo here with the customary *9 h3*.

9	...	♗g4
10	♗e3	exd4

Gligorich's *10...d5* is probably best. On the old *10...♘xe4!? 11 ♗d5 ♕d7 12 ♗xe4 d5 13 ♗xh7+! ♔xh7 14 dxe5*, White, according to Robert Byrne, can keep his extra Pawn and weather the attack.

11	**cxd4**	♘a5

11...d5 *12* e5 ♘e4 *13* ♘bd2 ♘xd2 *14* ♕xd2 ♗xf3 *15* gxf3 ♗b4 *16* ♕c2 ♗xe1 *17* ♕xc6 ♗b4 *18* ♗xd5 is known to favor White.

12	♗c2	...

KORCHNOI

Position after 12 ♗c2

FISCHER

12	...	♘c4

12...c5 may be better; *13* ♘bd2 cxd4 *14* ♗xd4 ♘c6 *15* ♗e3 d5 *16* exd5 ♘b4= (Yates-Bogolyubow, New York 1924.) Hence *13* dxc5 dxc5 *14* ♘bd2 seems the only try for an advantage.

13	♗c1	c5
14	**b3**	...

Interesting is *14* ♘bd2 ♘xd2 *15* ♕xd2 ♗xf3 *16* gxf3. (Geller-Panno, Amsterdam 1956.)

14	...	♘a5

Korchnoi is of a mind that the retreat *14*...♘b6 completely equalizes. But White can keep a pull after *15* ♘bd2 cxd4 (maybe better is *15*...♘fd7 *16* h3 ♗h5 *17* g4 ♗g6 *18* d5 ♗f6 *19* ♖b1 h5! Pietzsch-Szabo, 1962) *16* h3 ♗h5 *17* g4! ♗g6 *18* ♘xd4. (Pietzsch-Matanovich, Havana 1962.)

15	**d5!**	...

"A strong continuation which improves on *15* ♗b2 ♘c6! *16* d5 ♘b4 (Capablanca-Bogolyubow, London 1922) when Black gains the advantage of the pair of Bishops." (KORCHNOI.)

15	...	♘d7

On *15...*♘xe4 *16* ♖xe4 ♗xf3 *17* ♕xf3 ♗f6 *18* ♘c3 b4 *19* ♗b2 bxc3 *20* ♗xc3 ♗xc3 *21* ♕xc3 White has a big advantage.

16	♘bd2	♗f6

Aiming to strike on the dark squares before White can mobilize a K-side initiative.

17	♖b1	c4

Korchnoi considers this overambitious, believing that it creates too many Pawn weaknesses. He thinks Black ought to play *17...*♘e5 *18* h3 ♘xf3+ *19* ♘xf3 ♗xf3 *20* ♕xf3 b4; but after *21* ♗f4 ♖e8 (too passive is *21...*♘b7 *22* ♗d3, etc.) *22* ♕g3 ♗e5 *23* ♗xe5 ♖xe5 (if *23...*dxe5 *24* ♗d3) *24* f4 ♖e7 *25* ♖bd1 (threatening e5) maintains the pressure.

18	h3	...

"White does not fall for *18* b4? c3! *19* bxa5 cxd2 *20* ♗xd2 ♘e5 when the ensuing break-up of the Pawn protection of White's King more than compensates for his extra doubled Pawn." (KORCHNOI.)

18	...	♗xf3

"Giving White the two Bishops, but if *18...*♗h5 *19* b4! is now strong: *19...*c3 *20* bxa5 cxd2 *21* ♗xd2 ♘e5 *22* g4." (KORCHNOI.)

In this line simply *19...*♘b7 followed by ...a5 yields good counterplay. On *18...*♗h5 I intended *19* g4! (deadening Black's Bishop is worth this weakness). *19...*♗g6 *20* ♘f1-g3, etc.

19	♘xf3	cxb3

19...♖e8 *20* b4 ♘b7 *21* ♘d4 is strong. And *19...*c3? *20* a3! leaves the c-Pawn artificially isolated: White can encircle it by ♗e3-d4, ♖e3, etc.

Black's Knight on a5 is stranded; should it retreat to b7, then b4 smothers its future.

20	**axb3**	♕**c7**
21	♗**e3**	...

"Up to here, White has played in excellent style, but this inaccurate move considerably improves the Black position. White ought to play *21* ♗d2 or, still better, *21* ♖e2! protecting the KB and preparing the powerful maneuver ♘d4." (KORCHNOI.)

The truth is, White just doesn't have that much. After *21* ♗d2 or ♖e2 Black can still reply with ...♗c3.

21	...	♗**c3!**
22	♖**e2**	**b4**

"Now Black has sufficient play on the black squares." (KORCHNOI.)

23	♘**d4**	...

KORCHNOI

Position after 23 ♘*d4*

FISCHER

23	...	♖**fe8**

"Worried by his loose Pawn front and his scattered minor pieces, Black decides that he ought to get another piece into play rather than spend a move protecting his King's side. However, Fischer soon demonstrates that the White Knight obtains splendid prospects on the King's side, hence *23...g6* is much better." (KORCHNOI.)

On *23...g6 24* ♗d3 ♘c5 *25* ♖c2 ♘ab7 *26* ♘e2 ♗g7 the Bishop dances away and White has nothing.

24	♘**f5**	♘**b7**
25	♗**d4**	**g6**

The threat was ♘xg7.

| 26 | ♘h6+ | ♔f8 |
| 27 | ♖c1! | ... |

"This powerful move is a reminder to Black that he has problems on the c-file as well as in the neighborhood of his King." (KORCHNOI.)

| 27 | ... | ♖ac8 |

"In the event of White's exchanging Bishops, Black wants to be ready to recapture with a piece (Queen or Rook) rather than be left with a Pawn on c3 which will most likely be fatally weak." (KORCHNOI.)
Not 27...♗xd4 28 ♕xd4 f6 29 ♕xb4.

| 28 | ♗d3 | ... |

"This inaccuracy grants Black a fresh chance of recovery. A very strong continuation here was 28 ♖e3! with the threat of 29 ♗xc3 bxc3 30 ♕d4! f6 31 ♗b1 when the c-Pawn would fall." (KORCHNOI.)

| 28 | ... | ♕a5 |

On 28...♕d8 29 ♖ec2 maintains the pin.

| 29 | ♖ec2 | ♘e5 |
| 30 | ♗f1 | ♘c5 |

"Sacrificing a Pawn for the moment; but the Black pieces obtain excellent activity." (KORCHNOI.)

31	♗xc3	bxc3
32	♖xc3	♔g7
33	♘g4	♘xg4
34	♕xg4	♖b8

Breaking the pin and threatening the e-Pawn and/or the b-Pawn. Not 34...♖xe4?? 35 ♕xc8.

| 35 | ♖f3 | ... |

"White's best chance is to revive his attack on the King's wing." (KORCHNOI.)

35	...	♘xe4
36	♕f4	f5

"*36...♖b7 may be safer here.*" (KORCHNOI.)
The text weakens the K-side, but White can't exploit it.

37	♖e3	♖e5
38	♖c6	♖be8!?

"Short of time, I overlooked White's next move completely. Even so, the text is not bad, but for practical purposes Black ought to choose the simple *38...g5* maintaining a good position without risk." (KORCHNOI.)

After *38...g5 39 ♕f3 ♖be8 40 ♖xa6 ♕xd5 41 b4* the chances are approximately equal.

39	♖xd6!	...

KORCHNOI

Position after 39 ♖xd6!

FISCHER

39	...	♕a1?

"A bad error, after which Black is two Pawns behind with no compensation. Correct and necessary is *39...g5! 40 ♖d7+ ♔g6 41 ♕f3 ♕b6!* with the threat *42...♘xf2!*. For instance:

A] *42 ♗d3? ♘xf2 43 ♖xe5 ♘xd3 dis. ch.*

B] *42 g4? ♘xf2 43 ♖xe5 ♘xg4 dis. ch.*

C] *42 ♖xe4!* (best) *42...♖xe4 43 g4 ♖f4 44 gxf5+ ♔h6 45 ♕g3 ♖e5* with at least a draw.

"Instead, Black panics at the unexpected turn of events, and Fischer efficiently finishes the game in a few moves." (KORCHNOI.)

Incidentally, Korchnoi neglects to add that after *41...♕b6!* Black has the additional threat of ...♘f6 (as well as ...♘xf2) trapping the Rook. He also neglects to analyze the right defense: *42 ♕e2! ♘xf2* (What else? If *42...f4 43 ♖xe4 ♖xe4 44 ♕c2 ♔h6 45 ♖c7! wins*); *43 ♖xe5!*

♘e4+ (it's fascinating that Black has no better discovery; if *43...♘g4+ 44 ♖e3! ♖xe3 45 ♕xa6 ♕xa6 46 ♗xa6 ♘f6! 47 ♖d8 ♖xb3=*. But not *43...♘xh3++? 44 ♔h2 ♕g1+ 45 ♔g3! f4+ 46 ♔f3! ♖xe5 47 ♕xa6+!* wins) *44* ♔h2 ♖xe5 *45* ♕xa6 ♕xa6 *46* ♗xa6 ♘f6 regaining the d-Pawn with a draw in view.

40	♖xa6	♕d4
41	♖d3	♕b2
42	d6	g5
43	♕e3	f4
44	♕a7+	**Black resigns**

Black must lose a Rook after *44...♔f8 45 d7 ♖d8 46 ♕b6 ♔e7 47 ♕xd8+ ♔xd8 48 ♖a8+* followed by *49 d8=♕+*.

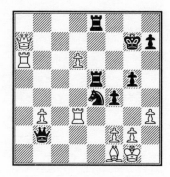

KORCHNOI

Final Position after 44 ♕a7+

FISCHER

37 Keres *[U.S.S.R.]* - Fischer

CURAÇAO 1962

SICILIAN DEFENSE

Only a draw

This contest brings to mind Emanuel Lasker's axiom: "When evenly matched opponents play 'correctly' the games seldom have any content and frequently end in draws." Here a little incorrect play provokes a series of brilliant moves leading to a most unusual draw.

Employing a slow, closed system against the Sicilian, Keres is strategically outplayed. By adjournment, however, he manages to achieve equality. Fischer refuses a draw, and the struggle flares anew. Working with a Rook against two minor pieces, he makes steady inroads. Each serpentine twist in the endgame, including the double error on move 56, is a joy, a revelation, and a study in itself. Keres' saving resources smack of sheer wizardry.

1	**e4**	**c5**
2	**♘e2**	**d6**
3	**g3**	**g6**

Sharper is *3*...d5! *4* ♗g2 dxe4 *5* ♗xe4 (on Lombardy's *5* ♘bc3 ♘f6 equalizes – but not *5*...f5 *6* d3 exd3 *7* cxd3 ♘f6 *8* 0-0) and White's attack is worth more than a Pawn) *5*...♘f6 *6* ♗g2 ♘c6 *7* 0-0 e6=.

4	**♗g2**	**♗g7**
5	**0-0**	**...**

Harmless. Correct is *5* c3 ♘c6 *6* d4 with a powerful center. If Black goes Pawn hunting now he gets shattered: *6*...cxd4 *7* cxd4 ♕b6? *8* ♘bc3 ♘xd4? *9* ♘d5 ♕c5 *10* ♘xd4 ♗xd4 *11* ♗e3! ♗xe3 *12* fxe3 ♕a5+ *13* b4 ♕d8 *14* ♖c1 ♖b8 *15* 0-0 ♗d7 *16* ♕d4 f6 *17* ♘c7+ ♔f7 *18* e5! with a strong attack. (Samarian-Wesen, corres. 1958.) The sober *6*...e5 *7* dxc5 dxc5 *8* ♕xd8+ ♘xd8 *9* ♘a3 allows White only a slightly better ending.

5	**...**	**♘c6**

6	c3	e5!
7	d3	...

Now White has to regroup in order to get in d4.

7	...	♘ge7
8	a3	...

A lemon, but already White must fight for equality. On *8* ♗e3 0-0 *9* d4 exd4 *10* cxd4 (Pachman-Tal, Amsterdam 1964) 10...cxd4 (also good is *10*...d5 *11* ♘bc3 ♗g4!) *11* ♘xd4 ♘e5 Black captures the initiative.

8	...	0-0

Deciding to ignore the Q-side. Keres hoped for *8*...a5 *9* a4! and White has tricked Black into weakening his b5 square.

9	b4	...

Probably played against Keres' better judgment, but I guess he wanted to justify his last move. One lemon leads to another.

9	...	b6
10	f4	exf4!

Abandoning the center to play against White's shaky Pawn structure.

11	gxf4	...

Not *11* ♘xf4? (or *11* ♗xf4 d5) 11...cxb4 *12* axb4 ♘xb4!

11	...	d5!

Wrong is *11*...cxb4 *12* axb4 ♘xb4? *13* f5! ♘ec6 *14* d4 ♘a6 *15* e5, etc.

12	e5	...

Poker-faced, as always, Keres made this move as though it were the most natural one on the board. But it was the last thing he wanted to do, since it exposes the poverty of White's strategy.

FISCHER

Position after 12 e5

KERES

| 12 | ... | ♗g4 |

Not bad, but *12...♘f5 à la* Nimzovich is even better. After *13 ♘g3 ♘ce7* maintains a solid blockade, and Black can break with ...f6 at his leisure.

| 13 | h3 | ♗xe2 |

Even stronger is *13...♗e6 14 ♘g3 ♕d7 15 ♔h2 f6.* The absence of Black's QB makes it difficult to exploit the white square weaknesses.

| 14 | ♕xe2 | f6 |
| 15 | b5 | ... |

The only way to keep the center from crumbling. After *15 e6 f5* the advanced e-pawn becomes a target.

| 15 | ... | ♘a5 |
| 16 | ♘d2 | ... |

Better is *16 ♖a2.* If then *16...fxe5 17 fxe5 ♖xf1+ 18 ♕xf1 ♗xe5 19 ♗g5!* is strong.

16	...	fxe5
17	fxe5	♖xf1+
18	♘xf1	...

Any recapture proves to be awkward. Also *18 ♗xf1 ♕c7! 19 ♘f3* (not *19 d4 cxd4 20 cxd4 ♕c3) 19...♘b3* is similar to the game.

18	...	♘b3
19	♖b1	♘xc1
20	♖xc1	♕c7!
21	♖e1	...

Still impossible is *21* d4? cxd4 and White can't recapture because of the pin. Despite the drawing tendency of the opposite colored Bishops, White has a difficult game: he's weak on all the squares and his King is somewhat exposed.

| | 21 | ... | ♖d8 |
| | 22 | ♘h2 | ... |

Black gets an iron grip after *22* d4 cxd4 *23* cxd4 ♘f5 followed by ...♗h6, etc.

	22	...	d4
	23	cxd4	cxd4
	24	♘f3?	...

A terrible boner, just when White could equalize with *24* ♘g4! ♖f8 *25* ♖f1.

| | 24 | ... | ♗h6! |

Keres probably underestimated the strength of this reply.

| | 25 | ♕a2+ | ♔h8 |
| | 26 | ♕e6 | ... |

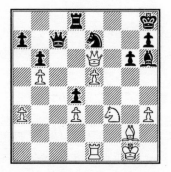

FISCHER

Position after 26 ♕e6

KERES

| | 26 | ... | ♘d5? |

Tempting but wrong. Correct is *26...♘f5! 27* ♕f6+ (if *27* ♘h2? ♗e3+ wins) *27...♗g7 28* ♕e6 ♖f8 followed by ...♗h6 again, and it's just a matter of time before Black invades on the weak dark squares. For example, *29* ♘g5 (not *29* ♘h2 ♕c3!) *29...♗h6 30* ♘e4 ♗e3+ *31* ♔h1 ♗f4 *32* ♘f6 ♕c3 *33* ♖d1 ♕c2, etc.

| | 27 | ♘h2! | ... |

The saving clause. Not *27* ♘xd4? ♕c5.

| 27 | ... | ♘e3 |

After 27...♘f4? 28 ♕f6+ ♔g8 29 ♘g4 White wins!

| 28 | ♗c6! | ... |

Now the Queen is hemmed in and Black has nothing. The Knight on e3 must coordinate with the heavy artillery to be really meaningful.

| 28 | ... | ♖f8 |
| 29 | ♘f3 | ♗f4 |

On 29...♕d8 30 ♕d6 holds. The chances are now even.

30	♘xd4	♗xe5
31	♘f3	♗d4!
32	♖xe3	...

Not 32 ♘xd4?? ♕g3+.

| 32 | ... | ♗xe3+ |

On 32...♕f4 33 ♔f2! holds.

33	♕xe3	♕g3+
34	♔f1	♕xh3+
35	♔e1	♕f5
36	d4	♔g7

36...h5? 37 ♕h6+ ♔g8 38 ♗d5+ ♕xd5 39 ♕xg6+ draws.

| 37 | ♔f2! | ... |

The right plan – the King must stay on the K-side to blockade Black's Pawns. Eventually Black, to make progress, must advance; but in so doing he will expose his King to perpetual check.

Worse is 37 ♕e5+ ♕xe5+ 38 dxe5 ♖f4 (intending ♖a4). White's e-Pawn can always be stopped by the King.

37	...	h5
38	♔g3	♕g4+
39	♔h2	♖f4

On 39...♕f4+ 40 ♕xf4 ♖xf4 41 ♔g3 holds. And not 39...h4? 40 ♕e7+ ♖f7 41 ♕xf7+!

40	♕e7+	♚h6

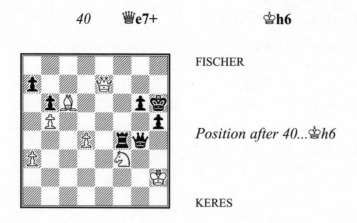

FISHER

Position after 40...♚h6

KERES

The game was adjourned and Keres sealed his move. Upon resuming the next day, he offered me a draw, which I rejected. I knew Black no longer had a winning advantage, but felt no harm could come from continuing since there was little danger of losing. Besides, winning this game would still have put me in contention for first place even as late as round 14, the halfway mark.

41	♕e2	♕f5
42	♕e3	g5
43	♔g2	♖g4+
44	♔f2	♖f4
45	♔g2	♕c2+

Beginning a series of exploratory checks to see if White goes to the wrong square. For instance, *46 ♔g3? ♖g4+ 47 ♔h3 ♕g2 mate*. Hope springs eternal!

46	♔h1	♕b1+
47	♔h2	♕a2+
48	♔h3	♕f7
49	♔h2	♕f6
50	♔g2	♔g7

Getting out of the potential pin. Not *50...g4? 51 ♔g3*. Black must strive to advance the Pawns so that they retain maximum mobility.

51	♔g3	h4+
52	♔g2	...

52 ♔h2? loses to 52...g4.

52	...	♖g4+

52...g4 is refuted by 53 ♘xh4!

53	♔h1	♖g3
54	♕e4	g4
55	♘h2	♕g5
56	♘f1?	...

A blunder on the last move of the second time-control. Perhaps Keres has allowed me to get a little too much out of the position, but he can still hold a draw with *56 ♕e5+! ♕xe5 57 dxe5* (threatening ♗d7) *57... ♖xa3 58 ♘xg4*, etc.

FISCHER

Position after 56 ♘f1?

KERES

| 56 | ... | ♖h3+? |

I had a feeling this might be a mistake, but time was short and I had to make a move – any move. "Patzer sees a check, gives a check." But now the game can no longer be won.

Correct is *56...♖xa3! 57 d5 g3 58 d6* (if *58 ♗d7 ♖a1 59 ♔g2 ♖a2+ 60 ♔g1 ♕f6 61 ♗f5 ♖f2*) *58...♖a1 59 ♕e7+* (if *59 ♔g1 ♕c5+ wins*) *59...♕xe7 60 dxe7 h3! 61 e8=♘+ ♔f8 wins.*

57	♔g1	♖xa3
58	d5	g3
59	♗d7!	♖a1

No longer gains a tempo, as in the last note.

| 60 | ♗f5! | ... |

The idea is to advance the Pawn to d6 without allowing ...♕c5+. I must confess that I still expected to win. But now Keres really starts to find moves!

| 60 | ... | ♕f6 |

61	♕f4	♖e1
62	d6	♖e5
63	♕g4+!	...

Not *63* d7? ♖xf5 *64* ♕xf5 ♕xf5 *65* d8=♕ ♕f2+ and mate next.

63	...	♔f8
64	d7	♖d5

Now *64*...♖xf5 *65* d8=♕+! ♕xd8 *66* ♕xf5+ draws.

FISCHER

Position after 64...♖d5

KERES

65	♔g2!	♖xd7!

On *65*...♕b2+ *66* ♔h3 ♕f2 *67* ♗e4! ♕xf1+ *68* ♗g2 ♕f2 *69* ♕b4+! holds.

66	♗xd7!	...

I thought this was a mistake at the time, but that he was lost anyway. Keres, however, has seen just one move further –

66	...	♕f2+
67	♔h3	♕xf1+
68	♔xh4	g2
69	♕b4+	♔f7!
70	♕b3+	♔g7
71	♕g3+	♔h7!

Haven – at last. Now I was sure I had him. Surely he would go in for *72* ♗f5+ ♕xf5 *73* ♕xg2 ♕f4+! *74* ♕g4 (on *74* ♔h3 ♕h6+! wins) *74*...♕xg4+ *75* ♔xg4 ♔g6! gaining the opposition and winning White's last Pawn by force.

72   ♕e5!!   ...

What's this? He makes no attempt to stop me from queening!?
Gradually my excitement subsided. The more I studied the situation,
the more I realized Black had no win.

FISCHER

Position after 72 ♕e5!!

KERES

72   ...   ♕h1+

The main line also draws – by a miracle: *72...♕f2+ 73 ♔h3 g1=♕*
(making a Knight with check also doesn't win) *74 ♗f5+ ♔h6*
(*74...♕xf5+ 75 ♕xf5+ ♕g6 76 ♕xg6+ ♔xg6 77 ♔g4!* is similar to the
final note) *75 ♕f6+ ♔h5 76 ♗g6+! ♕xg6 77 ♕g5+!! ♔xg5* Stalemate!

73   ♗h3   ♕xh3+

73...g1=♕ 74 ♕h5+ ♔g7 75 ♕g6+! forces stalemate or a perpetual.

74   ♔xh3   g1=♕
75   ♕e7+   ♔h8
76   ♕f8+   ♔h7
77   ♕f7+

Drawn

A last try might have been *77...♕g7 78 ♕xg7+! ♔xg7 79 ♔g3!*
holding the "distant opposition": e.g., *79...♔f6 80 ♔f4 ♔e6 81 ♔e4
♔d6 82 ♔d4 ♔c7 83 ♔d5 ♔b7 84 ♔c4 ♔c7 85 ♔d5 ♔d7 86 ♔e5* and
Black can't penetrate.

38 Fischer - Keres [*U.S.S.R.*]

CURAÇAO 1962

RUY LOPEZ

Detective story

Occasionally one comes across a miraculous victory in which, despite intensive post-mortems, there seems to be no losing move or pattern, no blunder on the part of the vanquished. But how can that be possible? A loser must make a mistake somewhere, however infinitesimal, however it may evade detection. Is it Keres' opening novelty which leads him to disaster? Could his defense have been improved afterward? If so: where? Whatever the answer, the reader is invited to share the magnifying glass with Fischer and hunt for that elusive error.

1	e4	e5
2	♘f3	♘c6
3	♗b5	a6
4	♗a4	♘f6
5	0-0	♗e7
6	♖e1	b5
7	♗b3	d6
8	c3	0-0
9	h3	...

For *9* d4 see game 36.

9	...	♘a5
10	♗c2	c5
11	d4	♘d7

"Now it is not easy to find a satisfactory continuation for White." (KERES.)

Keres' novelty, introduced on this occasion, has since become quite fashionable. I was – and still am – unimpressed. Black loses time redeveloping his knight to b6, but the K-side is weakened by its absence and it's questionable whether the Knight is not better where it stands originally.

KERES

Position after 11...♘d7

FISCHER

12	**dxc5!**	...

12 ♘bd2 was all the rage, but *12...cxd4 13* cxd4 ♘c6 may equalize. But not *12* dxe5 ♘xe5! with complete freedom.

"In spite of having won this game, it is probable that Fischer is not very convinced of the correctness of this continuation, because in a later game he closed the center with *12* d5." (KERES.)

According to that logic, Keres must not be convinced of the correctness of *11...♘d7* since he later varied with the old *11...♛c7* (against Gligorich at Hastings 1965).

12	...	dxc5
13	♘bd2	♛c7?

This is supposed to lead to trouble. If such a natural developing move is bad, then what kind of a position is this for Black? At the time Boleslavsky in his notes gave "*13...*f6!=" and this cryptic evaluation apparently cowed the chess world into abandoning *12* dxc5 – until very recently. After *13...*f6 *14* ♘h4 ♘b6 *15* ♘f5 ♖f7 (Fischer-Ivkov, Havana 1965) *16* ♛g4! (instead of my *16* ♘xe7+?) *16...*♚h8 *17* h4! threatening h5 followed by ♘f3-h4 is in White's favor: e.g., *17...*g6 *18* ♘h6 ♖g7 *19* ♛f3, etc.

14	♘f1	♘b6
15	♘e3	♖d8
16	♛e2	♝e6
17	♘d5!	...

The idea is to open lines and take advantage of Black's weakened K-side.

| 17 | ... | ♘xd5 |

On *17...♗xd5 18* exd5 f6 *19* h4! is strong. Now if *19...♘xd5* (*19...♘ac4 20* h5 ♘d6 *21* ♕d3! e4 *22* ♖xe4! ♘xe4 *23* ♕xe4 wins) *20* h5 (threatening *21* ♕e4) is powerful.

| 18 | **exd5** | **♗xd5** |
| 19 | **♘xe5** | ... |

KERES

Position after 19 ♘xe5

FISCHER

Since his early attacking days, Keres has switched to positional-defensive chess. But this type of position is too much even for him.

| 19 | ... | **♖a7** |

To defend the second rank. What else can Black do? White threatens to build up with ♗f4 and ♖ad1, and already sacrificial themes are in the air.

On *19...♗d6 20* ♕d3! ♗xe5 *21* ♕xh7+ ♔f8 *22* f4 wins. Or *19...♗e6 20* ♘xf7! Or *19...♗f8 20* ♕h5 g6 (if *20...h6 21* ♘g4) *21* ♕h4 ♗g7 (if *21...♗e7 22* ♕g3 threatening *23* ♘xg6) *22* ♘g4. Finally *19...f6* (*19...♖e8? 20* ♕d3) *20* ♕h5! fxe5 *21* ♗xh7+ ♔f8 *22* ♖xe5 ♗f7 *23* ♖f5 ♗f6 *24* ♖xf6! gxf6 *25* ♗h6+ ♔e7 *26* ♖e1+ ♗e6 (if *26...♔d6 27* ♗f4+ ♔c6 *28* ♗e4+ wins) *27* ♗f5 ♖d6 *28* ♗f4 wins.

| 20 | **♗f4** | **♕b6** |

The threat was *21* ♘g6. On *20...♕c8 21* ♖ad1 quietly continues the build-up.

| 21 | 罝ad1! | ... |

Threatening *22 罝xd5 罝xd5 23 豐e4*. Instead of seeking a "violent solution," my instinct told me to strengthen the position.

| 21 | ... | g6 |

Eliminating stock combinations against h7, but creating new weaknesses on the dark squares. What's better? On *21...奧xa2 22 罝xd8+ 豐xd8 (if 22...奧xd8 23 ♘c4! 豐e6 24 豐d1 罝d7 25 ♘d2) 23 b4! cxb4 24 cxb4 奧xb4 (the Knight can't move because of ♘c6) 25 豐e4! 奧xe1 26 豐xh7+ 當f8 27 豐h8+ 當e7 28 奧g5+ f6 29 ♘g6+ 當d7 30 奧f5+ 當c7 31 奧f4+* wins the Queen.

| 22 | ♘g4 | ... |

KERES

Position after 22 ♘g4

FISCHER

| 22 | ... | ♘c4 |

An attempt to bring this Knight toward the embattled sector. After *22...奧xa2 23 罝xd8+ 豐xd8 24 奧h6!* White has just too many threats. For example, *24...f5 (not 24...f6 25 b3! or 24...奧f8 25 豐e8 罝a8 26 ♘f6+ 當h8 27 奧xf8 wins) 25 豐e5! 奧d6 (if 25...奧f8 26 豐e8 豐xe8 27 罝xe8 罝f7 28 ♘e5 罝f6 29 ♘d7) 26 罝d1! ♘c4 (if 26...fxg4 27 罝xd6 罝d7 28 豐g7+!! wins) 27 豐e6+ 當h8 (if 27...罝f7 28 b3 fxg4 29 bxc4 豐h4 30 罝xd6 豐xh6 31 罝d8+ 當g7 32 豐e5+) 28 b3! fxg4 29 bxc4 罝d7 30 奧g5!* wins.

| 23 | 奧h6 | ... |

Some recommended the more direct *23 ♘h6+ ♔g7 24 ♖xd5 ♖xd5 25 ♘xf7*. I thought this might win at the time, but it looked speculative – and *25...♕f6!* refutes. Since Black is tied up in knots, I felt sure of a patient strategical victory.

<blockquote>23   ...   ♗e6</blockquote>

23...♘xb2 loses to *24 ♖xd5! ♖xd5 25 ♗e4 ♖d8 26 ♕xb2 f5 27 c4!* (threatening ♕g7 mate).

<blockquote>24   ♗b3!   ...</blockquote>

Pinning the Knight and piling on the pressure.

<blockquote>24   ...   ♕b8</blockquote>

To prevent White's Queen, in some variations, from penetrating to e5.

<blockquote>25   ♖xd8+   ♗xd8</blockquote>

Not *25...♕xd8? 26 ♗xc4 ♗xc4* (if *26...bxc4 27 ♕e5*) *27 ♘f6+! ♔h8 28 ♕e5*, etc.

<blockquote>26   ♗xc4   bxc4
27   ♕xc4!   ...</blockquote>

Cashing in! "Converting a spatial advantage into a material one." (See Evans' *New Ideas in Chess*.)

KERES

Position after 27 ♕xc4!

FISCHER

<blockquote>27   ...   ♕d6</blockquote>

Not *27...♕xb2 28 ♖xe6!* Or *27...♗xc4?? 28 ♖e8* mate.

<blockquote>28   ♕a4   ♕e7</blockquote>

29	♘f6+	♚h8
30	♘d5	♛d7
31	♛e4!	...

Back to the old stand, angling for e5 again.

| 31 | ... | ♛d6 |

31...♗xd5? 32 ♛e8+ mates. The weakness of Black's first rank has consistently proved to be his undoing throughout the mid-game.

| 32 | ♘f4 | ... |

32 c4 is also good.

| 32 | ... | ♖e7 |

Token resistance.

| 33 | ♗g5 | ... |

33 ♗f8! wins outright.

| 33 | ... | ♖e8 |
| 34 | ♗xd8 | ♖xd8 |

On 34...♛xd8 35 ♛e5+ f6 (not 35...♚g8 36 ♘d5!) 36 ♛xc5 ♗xa2 37 ♖xe8+ ♛xe8 38 c4 is the easiest path to victory.

| 35 | ♘xe6 | ♛xe6 |

On 35...♖e8 36 ♛e5+ is decisive.

36	♛xe6	fxe6
37	♖xe6	♖d1+
38	♚h2	♖d2
39	♖b6	♖xf2
40	♖b7!	♖f6
41	♚g3	**Black resigns**

Not only is Black a Pawn behind, but his King on the first rank is cut off as well. A likely winning line is 41...♚g8 42 b4 cxb4 43 cxb4 ♖d6 44 a4 ♖d3+ 45 ♚h2 ♖a3 46 a5 ♖a4 (if 46...♚h8 47 ♚g1 ♖a2 48 ♚f1 ♚g8 49 ♚e1 ♖xg2 50 b5 axb5 51 a6 ♖a2 52 a7) 47 ♚g3 and the King invades!

39 Botvinnik *[U.S.S.R.]* - Fischer

VARNA OLYMPIC 1962

GRUENFELD DEFENSE

The confrontation

This dramatic meeting between the generations took place on board I after it was rumored that Botvinnik would be given a "rest day" against the American team. But it was fated that Fischer, at last, albeit with Black, would have a crack at the world champion.
Walking into a prepared variation, Fischer promptly refutes it. "The reader can guess that my equanimity was wrecked," confesses Botvinnik, whose notes are incorporated here. Nervously, he proceeds to run his still tenable position downhill. But Fischer, instead of nursing his winning advantage, simplifies too quickly and reaches an adjournment where victory is problematical. After a sleepless night of analysis, Botvinnik finds a stunning defense. Fischer engages in a seemingly harmless transposition of moves (51...b5), and falls into a pit – throwing away the win he maintains was still there.

1	**c4**	**g6**
2	**d4**	**...**

If White so desires, he can prevent the Gruenfeld by *2 ♘c3 ♘f6 3 e4.*

2	**...**	**♘f6**
3	**♘c3**	**d5**

The spur of the moment. I could see by the glint in his eye that he had come well armed for my King's Indian.

4	**♘f3**	**...**

The sharpest try is *4 cxd5 ♘xd5 5 e4.*

4	**...**	**♗g7**
5	**♕b3**	**...**

The main line, but I don't believe this early development of the Queen can give White anything.

5	...	**dxc4**

A solid alternative is 5...c6.

6	**♕xc4**	**0-0**
7	**e4**	**♗g4**

Also interesting is Donald Byrne's provocative 7...♘c6.

8	**♗e3**	...

On 8 ♘e5 ♗e6 9 d5 ♗c8 followed by ...e6 equalizes.

8	...	**♘fd7**

Smyslov's Variation.

FISCHER

Position after 8...♘fd7

BOTVINNIK

So far theory has found no way to derive any clear advantage for White.

A] 9 0-0-0 ♘c6 10 ♗e2 ♘b6 11 ♕c5 ♕d6 12 h3 ♗xf3 13 gxf3 f5! (13...♖fd8? 14 e5! [Reshevsky-Evans, Las Vegas 1965], practically forces a won endgame for White, since if 14...♕d7? 15 d5! ♘xe5 16 f4) 14 d5 (if 14 e5 ♕xc5 15 dxc5 f4! is adequate) 14...♘e5 15 f4 (if 15 ♘b5? ♕f6 16 ♗d4 fxe4 17 fxe4 ♕f4+, etc.) 15...♘ed7 with a nice game.

B] 9 ♖d1 ♘c6 10 ♕b3 e5! 11 dxe5 ♗xf3 12 gxf3 ♘cxe5 13 ♗h3 ♘xf3+ 14 ♔e2! ♘fe5 15 ♗xd7 ♘xd7 16 ♕b5 c6 17 ♕xb7 ♖b8 18 ♕xd7 ♖xb2+ 19 ♔f1 ♕xd7 (Simagin's 19...♕f6 has also been analyzed to a draw) 20 ♖xd7 ♗xc3= Evans-Fischer, US Championship 1962-3.

9	♗e2	♘c6

Botvinnik thinks *9...♘b6* first is more accurate.

10	♖d1	♘b6

10...♗xf3 followed by *11...e5* also gives Black active play.

11	♕c5	♕d6!
12	h3	...

12 ♕xd6 is answered by *...cxd6!* improving Black's Pawn structure and neutralizing White's center.

12	...	♗xf3
13	gxf3	♖fd8

Wrong is *13...♕xc5 14 dxc5 ♗xc3+ 15 bxc3 ♘a4 16 ♔d2!* Botvinnik is of the opinion that *13...e6* (FURMAN) gives Black an equal game. But I feel it is not in the hypermodern spirit, which is precisely to tempt White into advancing his center Pawns in the hope they will become overextended.

14	d5	...

Opening the diagonal for Black's KB can't be right, but White is still striving for an opening advantage. On *14 e5 ♕xc5 15 dxc5 ♖xd1+ 16 ♔xd1 ♘d7 17 f4 g5! 18 fxg5 ♗xe5=.* Or *14 ♕xd6* (if *14 ♘b5 ♕xc5 15 dxc5 ♘a4!*) *14...cxd6=.*

14	...	♘e5
15	♘b5	...

"At once *15 f4* is not good because of *15...♘ec4 16 ♗xc4 ♕xc5 17 ♗xc5 ♘xc4 18 e5 ♘xb2 19 ♖d4 f6!* and White's central position breaks up." (BOTVINNIK.)

On *15 f4* also playable is simply *15...♘ed7 16 ♕b5* (*16 ♕xd6 cxd6* gives Black a comfortable ending) *16...e5! 17 f5* (*17 dxe6 e.p. ♗xc3+! 18 bxc3 ♕xe6*) with equal chances.

| 15 | ... | ♕f6! |

Weak is *15...♕xc5 16 ♗xc5 c6 17 ♘c7* (not *17 ♘xa7? ♘a4*) *17...♖ab8 18 ♗xe7 ♖d7 19 d6 ♘c8 20 ♘e8!* (not *20 f4 ♘xe7 21 fxe5 ♗xe5 22 dxe7 ♖xe7) 20...♘xe7 21 ♘xg7 ♚xg7 22 f4!*

| 16 | f4 | ♘ed7 |
| 17 | e5 | ... |

On *17 ♕xc7? ♕xb2* White can't castle and *18...♕b4+* is threatened.

FISCHER

Position after 17 e5

BOTVINNIK

"When I was preparing to meet Smyslov, I, of course, made a thorough analysis of the Smyslov System in general and of the position on the diagram in particular! Here I reckoned that whether the Black Queen went to h4 or f5, it would be in danger; for example, *17...♕f5 18 ♕b4 a5 19 ♕d4* threatening *20 ♗g4* or *17...♕h4 18 ♕c2 g5 19 ♖d4!*

Alas, my opponent found a third continuation!" (BOTVINNIK.)

| 17 | ... | ♕xf4! |

"A very unpleasant surprise – now White really had to start playing. Up to here I had only had to remember my analysis, though that was not so easy. I had a recollection of the Black Queen being trapped somewhere on the K-side; and following this track I managed to recall the whole variation. At last everything was in order – on the board was the familiar position; then suddenly it was obvious that in my analysis I had missed what Fischer had found with the greatest of ease at the board. The reader can guess that my equanimity was wrecked.

However, if you assess *17...*♕xf4 from an objective point of view, then although it is the best way out for Black, as you will see from what comes later, his position is still difficult." (BOTVINNIK.)

When I made this move, I felt sure he had overlooked it.

| 18 | ♗xf4 | ... |

Black's last is tactically justified after *18* ♕xb6 ♕e4! *19* f3 ♕h4+! *20* ♗f2 ♕b4+ followed by ...axb6! (toward the center).

18	...	♘xc5
19	♘xc7	♖ac8
20	d6	exd6
21	exd6	...

Not *21* ♖xd6? ♘cd7.

| 21 | ... | ♗xb2 |

"So Black has won a Pawn; but the Knight on c7 and the Pawn on d6 confine his Rooks – and also, White has two Bishops. The first thing White must do is complete his development." (BOTVINNIK.)

| 22 | 0-0 | ♘bd7 |

"A bad mistake; evidently, Black overestimated his possibilities. Of course, he had to prepare the move ...♗e5; the only way this could be done was by *22...*♘cd7 and after *23* ♗f3 ♗e5 *24* ♗xe5 ♘xe5 *25* ♗xb7 ♖b8 White has no more than a minimal advantage.

Now White has the two important squares d5 and c5 at his disposal and his spatial advantage becomes crushing." (BOTVINNIK.)

Needless to add, I couldn't disagree more. Why should Black return the Pawn?

| 23 | ♖d5 | ... |

Archives recommends *23* ♘d5 but after *23...*♔g7 the burden of proof rests with White – he's a Pawn down.

| 23 | ... | b6 |

FISCHER

Position after 23...b6

BOTVINNIK

| 24 | ♗f3? | ... |

"Feeble play. Actually, White had played quite consistently so far and here he could have deployed his force with maximum efficiency by *24 ♗c4!* with the threat of ♖e1-e7.

The bishop is out of it on f3 and merely becomes an object of attack. Black now frees himself, and a Pawn down White is in a critical position." (BOTVINNIK.)

After *24 ♗c4!* it is true that White has a bind, but with *24...♘e6* Black can practically force a draw, if he wants it, after *25 ♗h2 ♘d4* (threatening ...♘f6) *26 ♖b1 ♗c3 27 ♖c1 ♗b2*, etc.

| 24 | ... | ♘e6! |

"Apparently, this forces the exchange of the Knight on c7, for *25 ♗h2 ♘d4 26 ♗g2 ♘f6* is very bad for White. In fact, even here *26 ♖xd4!* (pointed out by Geller) *26...♗xd4 27 ♖e1* gave White a real chance to get out of all his troubles. A second error running makes his position hopeless." (BOTVINNIK.)

The reader is invited to judge for himself whether, in Geller's line, White has any real compensation for the exchange and a Pawn. Here *27...♗c5* followed by *...♘f6* or *...♘f8* should extricate Black.

| 25 | ♘xe6? | ... |

This really took me aback. After *25 ♗e3* at least White's still in the game.

| 25 | ... | **fxe6** |

26	♖d3	...

On *26* ♖dd1? (or *26* ♖d2? ♗c1 *27* ♖d4 e5) *26*...♖f8! *27* ♗g4 ♖xf4 *28* ♗xe6+ ♖f7 wins.

26	...	♘c5
27	♖e3	...

Bad is *27* ♖d2 ♖f8 *28* d7 ♖cd8.

27	...	e5

"The simplest. If *27*...♗d4 *28* ♖a3 e5 *29* ♗g5 ♖xd6 *30* ♗e7 ♖d7 *31* ♗g4 Black lost the exchange." (BOTVINNIK.)

28	♗xe5	...

Just leads to a dead lost ending. I expected *28* ♖xe5!? (hopeless though it is) to try and keep a little "dynamic imbalance."

28	...	♗xe5
29	♖xe5	♖xd6
30	♖e7	♖d7
31	♖xd7	...

On *31* ♖fe1 ♖cc7! flushes White off the 7th rank.

31	...	♘xd7
32	♗g4	...

"A pointless move, since White cannot go into the lost Rook and Pawn ending; he should have played at once *32* ♖e1 ♔f8 *33* ♖e3 (or *33* ♗d5) – Black would still have had technical difficulties." (BOTVINNIK.)

32	...	♖c7
33	♖e1	♔f7
34	♔g2	...

"And now *34* ♗e6+ was preferable, as the Bishop is poorly posted at g4." (BOTVINNIK.)

34	...	♘c5
35	♖e3	♖e7
36	♖f3+	...

"White's best practical chance consisted in an exchange of Rooks and a position with his King on d4 (or e3), his Bishop on c2 and his f-Pawn at f4. But all that is impossible – 36 ♔f3 h5! and White loses his Bishop." (BOTVINNIK.)

36	...	♔g7
37	♖c3	♖e4
38	♗d1	♖d4

"Before this I considered the game completely hopeless for me, but the text move gave me new heart; why had my opponent allowed my Bishop to get to a good post (and the only good one!) at c2? Surely, by 38...♖e1! (39 ♗c2 ♖c1) White's defenses could have been completely disorganized." (BOTVINNIK.)

After 38...♖e1 simply 39 ♗f3 is more logical.

| 39 | ♗c2 | ♔f6 |
| 40 | ♔f3 | ♔g5 |

"In general terms, d6 is the best square for the King; for then the Knight would not need to defend the b-Pawn and Black would win by advancing his Q-side Pawns. But this maneuver is also not bad." (BOTVINNIK.)

| 41 | ♔g3 | ... |

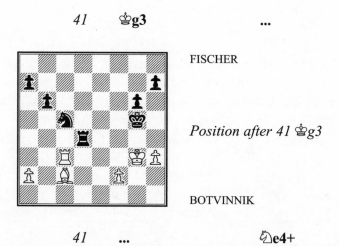

FISCHER

Position after 41 ♔g3

BOTVINNIK

| 41 | ... | ♘e4+ |

"Could have led to an immediate draw – and just at the very moment when Black was nearing his goal. You see, White was already in *zugzwang*: against a King move Black plays ...♔h4 and ...♘e6-f4(xh3); if ♗b1, the reply ...♖d1 wins; and if the White Rook moves from its place, then ...♖c4 is decisive. So after, for instance, *41...♖b4 42 a3 ♖d4 43 f3 a5* White would have had no satisfactory reply.

It is psychologically understandable why Black decided on the Rook and Pawn ending – earlier (see White's 23rd move) White had avoided it. But there is a difference between these two endings – the Black King is in a bad position on g5." (BOTVINNIK.)

Although I agree that Black can win by keeping the minor pieces and gradually improving his position, the text should also produce the same result, if only by a hair's breadth.

42	♗xe4	♖xe4
43	♖a3	...

"Natural and bad. White is now in danger of defeat again. *43 ♖c7!!* was essential, and White gets a draw as in the game. The fact that his Pawn is on a2 and not a4 has no significance." (BOTVINNIK.)

After *43 ♖c7 ♖a4 44 ♖xh7 ♖a3+! 45 f3* (if *45 ♔g2 ♖xa2 46 ♖b7 ♖a1 47 ♔f3 ♔f5 48 ♖f7+ ♔e5 49 ♖g7 b5* gains a tempo over the game because White's pawn is on h3 instead of h4) *45...♖xa2 46 h4+* leads to the same ending as the game, except White has already played f3 which Botvinnik, for some reason, carefully avoided. So the difference may be significant.

43	...	♖e7

"Perhaps *43...a5! 44 ♖b3 ♖b4* was better; Black obtained either a won Rook and Pawn ending or – after *45 ♖xb4 axb4 46 f4+ ♔f5 47 ♔f3 ♔e6 48 ♔e4* (*48 ♔g4 h6*) *48...♔d6 49 ♔d4 b5 50 ♔d3 ♔d5* – a probably won Pawn ending." (BOTVINNIK.)

44	♖f3	♖c7

"His last chance consisted in improving the position of his King by the maneuver ...♔h6-g7." (BOTVINNIK.)

45	a4	...

FISCHER

Position after 45 a4

BOTVINNIK

"Here Black sealed a move. White's threat is to exchange a pair of Pawns on the Q-side by a5 (for example, *45...♖c4 46* a5 bxa5 [or *46...b5 47 ♖f7*] *47 ♖f7* a6 *48* h4+ ♔h6 *49 ♖d7*) after which the weakness of Black's h-Pawn together with the unfortunate position of his King would guarantee the draw.

The most subtle move was *45...♔h6*, although even then Black gets nowhere after *46 ♖d3! ♖c5 47* h4 ♖a5 *48 ♖d4*.

What happened in the game is also most probably a draw." (BOTVINNIK.)

The game was officially "drawn" at breakfast. The Russian team had a table near the American team. Someone inquired of Botvinnik what he thought of the adjourned position. Hardly looking up from his plate, the world champion shrugged, *"Nichia"* (draw). The word quickly spread, and I overheard someone at the English table saying: "The Russians said Fischer could have won before adjournment..."

45	...	♖c5
46	♖f7	♖a5
47	♖xh7!	...

"A very fine idea, found during overnight analysis by Geller. Because of his bad King position Black finds it difficult to mobilize his connected passed Pawns." (BOTVINNIK.)

This was the first defense I had considered! Passive play is hopeless: e.g., *47 ♖f4 ♖f5 48 ♖c4 ♖f7* followed by ...♔f5 and Black brings his King to the Q-side.

47	...	♖xa4
48	h4+!	...

I had analyzed mainly *48* f4+ but Botvinnik's line is best and also contains a sly trap.

| 48 | ... | ♚f5 |

"Or *48*...♚f6 *49* ♖b7! ♖a5 *50* ♚g4 b5 *51* f4 a6 *52* ♖b6+ ♚f7 *53* ♖b7+ and White is quite safe." (BOTVINNIK.)

| 49 | ♖f7+ | ♚e5 |
| 50 | ♖g7 | ... |

"The weakness of the g-Pawn and the a-Pawn gives White sufficient counterplay." (BOTVINNIK.)

| 50 | ... | ♖a1 |
| 51 | ♚f3 | ... |

FISCHER

Position after 51 ♚f3

BOTVINNIK

| 51 | ... | **b5?** |

Originally Botvinnik wrote in *Chess Life*: "This is a mistake in analysis. But even after *51*...♚d5! *52* ♖xg6 b5 *53* ♚e2 ♚c4 *54* h5 b4 *55* ♖g4+ ♚b5 (if *55*...♚c3 or *55*...♚b3 then *56* ♖h4 followed by h6-h7 is very strong) *56* ♚d3 the White King reaches the Q-side and it is easy to credit the draw."

Later in the 1962 Russian *Yearbook*, he analyzed the entire ending more exhaustively and came to the conclusion, after considerable soul-searching, that it was drawn even against the best line: *51*...♚d4! The bracketed comments are mine. "*52* ♖xg6 b5 *53* h5 b4 *54* ♚g2 b3 *55* h6 b2 *56* h7 ♖h1! *57* ♚xh1 b1=♕+ *58* ♚h2 ♕b8+ *59* ♚g1 ♕h8 [*59*...♕e5! seems to do the trick: if *60* ♖g8 ♕e1+ *61* ♚h2 ♕xf2+ *62* ♚h3 ♕f3+! forces the win of the h-pawn or if *60* ♚f1 ♕h2 *61* ♖g7 a5 *62* ♖a7 ♚d3!] *60* ♖g4+ ♚c3 *61* ♖h4 a5 *62* ♚g2 ♚b3 *63* ♖h3+ ♚c2

64 Rh4 a4 *65* Rxa4 Qg7+! (if *65...*Qxh7 *66* Rg4-g3 and the Rook holds the third rank, shuttling to e3, if necessary, keeping Black's King out – with a draw); *66* Kf1 Qxh7 wins, since White can't get his Rook back to the third rank: e.g., *67* Ra2+ Kb3 [*68* Ra5 seems to hold here] or *67* Ra3 Qh1+ *68* Ke2 Qd1+ *69* Ke3 Qc1+ wins the Rook. Or *67* Rg4 Qh1+ *68* Rg1 (if *68* Ke2 Qd1+ wins the Rook) *68...*Qh3+ *69* Rg2 (if *69* Ke1 Qf3 forces mate) *69...*Kd2 *70* Kg1 Ke1 wins (*71* Rg3 Qf1+).

Was it really true that the adjourned position was lost? Was I mistaken?" (BOTVINNIK.)

Botvinnik then went on to give a corrected analysis which, as we shall see, also falls short. *51...*Kd4! *52* Rxg6 b5 *53* h5 b4 *54* h6! (instead of his previous *54* Kg2) *54...*b3 (if *54...*Rh1 *55* Kg2! Rh5 *56* Ra6 b3 *57* Rxa7 Rxh6 *58* Rb7 Kc4 *59* Kf3 leads to a theoretical draw) *55* Rg4+ (if *55* h7 Rh1 *56* Rg7 a5 wins) *55...*Kc5! (not *55...*Kc3? *56* Rh4 and White queens with check; or *55...*Kd3? *56* Rb4 Kc2 *57* Rc4+ draws) *56* Rg5+ Kc6! [Here I break camp with Botvinnik, only to meet at the next diagram. He gives *56...*Kb4 overlooking that White can obtain an immediate draw with *57* Rg7! b2 (*57...*a5? loses to *58* Kg2!) *58* h7 Rh1! *59* Rxa7 Kb3 *60* Rb7+ Kc2 *61* Rc7+ Kd2 *62* Rb7, etc.] *57* Rg6+ Kb7! *58* Rg7+ (if *58* Rg4 a5 wins) *58...*Ka6! (the idea is to keep the King off the b-file so that White's Rook can't check from behind) *59* Rg6+ (if *59* Kg2 b2 *60* h7 b1=Q *61* h8=Q Qe4+! and White is bombarded with checks which lead to probable mate, certainly win of material) *59...*Ka5! (not *59...*Kb5? *60* Rg7 a5? *61* Kg2! wins) *60* Rg5+ (if *60* Rg7? b2 *61* Rxa7+ Kb6 wins) *60...*Ka4! (finally Black has crawled up along the a-file) *61* Rg4+ (*61* Rg7 a5 *62* Rb7 Rh1 is easy; or *61* Rh5 b2 *62* h7 b1=Q *63* h8=Q Qd3+ *64* Kf4 Re1! is the pause that refreshes – White is checkless – if *65* Re5 Qd4+ *66* Kf5 Qxf2+ *67* Ke6 Qb6+ is decisive) *61...*Ka3 *62* Rh4 b2 *63* h7 b1=Q *64* h8=Q.

FISCHER

*Possible position after 64 h8=*Q
(analysis)

BOTVINNIK

Botvinnik also reached this position in his analysis independently, and concluded that it was a draw. However, it is precisely here, in this barren wilderness, that Black can wend his way to a win.

Correct is *64...♕b3+! 65 ♔e2* (if *65 ♔f4 ♕f7+* or *65 ♔g2 ♕d5+ 66 f3 ♕d2+) 65...♕d1+ 66 ♔e3 ♖b1!! 67 ♕f8+* (not *67 ♕c3+? ♖b3* or *67 ♖h3 ♔a2! 68 ♕g8+ ♕b3+* wins) *67...♔a2* and White's King will be without shelter from the coming avalanche of checks.

Now to return to the dreary (for me) game.

| | 52 | **h5!** | ... |

"Now Black is left with two RP's and the draw becomes a question of theory." (BOTVINNIK.)

The move I overlooked. *52 ♖xg6 ♔d4* transposes into the note to Black's 51st.

52	...	**♖a3+**
53	**♔g2**	**gxh5**

Botvinnik visibly relaxed. I had played right into his hands.

54	**♖g5+**	**♔d6**
55	**♖xb5**	**h4**
56	**f4**	**♔c6**
57	**♖b8!**	**h3+**
58	**♔h2**	**a5**
59	**f5**	**♔c7**
60	**♖b5**	**♔d6**

FISCHER

Position after 60...♔d6

BOTVINNIK

"Generally speaking, this ending would be drawn even without the f-Pawn – any textbook on the endgame will tell you this." (BOTVINNIK.)

61	**f6**	**♔e6**
62	**♖b6+**	**♔f7**
63	**♖a6**	**♔g6**
64	**♖c6**	**a4**
65	**♖a6**	**♔f7**
66	**♖c6**	**♖d3**
67	**♖a6**	**a3**
68	**♔g1**	

Drawn

"'Too many mistakes?' the reader may justly ask. Yes, there were rather a lot!" (BOTVINNIK.)

FISCHER

Final Position after 68 ♔g1

BOTVINNIK

40 Fischer - Najdorf *[Argentina]*

VARNA OLYMPIC 1962

SICILIAN DEFENSE

The Najdorf Variation

The durable Najdorf Variation remains Fischer's favorite, and he constantly experiments when confronted with it. Here, against the originator of the defense, he employs an unorthodox continuation. Najdorf counters sharply, launching an early struggle.

In order to preserve the initiative, Fischer gambits a Pawn with 7 ♘d5. Najdorf unwisely declines, only to accept three moves later under more unfavorable circumstances. He loses his way in the complications, allowing a devastating sacrifice which pins his King in the center. Although Najdorf defends with precision, it is too late to compensate for his earlier dilatory tactics. He finds himself ensnarled in a mating net after twenty-four moves. Rather than prolong his agony, the grand old master tenders his resignation.

1	e4	c5
2	♘f3	d6
3	d4	cxd4
4	♘xd4	♘f6
5	♘c3	a6
6	h3	...

For *6* ♗g5 see games 9 and 15. For *6* ♗e2 see games 4 and 42. For *6* ♗c4 see games 17, 55, 58.

6	...	b5!?

The sharpest reply. For *6...*g6 see game 43. For *6...*♘c6 see game 35.

7	♘d5!?	...

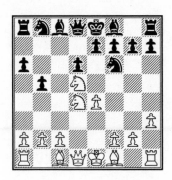

NAJDORF

Position after 7 ♘d5!?

FISCHER

The idea is to exploit the hole on c6. Najdorf apparently underestimated the strength of this "eccentric" move which appears to violate principle by moving the same piece twice.

A good alternative was *7 a4.*

7 ... ♗b7?

Black's subsequent troubles can be traced to this. No better is *7...♘bd7??* *8 ♘c6* winning the Queen. And on *7...♘fd7* *8 ♗g5! h6?* *9 ♘e6!*

On *7...e6* *8 ♘xf6+ ♕xf6* *9 c4 b4* Black's Queen is misplaced and his Q-side has been weakened.

Unclear are the complications stemming from *7...♘xe4!* *8 ♕f3 ♘c5* and White is confronted with 2 main lines:

A] *9 ♘f6+? gxf6* *10 ♕xa8 ♗b7* *11 ♕a7 ♕c7* (or *11...e5* *12 b4 exd4* *13 bxc5 ♕e7+* *14 ♗e2 ♘c6* *15 ♕b6 dxc5* *16 0-0!* is good for White) *12 b4 ♘cd7* and Black has excellent play for the exchange.

B] *9 b4! e6* (not *9...♘b7?* *10 ♕c3!* but interesting is *9...♘cd7* *10 ♕c3! ♖a7* *11 ♗g5!?* or even *11 ♗xb5*) *10 bxc5* (if *10 ♘f6+ ♕xf6* *11 ♕xa8 ♕xd4* *12 ♕xb8 ♕xa1* *13 ♕xc8+ ♔e7*) *10...exd5* *11 ♕xd5 ♖a7=.*

8 ♘xf6+ gxf6
9 c4! ...

White must play sharply, else his advantage evaporates. After the tame *9 ♗d3, ♘d7* is tenable.

9 ... bxc4

Had Najdorf correctly evaluated the results of this decision, he would have chosen *9...b4.* The 1962 Russian *Yearbook* gives *9...♗xe4*

10 cxb5 ♗g7 *11* ♕g4 ♗g6 *12* ♘f5 with advantage. But *12*...0-0 is unclear.

| *10* | ♗xc4 | ♗xe4 |

On *10*...♕a5+ *11* ♗d2 ♕e5 *12* ♕b3! ♕xe4+ *13* ♔d1 White has a very strong attack.

| *11* | **0-0** | **d5** |
| *12* | **♖e1!** | **...** |

NAJDORF

Position after 12 ♖e1!

FISCHER

| *12* | **...** | **e5** |

A] *12*...♖g8 *13* ♖xe4! dxe4 *14* ♕h5 ♖g7 (if *14*...♖g6 *15* ♕xh7 ♖g7 *16* ♕xe4 ♖a7 *17* ♘f5 or ♗f4) *15* ♘f5, etc.

B] *12*...e6 *13* ♕h5 ♗g6 *14* ♕xd5 ♕xd5 *15* ♗xd5 ♖a7 *16* ♗f4 ♖d7 *17* ♘xe6 fxe6 *18* ♗xe6 ♘c6 *19* ♖ac1, etc.

C] *12*...h5 *13* ♖xe4! dxe4 *14* ♕b3! ♕xd4 *15* ♗e3 with a winning attack.

D] *12*...♘d7 *13* ♘c6 ♕c7 *14* ♗xd5, etc.

E] *12*...♗xg2 *13* ♔xg2 dxc4 *14* ♕f3 ♘d7 *15* ♘f5 ♖g8+ (if *15*...e6 *16* ♖xe6+! fxe6 *17* ♕h5 mate) *16* ♔h1 e5 (if *16*...e6 *17* ♕c6 threatening *18* ♖xe6+) *17* ♗e3 with a winning bind despite the two-Pawn deficit.

F] Relatively best is *12*...dxc4 *13* ♖xe4 ♕d5 *14* ♕f3 e6.

| *13* | **♕a4+!** | **...** |

Inferior is *13* ♖xe4 dxe4 *14* ♕a4+ ♕d7 *15* ♗b5 axb5 *16* ♕xa8 exd4 *17* ♕xb8+ ♔e7, etc.

| 13 | ... | ♘d7 |

On *13...*♕d7 *14* ♗b5! axb5 *15* ♕xa8 ♗d6 *16* ♖xe4! dxe4 *17* ♕xe4 followed by ♘f5 with a powerful bind.

NAJDORF

Position after 13...♘d7

FISCHER

| 14 | ♖xe4! | **dxe4** |

14...dxc4 15 ♘f5 leads to the same type of position as the game, except Black is without any material compensation.

| 15 | ♘f5! | ... |

Perhaps Black had hoped for *15* ♕b3 ♕b6 *16* ♗xf7+ ♔d8 with some chances for survival.

| 15 | ... | ♗c5 |
| 16 | ♘g7+! | ♔e7 |

On *16...*♔f8 *17* ♗h6 ♔g8 *18* ♕b3 is murder.

| 17 | ♘f5+ | ♔e8 |

Back where we started – but Black has lost the right to castle.

| 18 | ♗e3 | ... |

Tal suggested *18* ♗h6 but after *18...*♖a7 *19* ♖d1 ♕b6 Black is still alive. The text robs Black of any possible counterplay.

| 18 | ... | ♗xe3 |

| 19 | fxe3 | ... |

The exchange of Bishops has failed to ease Black's defensive task. The threat of ♘d6+ is now in the offing.

| 19 | ... | ♕b6 |
| 20 | ♖d1! | ... |

Again after 20 ♗xf7+ ♔d8! 21 ♖d1 ♕b5 White has no immediate forced win.

| 20 | ... | ♖a7 |
| 21 | ♖d6! | ... |

The crusher! Either 21 ♗xf7+ ♔d8 or 21 ♘d6+ ♔e7 allow resistance.

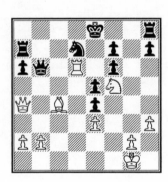

NAJDORF

Position after 21 ♖d6!

FISCHER

| 21 | ... | ♕d8 |

Best under the circumstances. On *21...♕c7 22 ♖xf6* wins. And on *21...♕xb2 22 ♗xf7+* (finally!) *22...♔xf7* (if *22...♔d8 23 ♕a5+ ♔c8* [*23...♖c7 24 ♗e6* wins] *24 ♘e7+ ♔b8 25 ♘c6+ ♔a8 26 ♘xa7*) *23 ♖xd7+ ♖xd7 24 ♕xd7+ ♔g6 25 ♕g7+ ♔xf5 26 ♕g4* mate.

| 22 | ♕b3 | ♕c7 |

On *22...♖f8 23 ♘g7+ ♔e7 24 ♕a3!* is very decisive.

| 23 | ♗xf7+ | ♔d8 |

On *23...♔f8 24 ♗h5* and mates.

24	♗e6	...

NAJDORF

Final Position after 24 ♗e6

FISCHER

24	...	**Black resigns**

Najdorf has no taste for prolonging the torture. If, for example, *24...♖b7 25 ♕a4 ♕c8 26 ♕a5+ ♔e8 27 ♕xa6 ♔d8 28 ♗xd7 ♖xd7 29 ♖xd7+ ♕xd7 (29...♔xd7 30 ♕d6+ ♔e8 31 ♕e7 mate) 30 ♕xf6+ ♔c7 31 ♕xe5+ ♔b6 32 ♕xh8* with a winning endgame.

41 Fischer - Robatsch [Austria]

CENTER COUNTER DEFENSE

A bright cameo

Facing one of Robatsch's pet lines, Fischer proceeds to institute such a crisp attack that one is reminded of Morphy in his heyday. Noteworthy are White's 5th and 6th, practically refuting the whole variation.

Seeking safety for his King, Robatsch makes the mistake of castling too early. Fischer, already castled on the opposite wing, incurs no risk advancing his K-side Pawns, using them as battering rams to pry open the g-file. Robatsch is unable to effect a closure and Fischer rushes into the breach — compelling resignation in only twenty moves.

1	e4	d5
2	exd5	♕xd5

This old move is considered weak but Black has a new twist in mind. The modern way is 2...♘f6. Then White has the choice of either 3 c4 or 3 ♗b5+ to hold the Pawn, or simply 3 d4. Against Bergrasser at Monaco 1967, I chose 3 ♗b5+ ♗d7 4 ♗c4 ♗g4 5 f3 ♗f5 (safer is 5...♗c8) 6 g4! ♗c8 7 ♘c3 ♘bd7 8 g5 ♘b6 9 ♗b5+ ♘fd7 10 f4 ♘xd5 11 ♘xd5 c6 12 ♗c4 cxd5 13 ♗xd5 and White's extra Pawn should prevail.

3	♘c3	♕d8

A hypermodern approach, championed by Bronstein. The idea is to give up the center and then play against it. Seidman, as Black, played the more traditional 3...♕a5 against me in the 1958-9 US Championship, which continued: 4 d4 ♘f6 5 ♘f3 ♘c6 6 d5!? (possibly an improvement over the usual 6 ♗b5) 6...♘b4 7 ♗b5+ c6 (more crucial is 7...♗d7 8 ♗xd7+ ♘xd7 9 a3 ♘f6 10 axb4 ♕xa1 11 0-0 ♕a6 12 ♖e1 with a terrific attack. Not 12...0-0-0? 13 ♘e5) 8 dxc6 bxc6 9 ♗a4 ♗a6? (9...♗d7 is necessary) 10 a3! ♖d8 11 ♗d2 ♕f5 12 axb4 ♖d6 13 ♗b3 ♘e4 14 ♖xa6 ♖xd2 15 ♕c1 ♘xc3 16 bxc3 ♖d6 17 0-0 Black resigns.

| *4* | **d4** | **g6!?** |

The idea is to reserve the option of developing the KN to h6 followed by ...♘f5 with pressure on the d-Pawn. After the game Robatsch told me he'd enjoyed excellent results with this system.

| *5* | **♗f4!** | ... |

Against the pedestrian *5* ♘f3 (or *5* ♗c4 ♗g7 *6* ♘f3 ♘h6) *5...*♗g7 *6* h3 ♘f6 (not *6...*♘h6 *7* g4! Sokolsky) White holds no more than a minimal edge.

| *5* | ... | **♗g7** |

On *5...*♘h6 *6* ♗e5! f6 *7* ♗f4 messes up Black's Pawns.

| *6* | **♕d2!** | ... |

Ignoring the "threat." Weak is *6* ♘b5 ♘a6 followed by ...c6, etc. (Bronstein-Kholmov, USSR 1959). And *6* ♘f3 ♘h6 would permit Black the setup he is striving for.

ROBATSCH

Position after 6 ♕d2!

FISCHER

| *6* | ... | **♘f6** |

Stymied, Black can no longer play ...♘h6.

The main line is *6...*♕xd4 *7* ♕xd4 ♗xd4 *8* ♘b5 ♗b6 (forced) *9* ♘xc7+ ♗xc7 *10* ♗xc7 with the two Bishops and all the chances. Another possibility is *6...*♗xd4? *7* 0-0-0 ♘c6 *8* ♗b5 ♗d7 *9* ♘d5! (not *9* ♗xc6? ♗xc6 *10* ♕xd4? ♕xd4 *11* ♖xd4 ♗xg2) *9...*e5 *10* ♘f3 and Black will never get out of the opening alive.

7	**0-0-0**	**c6**

Better is *7...*♘d5 *8* ♗e5 (*8* ♗h6!? ♗xh6 *9* ♕xh6 ♘xc3 ruptures White's Pawns) *8...0-0 9* h4 h5 *10* ♘ge2 with a clear advantage but no forced win.

8	♗**h6**	**0-0?**

Castling into it – with a vengeance. Black should strive to castle long with *8...*♗xh6 *9* ♕xh6 ♗f5.

9	**h4**	♕**a5**
10	**h5!**	...

The attack plays itself. My experience with this line dates back to the Dragon-slaying days (see game 2).

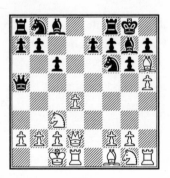

ROBATSCH

Position after 10 h5!

FISCHER

10	...	**gxh5**

Horrible, but Black must keep the h-file closed one way or another. On *10...*♖d8 *11* hxg6 fxg6 *12* ♗xg7 ♔xg7 *13* ♕h6+ ♔g8 *14* ♘f3-g5 is slaughter.

Or *10...*♘xh5 *11* ♗e2 ♘f6 *12* ♗xg7 ♔xg7 *13* ♕h6+ ♔g8 *14* g4! ♖d8 *15* g5 ♘h5 *16* ♗xh5 gxh5 *17* ♖xh5 ♗f5 (or *17...*♕f5 *18* g6! ♕xg6 *19* ♖g5) *18* g6! wins.

On *10...*♗f5 *11* f3 (threatening g4) *11...*♗xh6 (*11...*gxh5? *12* ♕g5 wins) *12* ♕xh6 gxh5? *13* ♕g5+ ♔h8 *14* ♗d3 wins a piece.

11	♗d3	...

It's important to exclude Black's Bishop from f5.

11	...	♘bd7

Not *11...♗f5? 12 ♕g5*.

12	♘ge2	...

Taking advantage of the lull to bring out the reserves.

12	...	♖d8
13	g4!	♘f8

On *13...♘xg4 14 ♖dg1!* (threatening both f3 and/or ♖xg4+) wins at least a piece. Black hopes to hang on by clustering minor pieces around his King.

14	gxh5	...

Now the open g-file becomes the new base of operations.

14	...	♘e6
15	♖dg1	♔h8

Also hopeless is *15...♔f8 16 ♗xg7+ ♘xg7 17 ♕h6 ♘g4 18 ♕xh7*.

16	♗xg7+	♘xg7
17	♕h6	♖g8

Or *17...♘e6 18 ♘f4!* forces mate.

18	♖g5	♕d8

Or *18...♘f5 19 ♖xg8+ ♘xg8 20 ♕f8* followed by ♖g1 is tasty.

19	♖hg1	...

ROBATSCH

Position after 19 ♖hg1

FISCHER

| 19 | ... | ♘f5 |

Blundering a piece. But Black is completely tied up, and it's a pity he didn't allow the prettier finish after *19...♕f8 20* d5! ♗d7 (if *20...*cxd5 *21* ♘xd5 ♘xd5 *22* ♕xh7 mate) *21* d6! ♘f5 *22* ♕xf8 ♖axf8 (or *22...*♖gxf8 *23* ♗xf5 h6 *24* dxe7 ♖fb8 *25* ♖g7 ♗xf5 *26* ♖xf7, etc.) *23* ♗xf5 ♖xg5 *24* ♖xg5 h6 *25* dxe7 ♖b8 *26* ♖g3! ♗xf5 *27* ♖f3 winning a piece.

| 20 | ♗xf5 | **Black resigns** |

42   Unzicker *[W.Germany]* - Fischer

VARNA OLYMPIC 1962

SICILIAN DEFENSE

Playing by ear

> This game illustrates the hazard of trying to rely solely on natural
> talent, without detailed knowledge of the latest opening innovations.
> Seldom is a chess master so drastically punished, as is Unzicker here,
> for failing to do his homework.
>
>   Disastrously pursuing a line with which Tal had just barely survived
> against Fischer, Unzicker blunders further through apparent
> unfamiliarity with Geller's improvement (15 ♔h1!). That had
> previously defeated Fischer at Curaçao. Unzicker simply puts his trust
> in "natural moves" and drifts into a constrained position, allowing
> Fischer to penetrate neatly on the weakened squares. The early
> decision, on move 26, comes as a surprise only to Unzicker.

1	e4	c5
2	♘f3	d6
3	d4	cxd4
4	♘xd4	♘f6
5	♘c3	a6
6	♗e2	...

On and off, White resorts to this solid and still respected system
(championed by Smyslov) whenever the sharper tries fail.

6	...	e5

Black's expectation in this Najdorf Variation is that his control of
important squares, with possibilities of Q-side expansion, will more
than compensate for the slight weakness of his backward d-Pawn.

7	♘b3	♗e6

To provoke f4-f5, weakening White's e-Pawn. For the non-committal
7...♗e7 see game 4.

8	**0-0**	♘bd7
9	**f4**	♕c7
10	**f5**	♗c4
11	**a4**	...

To hinder ...b5.

11	...	♗e7

Better than *11...♖c8? 12* a5 ♗e7 *13* ♗xc4 ♕xc4 *14* ♖a4! ♕c7 *15* ♗e3 h6 *16* ♖f2 with a bind. (Schmid-Evans, Varna 1962.)

12	♗e3	0-0

FISCHER

Position after 12...0-0

UNZICKER

13	**a5**	...

A critical alternative is *13* g4 d5! *14* exd5 (if *14* g5 d4! or *14* ♘xd5 ♘xd5 *15* exd5 ♘f6 *16* d6? ♗xd6 *17* ♗xc4 ♕xc4 *18* ♕xd6? ♕xg4+ *19* ♔h1 ♕e4+) *14...♗b4 15* g5 ♗xc3 *16* gxf6 ♗xb2 *17* fxg7 ♖fd8 *18* ♖b1 ♗c3. White's Pawns are overextended and his King is exposed.

13	...	**b5**

Too passive is *13...h6 14* g4 ♘h7 *15* ♗f2 followed by h4.

14	**axb6** *e.p.*	♘xb6
15	**♗xb6?**	...

At Curaçao 1962, Geller had found the right line: *15* ♔h1! ♖fc8 *16* ♗xb6 ♕xb6 *17* ♗xc4 ♖xc4 *18* ♕e2 ♖b4 *19* ♖a2! and Black is hard-pressed to defend his a-Pawn, but *19*...h6! *20* ♖fa1 ♗f8 *21* ♖xa6 ♖xa6 *22* ♖xa6 ♕b7 *23* ♘a5 ♕c7 *24* ♘b3 ♕b7 (ZUCKERMAN) =.

15	...	♕xb6+
16	♔h1	♗b5!

Intending ...♗c6 followed by ...a5.

17	♗xb5	...

White has already dissipated his theoretical advantage. He should settle for *17* ♘xb5 axb5 *18* ♕d3 with opposite colored Bishops.

17	...	axb5
18	♘d5	♘xd5
19	♕xd5	♖a4!

Avoids conceding the a-file and puts pressure on the e-Pawn.

20	c3	♕a6

FISCHER

Position after 20...♕a6

UNZICKER

21	h3	...

It's hard for White to hit upon a constructive plan. At Curaçao 1962, Tal played against me *21* ♖ad1 ♖c8 *22* ♘c1 b4 *23* ♘d3!? (White's in a bad way anyhow) *23*...bxc3 *24* bxc3 and now *24*...♖xc3 (instead of my *24*...♖a5 lemon) wins outright. If *25* ♘xe5 dxe5 *26* ♕xe5 (*26* ♕d8+ ♗f8!) *26*...♗b4! *27* ♕xc3 ♕xf1+! (KMOCH).

| 21 | ... | ♖c8 |
| 22 | ♖fe1 | h6! |

A handy *luft*, as becomes apparent later.

| 23 | ♔h2 | ♗g5 |
| 24 | g3? | ... |

Creating more K-side weaknesses. Better is *24* ♖ad1.

24	...	♛a7!
25	♔g2	♖a2
26	♔f1	...

What else? On *26* ♖xa2 ♛xa2 *27* ♖e2 ♖xc3!

FISCHER

Position after 26 ♔f1

UNZICKER

Now Black has a decisive shot.

| 26 | ... | ♖xc3! |

White resigns

27 ♖xa2 (*27* bxc3? ♛f2 mate) *27*...♖f3+ *28* ♔e2 ♖f2+ *29* ♔d3 ♛xa2 *30* ♖a1 ♛xb2 wins. Black's first rank is no longer vulnerable since the King can escape to h7 on the check.

43 Fischer - Reshevsky *[U.S.A.]*

USA CHAMPIONSHIP 1962-3

SICILIAN DEFENSE

The missing link

Many critics have dubbed this the "12th game" of the unfinished match, which had ended in a 5½-5½ tie. It is as adventurous and as bitterly contested as their earlier ones.

This time Reshevsky is well prepared for Fischer's opening, countering forcefully and equalizing without difficulty. However, instead of maintaining tension, he strives inconsistently for simplifications, forcing an exchange of Queens which leaves him with a strategically weak ending. Working with simultaneous threats on both wings, Fischer, despite the reduction in material, succeeds in exploiting several of his opponent's targets (backward Pawns on open files). Reshevsky defends this passive position with his usual tenacity, but is unable to prevent an eventual breakthrough.

1	e4	c5
2	♘f3	d6
3	d4	cxd4
4	♘xd4	♘f6
5	♘c3	a6
6	h3	g6

A good reaction. So is 6...b5 (see game 40).

By transposing into a Dragon Variation, Black hopes to render h3 useless, since in the normal Yugoslav Attack White will be forced to advance this Pawn again, thereby losing a tempo.

7	g4	♗g7
8	g5!?	...

Consistent, but perhaps premature. However, no other method offers more: e.g., 8 ♗e3 0-0 9 g5 ♘e8! Or 8 ♗g2 0-0 9 0-0 ♘c6=.

8	...	♘h5!

On 8...♘fd7 9 ♗e3 ♘c6 10 ♕d2 Black is slightly bottled up.

9	♗e2	e5

I had intended to answer *9...♘c6!?* with *10 ♘b3* (and not *10 ♘xc6 bxc6 11 ♗xh5 gxh5 12 ♕xh5 ♖b8* with good compensation for the Pawn).

10	♘b3	...

Bad is *10 ♘f5 gxf5 11 ♗xh5 f4* shutting out White's QB.

10	...	♘f4
11	♘d5	...

11 ♗g4 ♘c6 12 ♘d5 might transpose to the game.

RESHEVSKY

Position after 11 ♘d5

FISCHER

Objectively speaking, White has no opening advantage.

11	...	♘xd5

Instead of simplifying so readily, Black could try to exploit the weakened K-side. Tal says more "logical" is *11...0-0 12 h4 f5* (or the interesting Pawn sac *12...♘d7!? 13 ♘xf4 exf4 14 ♕xd6 ♗e5*).

Another possibility is *11...♘xe2* (not *11...♘xh3? 12 ♗e3* and the threat of *13 ♗b6* wins material) *12 ♕xe2 ♗e6=*.

12	♕xd5	♘c6

Tal gives the dubious sac *12...♗e6!? 13 ♕xb7 ♘d7* but *14 ♗e3* keeps the upper hand. But there's no need for Black to gamble. His position is basically sound.

13	♗g4	♗xg4

Tal gives *13...f5 14* gxf6 *e.p.* (if *14* exf5 ♘e7! *15* ♕d3 gxf5 *16* ♗h5+ ♘g6, etc.) *14...*♕xf6 *15* ♗xc8 ♖xc8 *16* c3 ♖c7, but after *17* ♗e3 followed by 0-0-0 White stands better.

14	hxg4	♕c8!

With the double threat of ...♕xg4 and/or ...♘b4.

15	♕d1	...

On *15* ♕xd6 ♕xg4 *16* ♕d3 ♖d8 *17* ♕e2 ♕g2 *18* ♖f1 h6 Black wrests the initiative.

RESHEVSKY

Position after 15 ♕d1

FISCHER

15	...	♘d4!

Apparently intent on simplifying at all cost. Reshevsky steers for an inferior ending. Tal gives *15...*♕e6 *16* ♗e3 0-0-0=.

A Bulgarian magazine gives the sharp *15...d5!?* as best, since it dissolves the backward d-Pawn immediately. The tactical justification shows up after *16* exd5 (if *16* ♕e2 or 16 c3, ...d4) *16...*♘b4 *17* c3 (if *17* 0-0 ♘xc2 *18* ♖b1 0-0 foils White's strategy) *17...*♕c4! and now there are two main lines:

A] *18* cxb4? ♕e4+ *19* ♔d2 ♖d8 *20* ♔c3 ♗f8! *21* a3 (if *21* ♘c5 ♗xc5 *22* bxc5 ♖xd5 wins) *21...*♖c8+ *22* ♔d2 (not *22* ♘c5? ♗xc5 *23* bxc5 ♖xc5+ *24* ♔b3 ♕c4 mate) *22...*♗e7! with a continuing attack.

B] *18* ♖h3 ♘xd5 (if *18...*♕e4+ *19* ♔f1 ♘c2? *20* ♘d2 wins) *19* ♕e2 ♕c7=.

16	c3	♘xb3
17	axb3	♕e6
18	♖a5!	f6?

Leads to a lifeless ending. Better chances are offered by *18...0-0* (or *18...b5 19* ♕d5 ♕xd5 *20* exd5 ♚d7) *19* ♖d5 ♖ad8 followed by ...f5.

| 19 | ♕d5! | ♕xd5 |

Not *19...*♕xg4? *20* ♕xb7 0-0 *21* gxf6.

20	♖xd5	♚d7
21	gxf6	♗xf6
22	g5	♗e7
23	♚e2	...

Now it's clear that Black's game is, at best, barely tenable. Both his d-Pawn and h-Pawn are ugly weaknesses exposed on open files.

23	...	♖af8
24	♗e3	♖c8
25	b4	...

More accurate possibly is *25* c4 ♚c7 *26* b4 and Black has constantly to worry about breaks with c5, b5, or even f4.

RESHEVSKY

Position after 25 b4

FISCHER

| 25 | ... | b5!? |

Many annotators criticized this because it creates a fresh weakness (the a-Pawn). But if Black just waits he ultimately should get squeezed to death after ♔d3 followed by c4, etc. Reshevsky apparently feels more comfortable living with his new weaknesses, rather than with the uncertainties which would be created after an eventual c4.

	26	♖dd1	...

White cannot keep d5 under control indefinitely. In order to make progress, the Rooks must strike at the backward RPs.

26	...	♔e6
27	♖a1	♖c6
28	♖h3	...

On *28 ♖h4?* h5! eliminates the weakness.

RESHEVSKY

Position after 28 ♖h3

FISCHER

	28	...	♗f8

28...d5!? loses a Pawn but offers a slight ray of hope: e.g., *29 exd5+ ♔xd5 30 ♖ah1 ♔c4 31 ♖xh7 ♖xh7 32 ♖xh7 ♖e6 33 ♔d2 (33 ♔f3? e4+! 34 ♔f4 ♔b3) 33...♔b3 34 ♔d3 ♔xb2 35 ♔e4! ♗f8 (if 35...♔xc3 36 ♔d5 ♖d6+ 37 ♔xe5 ♗f8 38 ♖c7+! ♔b3 39 ♖c8 ♗e7 40 ♖e8 ♖d7 41 ♔e6 wins a piece) 36 ♖h8 ♗g7 37 ♖g8 ♖e7 38 ♖c8!* followed by ♖c6 should win.

	29	♖ah1	♖c7

Now on *29...d5? 30 exd5+ ♔xd5 31 ♖xh7 ♖xh7 32 ♖xh7 ♔c4 33 ♖f7 ♖c8 34 ♖f6 ♔b3 35 ♖xa6 ♔xb2 36 ♗d2*, etc.

	30	♖h4!	...

The critical position. Black is virtually in *zugzwang*. The Rook on h4 serves a valuable function, as will become apparent.

30	...	d5

On *30...♖c4* (if *30...♖f7 31 ♖a1*) *31* f3 ♖c7 *32* ♔f2! d5 *33* ♖a1 ♖c6 *34* exd5+ ♔xd5 *35* ♖d1+ ♔e6 *36* ♖d8 should win.

31	♖a1!	...

Reshevsky doubtlessly underestimated this interpolation. He probably expected *31* exd5+ ♔xd5 *32* ♖d1+ ♔e6 *33* ♖d8 ♗g7!

31	...	♖c6

Or *31...dxe4 32* ♖xa6+ ♔d5 *33* ♖b6 wins.

32	exd5+	♔xd5
33	♖d1+	♔e6

The merit of the Rook on h4 is that it prevents the King from entering at c4.

34	♖d8	♔f5

With Black's Rook on c6 (instead of c7, as before) he no longer has the reply ...♗g7. And on *34...♖c7 35* ♖a8 is decisive.

35	♖a8	♖e6
36	♖h3!	...

RESHEVSKY

Position after 36 ♖h3!

FISCHER

36	...	♗g7

Equally useless is *36...♔g4 37* ♖g3+ ♔h5 *38* ♖f3 ♗g7 *39* ♖xh8 ♗xh8 *40* ♖f8 ♗g7 *41* ♖f7. Or *36...♔e4 37* ♖f3 ♗g7 *38* ♖xh8 ♗xh8 *39* ♖f8 ♗g7 *40* ♖f7 ♗h8 *41* f3+ ♔d5 *42* ♖xh7 ♖e8 *43* ♔d3.

37	♖xh8	♗xh8
38	♖xh7	♖e8
39	♖f7+	♔g4

Or *39...♔e4 40 f3+ ♔d5 41 ♔d3* wins.

40	f3+	♔g3
41	♔d3?	...

A buzz began to circulate in the playing hall and I wondered what it was all about. Later they told me *41 ♔f1!* (threatening *42 ♗f2+*) forces at least the win of a piece. Of course the text move also wins, but it takes ten moves longer.

41	...	e4+

Throwing another Pawn to the winds in order to get the Bishop into play. On *41...♖c8 42 ♗c5* also is easy.

42	fxe4	♖d8+
43	♗d4	♔g4
44	♖f1	♗e5

On *44...♔xg5 45 ♖g1+ ♔f4 46 ♖xg6*, etc.

45	♔e3	♗c7

After *45...♗xd4+ 46 cxd4 ♔xg5 47 e5* the center Pawns are irresistible.

46	♖g1+	♔h4
47	♔f3	♖d7

Or *47...♖f8+ 48 ♗f6 ♔h3 49 ♖h1+ ♗h2 50 e5 ♖e8 51 ♔e4*, etc. The rest is silence.

48	e5	♖f7+
49	♔e4	♖f5
50	e6	♗d8
51	♗f6!	♗xf6
52	gxf6	♖xf6
53	♔d5	♖f2
54	♖e1	**Black resigns**

44 Fischer - Fine [U.S.A.]

NEW YORK 1963: Skittles Game

EVANS GAMBIT

Shock treatment

Having become one of the leading players in the world, Fine quit chess at the height of his career (1945) to become a practising psychoanalyst; but he has lost none of his love for the game and little of his brilliance. The following is one of seven or eight offhand games played at his home in New York. As far as can be ascertained, Dr. Fine very nearly held his own.

Here, departing for the first time from his beloved Ruy Lopez, Fischer employs the daring gambit introduced by Captain Evans a century ago. This ploy has all but disappeared from the arena. Fine, although the author of several opening manuals, is understandably rusty, and he gets caught in a vise from which he never escapes. Fischer uncorks a sparkling finish in seventeen moves.

1	e4	e5
2	♘f3	♘c6
3	♗c4	♗c5
4	b4!?	♗xb4

Safer is *4...♗b6*, but that is hardly the way to refute the gambit.

5	c3	♗a5

For *5...♗e7* see game 50.

6	d4	exd4

6...d6 7 0-0 (better is 7 ♕b3) 7...♗b6 is the famous Lasker's Defense, which put the Evans out of commission last century.

7	0-0	...

FINE

Position after 7 0-0

FISCHER

7	...	**dxc3**

"A little too greedy." (*MCO*, 10th Ed.)

7...♗b6 *8* cxd4 d6 leads to the so-called "normal variation" which is tenable. After 7...d6 *8* ♕b3 (Waller's Attack) someone played *8*...♕d7 against me at an exhibition (Davis College 1964) *9* cxd4 ♗b6 *10* ♗b5 ♚f8! *11* d5 ♘a5 and Black saves the piece.

8	**♕b3**	**♕e7**

More usual is *8*...♕f6 *9* e5 ♕g6 *10* ♘xc3 ♘ge7 and now either *11* ♘e2 or ♗a3 leads to complicated positions which Tchigorin, for example, thought were playable for Black.

9	**♘xc3**	...

FINE

Position after 9 ♘xc3

FISCHER

9	...	**♘f6?**

On 9...♗xc3 *10* ♕xc3 f6 (if *10*...♘f6 *11* ♗a3 d6 *12* e5 ♘e4 *13* ♕b2 and against *13*...♘xe5 *14* ♘xe5 ♕xe5 *15* ♖fe1! wins a piece) *11* ♗a3 d6 *12* ♗d5! ♗d7 *13* ♖ab1 0-0-0 *14* ♘d4 is crushing.

The best defense follows an old analysis from Freeborough and Ranken (1893); *9...♕b4! 10 ♗xf7+ ♔d8 11 ♗g5+* (if *11 ♗xg8? ♕xb3!* holds) *11...♘ge7 12 ♘d5 ♕xb3 13 axb3 ♗b6* (*13...♗b4!* looks better) *14 ♖fc1 h6 15 ♖xc6 hxg5 16 ♘xb6 cxb6 17 ♖xb6*, etc.

	10	♘d5!	♘xd5

Necessary is *10...♕xe4;* but *11 ♘g5* produces a violent attack.

	11	exd5	♘e5

On *11...♘d8 12 ♗a3* is decisive (*12...d6 13 ♕b5+*).

	12	♘xe5	♕xe5
	13	♗b2	♕g5

FINE

Position after 13...♕g5

FISCHER

	14	h4!	...

Deflecting the "overloaded" Queen.

	14	...	♕xh4

On *14...♕h6 15 ♕a3* (threatening *♖fe1+*) wins. Or *14...♕g4 15 ♖fe1+ ♗xe1* (if *15...♔d8 16 ♕e3 ♗b4 17 ♕h6!! gxh6 18 ♗f6+ ♗e7 19 ♗xe7+ ♔e8 20 ♗g5+! ♔f8 21 ♗xh6+ ♕g7 22 ♖e8+!! ♔xe8 23 ♗xg7* wins) *16 ♖xe1+ ♔d8 17 ♕e3 ♕xh4 18 g3!* and Black's Queen must relinquish its guard of e7.

	15	♗xg7	♖g8

| 16 | ♖fe1+ | ♚d8 |

16...♗xe1 17 ♖xe1+ leads to the same finale.

| 17 | ♕g3! | ... |

FINE

Position after 17 ♕g3!

FISCHER

| 17 | ... | **Black resigns** |

17...♕xg3 18 ♗f6 mate.

45 Fischer - Bisguier *[U.S.A.]*

NEW YORK STATE CHAMPIONSHIP 1963
TWO KNIGHTS' DEFENSE

Ghosts

Steinitz, nicknamed "the Austrian Morphy" (although two styles could hardly be more dissimilar), apparently exercises a great influence on Fischer, who has restored several of his pet lines to prominence. One of these is the bizarre 9 ♘h3!?, found wanting at the turn of the century, and perhaps best left there.

Bisguier appears unimpressed, regaining his gambit Pawn with a strong initiative. But he misses several opportunities to gain an advantage and is gradually outplayed. Just at the critical moment, when the chances are roughly equal, he commits the same kind of gross oversight that had doomed Fischer against Spassky (game 18). He suffers the same fate.

1	e4	...

Best by test.

1	...	e5
2	♘f3	♘c6
3	♗c4	...

The last time I played this move in a tournament was when I was 12, at the 1955 US Junior Championship.

3	...	♘f6!?

Steinitz considered this to be an unsound sacrificial continuation!

4	♘g5	...

Tarrasch branded this a "duffer's move" and Panov called it "primitive." But there is no other way for White to try for an advantage.

4 d3 is tame. And after *4* 0-0 ♘xe4 *5* ♘c3 ♘xc3 *6* dxc3 ♕e7! White has no compensation for the Pawn. Finally, *4* d4 leads to the Max Lange attack.

4	...	d5
5	**exd5**	**♘a5**

5...♘d4!? (FRITZ) and *5...b5!?* (ULVESTAD) are both interesting but unsound. On *5...♘xd5 6* d4! (*6* ♘xf7!? is the "Fried Liver Attack") is so strong that *5...♘xd5* is practically extinct.

6	**♗b5+**	**c6**
7	**dxc6**	**bxc6**
8	**♗e2**	**h6**
9	**♘h3!?**	...

BISGUIER

Position after 9 ♘h3!?

FISCHER

To my knowledge, this is the first time that this move had been employed in Grandmaster chess for over seventy years. It is one of Steinitz's many unique opening contributions. The famous cable match game in 1891 between Steinitz and Tchigorin, which ended in a victory for Black, apparently caused the chess world to shy away from this variation.

9	...	**♗c5**

A] *9...♗d6* (STEINITZ) might be worth investigating. If *10* d4 (TCHIGORIN) then 10...e4 (FISCHER).

B] *9...♗f5* is too crude: *10* 0-0 ♕d7 *11* ♖e1 ♗xh3 *12* gxh3 ♕xh3 *13* ♗f1 and Black is busted, e.g., *13...♕g4+?* *14* ♕xg4 ♘xg4 *15* h3 wins a piece (STEINITZ).

C] *9...g5* *10* d3 g4 *11* ♘g1 ♗c5 *12* ♘c3 effectively wards off the threats (*12...♕b6* is answered by *13* ♘a4!).

10	**0-0**	**...**

Played by Steinitz in the 6th game of his second match with Tchigorin in 1892. Better is *10* d3! 0-0 *11* ♘c3 ♖e8 *12* 0-0 ♗xh3 *13* gxh3 ♕d7 *14* ♗g4 ♘xg4 *15* hxg4, etc., as I played vs. Radoicich here in a later round.

BISGUIER

Position after 10 0-0

FISCHER

10	**...**	**0-0**

Dr. Gottschall, in the 1892 *Deutsche Schachzeitung*, suggests *10*...g5, remarking it strange that a player as aggressive as Tchigorin did not chance it. Gottschall gives *11* ♔h1 g4 *12* ♘g1 ♘e4 *13* ♗xg4! ♘xf2+ *14* ♖xf2 ♗xf2 and, although Black has won the exchange, prefers White's practical chances.

After *10*...g5 *11* ♔h1 g4 *12* ♘g1 ♘e4 let us suppose White tries to avert material loss with *13* b4 (of no avail is *13* ♕e1 ♕d4 *14* ♗d1 ♘xf2+ *15* ♖xf2 ♕xf2 *16* ♕xe5+? ♗e6) *13*...♘xf2+ (or Gottschall's *13*...♗xf2 *14* d3 ♕h4 *15* dxe4 ♗g3 *16* ♘h3 [if *16* h3 gxh3 *17* gxh3 ♖g8] *16*...♗xh2! *17* ♔xh2 g3+ *18* ♔g1 ♗xh3, etc.) *14* ♖xf2 ♗xf2 *15* bxa5 ♕h4! *16* ♕f1 ♗g3 *17* h3 ♖g8 with a crushing attack.

11	**d3**	**♗xh3**

This certainly seems an improvement over the aforementioned Steinitz-Tchigorin match game which continued: *11*...♘d5 (Gottschall's *11*...♘h7 also merits attention) *12* c4 ♘e7 *13* ♔h1 ♗xh3 *14* gxh3 ♘f5 *15* f4 exf4 *16* ♗xf4 ♘e3 *17* ♗xe3 ♗xe3 *18* ♘c3 and White won easily with his Q-side majority.

12	**gxh3**	**♕d7**

| 13 | ♗f3 | ... |

A difficult choice. I rejected *13* ♔g2 since this was the square I had reserved for my Bishop. On *13* ♗g4 ♘xg4 followed by ...f5 gives fair attacking chances.

| 13 | ... | ♕xh3 |

So Black regains the Pawn, but I have faith in my two Bishops.

| 14 | ♘d2 | ... |

It would be a mistake to play for the win of a Pawn by *14* ♗g2 ♕h4! *15* ♕e1 ♖fe8! *16* ♕xa5 ♘g4 *17* h3 ♗xf2+ *18* ♖xf2 (if *18* ♔h1 ♕g3) *18*...♕xf2+ *19* ♔h1 e4! *20* hxg4 (if *20* dxe4 ♖xe4) *20*...exd3 with a winning attack.

| 14 | ... | ♖ad8 |

Not *14*...e4? *15* ♘xe4 ♘xe4 *16* ♗xe4 ♗d6 *17* f4, etc.

| 15 | ♗g2 | ♕f5 |

The Queen is forced off the h-file. On *15*...♕h4? *16* ♘f3 ♕h5 *17* ♕e1 wins a Pawn.

| 16 | ♕e1 | ... |

Perhaps better is *16* ♕f3 with possibilities of a slightly favorable ending.

16	...	♖fe8
17	♘e4	♗b6
18	♘xf6+	...

I was worried about the maneuver ...♘d5-f4. But sharper is *18* b4 ♘b7 *19* b5.

| 18 | ... | ♕xf6 |
| 19 | ♔h1 | c5 |

Stronger is *19*...g5 preventing White's break on f4 once and for all. Then by bringing his Knight to h4(!) Black could get a good game.

| 20 | ♕c3! | ... |

Serves the double purpose of preventing ...c4 and of enforcing f4. For all the good it does, Black's Bishop on b6 might just as well be a Pawn for the rest of the game.

BISGUIER

Position after 20 ♕c3!

FISCHER

| 20 | ... | ♘c6 |

Too late now is *20...g5? 21* f4!

| 21 | f4 | ♘d4 |
| 22 | ♕c4 | ... |

To prepare c3, driving the Knight away from d4. I didn't like the looks of *22* fxe5 ♕xe5 *23* ♗f4 ♕e2, etc.

| 22 | ... | ♕g6 |

Intending ...♕h5 followed by ...♘f5. (Not *22...*♕e6 *23* ♕a4 ♕d7? *24* ♕xd7 ♖xd7 *25* c3 ♘c2 *26* ♗c6!)

| 23 | c3 | ... |

After the game a kibitzer suggested *23* ♗e4 ♕h5 *24* f5 but this allows Black to turn the tables by *24...*♕e2 *25* ♖g1 ♘f3!

| 23 | ... | ♘f5 |

On *23...*♘e2 *24* f5 ♕f6 (*24...*♕h5? *25* ♗f3!) *25* ♗e3 ♘f4 *26* ♗e4 is tremendous.

| 24 | fxe5 | ... |

After *24* ♗e4 ♕h5 just who has got the attack is not quite clear!

| 24 | ... | ♖xe5 |
| 25 | ♗f4 | ... |

25 ♕f4 turns out badly after 25...♗c7! 26 ♗e4 ♕h5!

| 25 | ... | ♖e2 |

Black is playing for an advantage. 25...♘e3 26 ♗xe3 ♖xe3 is absolutely equal.

| 26 | ♗e4 | ... |

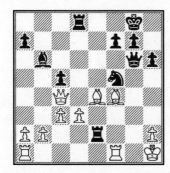

BISGUIER

Position after 26 ♗e4

FISCHER

The critical position.

| 26 | ... | ♖xb2? |

A pity that just when the game was getting interesting, Black has to make this terrible mistake.

Correct is 26...♖e8! (threatening ...♖8xe4). Bad would be 27 ♖g1 ♕h5 28 ♖af1 ♘e3! 29 ♕b5 ♖xe4 30 dxe4 ♘xf1 31 ♕e8+ (if 31 ♖xf1 ♕g4 wins) 31...♔h7 32 ♖xg7+ ♔xg7 33 ♗e5+ ♕xe5 34 ♕xe5+ f6 35 ♕e7+ ♔g6 36 ♕e8+ ♔g5 escaping the perpetual and should win.

After 26...♖e8! therefore, the best White has is 27 ♗f3 (to prevent ...♕h5) 27...♖xb2 28 ♖ae1 with even chances, owing to the Bishop pair.

| 27 | ♗e5! | ... |

Bisguier slumped and his chest collapsed, as he saw that Black cannot avert the loss of a piece.

27	...	♖e8
28	♖xf5	♖xe5
29	♖xe5	**Black resigns**

46 Fischer - Benko *[U.S.A.]*

USA CHAMPIONSHIP 1963-4

PIRC-ROBATSCH DEFENSE

Romp

Chess Life, *January 1964, reported:*
"In the later stages of the tournament some of Fischer's opponents did almost as much to guarantee his 11-0 score as Bobby did. The building tension worked to Fischer's advantage...On Monday, December 30, Fischer won his last game of 1963 – defeating Pal Benko with a neat little combination, after Benko had shown some suicidal tendencies in the management of his defense."
And so, in twenty-one moves, another Grandmaster is demolished. Benko misses a chance to simplify (on move 15) in order to reach an inferior but possibly tenable ending. This is fortunate for the reader, who otherwise would be cheated of White's scintillating 19th move. That alone is worth the price of admission!

1	e4	g6
2	d4	♝g7
3	♞c3	...

3 c4 d6 4 ♞c3 transposes to a King's Indian. An unorthodox try is 3 h4!?

| 3 | ... | d6 |
| 4 | f4 | ... |

Sharpest. Another build-up is *4 ♝e3 ♞f6 5 f3*, etc.

4	...	♞f6
5	♞f3	0-0
6	♝d3	...

An improvement over 6 ♝e2 which I played against Korchnoi at Curaçao 1962. That game continued: 6...c5 7 dxc5 ♛a5 8 0-0 ♛xc5+ 9 ♚h1 ♞c6 10 ♞d2 a5! 11 ♞b3 ♛b6 12 a4 ♞b4 13 g4 ♝xg4! with a big advantage.

6   ...   ♗g4?

Preparing to sac the "minor exchange." Interesting is Valvo's 6...♘a6!? 7 e5 dxe5 8 fxe5 ♘d5 9 ♘xd5 ♕xd5 about equal. (Bisguier-Benko, match 1964.)

The book gives 6...♘bd7 7 0-0 (7 e5 is best) 7...e5 8 dxe5 dxe5 9 fxe5 ♘xe5 10 ♘xe5 ♕d4+ 11 ♔h1 ♕xe5 12 ♗f4 ♕c5 with a tenable game.

Fischer-Perez, Havana 1965 continued; 6...♘c6!? 7 e5 dxe5 8 fxe5 ♘d5 (Spassky's 8...♘g4 or maybe even 8...♘h5 is better) 9 ♘xd5 ♕xd5 10 c3 ♗g4 11 ♕e2! with a pull.

7   h3   ♗xf3
8   ♕xf3   ...

I overheard someone explaining this game to a beginner: "You take off the Knight here, another piece comes out to replace it, so Black hasn't really stopped White's development..."

8   ...   ♘c6
9   ♗e3   e5

On 9...♘d7 10 e5 keeps Black cramped.

10   dxe5   dxe5
11   f5   ...

Already threatening to obtain a winning bind with g4-g5.

BENKO

Position after 11 f5

FISCHER

11   ...   gxf5

Best. My original note said: "If immediately 11...♘d4 12 ♕f2 gxf5 13 exf5 with a quick crush in sight." This verdict was later confirmed in Bednarsky-Kraidman, Tel Aviv 1964, which continued: *13*...b5 *14* 0-0 c5 *15* ♘e4 c4 *16* ♘xf6+ ♕xf6 *17* ♗e4 ♖ad8 *18* c3 ♖fe8 *19* ♔h1 ♔h8 *20* ♖ae1 b4 *21* cxd4 exd4 *22* ♗c1 d3 *23* b3 ♗h6 *24* ♗xh6 ♕xh6 *25* ♗f3 ♖xe1 *26* ♕xe1 c3 *27* ♕e7! and White won in ten more moves.

| *12* | ♕xf5 | ... |

After *12* exf5 e4! Black gets good counterplay.

| *12* | ... | ♘d4 |

Benko is willing to gamble a Pawn to drive White's Queen from its dominating post. *12*...♕d7 is safer, however.

BENKO

Position after 12...♘d4

FISCHER

| *13* | ♕f2 | ... |

I was tempted to accept the dare with *13* ♕xe5! ♘g4 *14* ♕xg7+! ♔xg7 *15* hxg4 with threats all over the place. For example, if *15*...♘e6 *16* e5 ♖h8 *17* ♗h6+ ♔g8 *18* ♘e4 wins. But *15*...♘c6 is hard to crack.

| *13* | ... | ♘e8 |

More active than *13*...♘d7 *14* 0-0-0 ♘c5 *15* ♔b1 followed by ♘e2 and c3 driving out the Knight. Now with ...♘d6 pending, Black threatens either to break with ...f5 or, in some lines, to advance with ...c5-c4.

| *14* | 0-0 | ... |

An alternative is *14* 0-0-0 ♘d6 *15* ♘e2. I thought White's King would be safer after the text – the drawback is the K-side Pawns can no longer safely advance.

14	...	♘d6

Sharp! I had expected *14...c6 15 ♘e2* after which Black must either exchange his only well-placed piece or allow White's Knight to scramble to g3 followed by h5 or f5.

15	♕g3	...

The only way to sustain the initiative. On *15 ♘d5 f5 16 ♗xd4 ♘xe4!* *17 ♗xe4 fxe4* wins a Pawn. And after *15 ♘e2 f5* gives Black active counterchances.

15	...	♚h8

On *15...f5 16 ♗h6 ♕f6 17 ♗xg7 ♕xg7 18 ♕xg7+ ♚xg7 19 exf5* *♘6xf5 20 ♖ae1 ♖ae8 21 ♘e4* with a comfortable edge, but certainly no forced win.

16	♕g4	...

To prevent ...f5.

16	...	c6

Too passive. Black should seize the opportunity for *16...c5!*

17	♕h5	...

Threatening *18 ♗xd4 exd4 19 e5*.

17	...	♕e8?

Either *17...♘e6* or ...c5 is essential.

18	♗xd4	exd4
19	♖f6!	...

The *zwischenzug* Benko missed. He had expected *19 e5 f5!*

BENKO

Position after 19 ♖f6!

FISCHER

A bolt from the blue!

| 19 | ... | ♔g8 |

Forced. On *19...dxc3 (or 19...♗xf6) 20* e5 mates.

| 20 | e5 | h6 |
| 21 | ♘e2! | ... |

Black was hoping for *21* ♖xd6 ♕xe5! and he survives to an ending.

| 21 | ... | **Black resigns** |

There is no defense to the threat of *22* ♖xd6. On *21...♘b5 22* ♕f5 wins. Or *21...♗xf6 22* ♕xh6 forces mate.

47 Fischer - Bisguier *[U.S.A.]*

USA CHAMPIONSHIP 1963-4

RUY LOPEZ

The Indian sign?

Bisguier is the one Grandmaster who consistently obtains decent positions against Fischer, only to throw them away for no apparent reason. Out of something like a dozen encounters, he has squeezed but a single draw.

Here is the only game in which Bisguier is outplayed from the start. Still, he does catch Fischer napping and nearly escapes. Describing his sensations before the game, Bisguier wrote:

"For the first time I was really in doubt as to what Bobby would play against me as White...I was hoping to play the Black side of the King's Gambit or the Two Knights' Defense, but he 'surprised' me with the Ruy Lopez...taken by surprise I was not so prepared or comfortable as I would like to have been. Now that Bobby has added psychology to his arsenal of weapons he is a much more dangerous opponent than ever before."

1	e4	e5
2	♘f3	...

In a previous round, against Evans, I had hazarded a King's Gambit: *2 f4 exf4 3 ♗c4 ♕h4+ 4 ♔f1* and White won only after some uneasy moments.

2	...	♘c6
3	♗b5	a6
4	♗a4	♘f6
5	0-0	♗e7
6	♖e1	b5
7	♗b3	0-0
8	c3	d6

Bernstein tried the Marshall Attack against me in the 1959-60 US Championship, and an interesting struggle developed: *8...d5!? 9 exd5 e4 (in place of the usual 9...♘xd5) 10 dxc6 exf3 11 ♕xf3 ♗g4 12 ♕g3 ♗d6 13 ♕h4 ♖e8 14 f3 ♗f5 15 d4 ♗xh2+ 16 ♔xh2 ♘g4+ 17 ♔g3*

♕xh4+ *18* ♔xh4 ♖xe1 *19* fxg4 ♖xc1 *20* gxf5 ♖d8 *21* a4! White won shortly.

9	**h3**	♘**a5**
10	**♗c2**	**c5**
11	**d4**	♕**c7**

For *11...*♘d7 see game 38.

12	♘**bd2**	♘**c6**
13	**dxc5**	...

The Rauzer Attack. White gives up the center in order to exploit Black's weakened squares on d5 and f5.

13	...	**dxc5**
14	♘**f1**	♖**d8**

Risky. Better is the usual *14...*♗e6 *15* ♘e3 ♖ad8 *16* ♕e2 g6, etc.

15	♕**e2**	♘**h5**

An old line rehabilitated by Reshevsky against Bronstein at Zurich 1953. If now *15...*♗e6 *16* ♘e3 g6 *17* ♘g5 ♗c8 *18* ♘d5! ♘xd5 *19* exd5 ♗xg5 (*19...*♖xd5 *20* ♕f3! ♗e6 *21* ♘xe6 fxe6 *22* ♕g4!) *20* ♗xg5 ♖xd5 *21* ♖ad1 with a plus (LIPNITZKY).

16	**g3!**	...

Bronstein's move – after first interpolating *16* a4 ♖b8.

BISGUIER

Position after 16 g3!

FISCHER

This idea bankrupts Black's strategy. The slight weakening of the K-side is inconsequential, but Black's loss of time with his KN is.

Actually the sharpest continuation is *16* a4! as I played against Eliskases at Mar del Plata 1960 (I simply forgot to interpolate it here) *16...*♖b8 *17* axb5 axb5 *18* g3! g6 *19* h4! ♗e6 *20* ♘e3 c4 *21* ♘g5 ♗xg5 *22* hxg5 ♘a5 *23* ♘g4 ♗xg4 *24* ♕xg4 ♘b3 *25* ♗xb3 cxb3 *26* ♗e3 with a great advantage.

16	...	**g6**

Simply *16...*♘f6 may be best. Then on *17* h4 h6 *18* ♘e3 ♗e6.

16...♗xh3 is bad owing to *17* ♘g5 ♗xg5 (if *17...*♗xf1 *18* ♕xh5 ♗xg5 *19* ♗xg5 f6 *20* ♗xf6! gxf6 *21* ♔xf1 White's better) *18* ♗xg5 ♘f6 (not *18...*♗xf1? *19* ♗xd8) *19* ♗xf6 gxf6 *20* ♘e3 White has more than enough for the Pawn.

17	**h4!**	...

Bronstein's *17* ♔h2 and Weinstein's *17* ♔g2 are time-consuming and hence weaker.

When I told Bronstein (at Mar del Plata 1960) that the text was a tremendous improvement over his game with Reshevsky, he replied: "Of course. After seven years one must find an improvement."

17	...	**♗e6**
18	**♘e3**	**f6**

Probably best. *18...*c4 *19* ♘g5! is similar to the quoted game with Eliskases.

19	**♘d5!**	...

Of course! Chess is a matter of timing. Given another move or two Black would be able not only to defend himself against this invasion, but even try for the initiative.

BISGUIER

Position after 19 ♘d5!

FISCHER

| 19 | ... | ♕b7 |

Prudent. "Winning" the Pawn would allow White's Bishop-pair to enter the game with powerful effect: e.g., *19...♗xd5 20 exd5 ♖xd5 21 c4! ♘d4 22 ♘xd4 ♖xd4 23 cxb5 axb5 24 ♕xb5* and now Eliskases recommends *24...c4* but I fail to see how this improves matters since *25 ♗e3 ♖b8 26 ♕a4 ♖b4?* is answered by *27 ♕e8+.*

| 20 | ♘xe7+ | ♕xe7 |

White has the two Bishops – or a "half point" advantage.

| 21 | ♘h2 | ... |

This Knight is also bound for d5.

21	...	♘g7
22	♘g4	c4
23	♕f3!	...

Winning the second "minor exchange." On *23...♖f8 24 ♘e3* the Knight is ready to pounce on d5, especially after Black's Rook has been deflected from the d-file.

23	...	♗xg4
24	♕xg4	♘e6
25	h5?	...

More accurate is *25 ♗e3 (25...♘c5? 26 ♗xc5 ♕xc5 27 ♕e6+ ♔g7 28 ♖ad1* penetrates decisively).

| 25 | ... | ♔h8! |

Alert. I had expected *25...g5* whereupon *26 ♗e3* is even more devastating than before.

| 26 | &g2! | ... |

On *26* hxg6 &g8 White is in trouble!

| 26 | ... | g5 |

Forced – eventually. On *26...&g8 27 &h1* gxh5? (*27...g5* is better) *28* &xh5 &f4+ *29* &xf4 exf4 *30* e5! &g7 *31* exf6 &xf6 *32* &xh7 wins.

| 27 | &e3 | &f4+! |

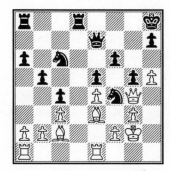

BISGUIER

Position after 27...&f4+!

FISCHER

| 28 | &h2! | ... |

28 gxf4? gxf4 threatening *29...&g8* as well as *29...*fxe3 regains the piece advantageously.

| 28 | ... | &d3 |
| 29 | &xd3 | cxd3? |

Now the advanced soldier must fall. Exchanging a pair of Rooks would make it more difficult, but White still maintains his grip after *29...&xd3 30* &ed1 &ad8 *31* &xd3 cxd3 (*31...&xd3? 32* &c8+ &d8 *33* &xa6) *32* &d1 &d7 *33* &d2 threatening a winning bind with *34* &c5.

| 30 | &ed1 | &d7 |

On *30...b4 31* &d2 bxc3 *32* bxc3 &a3 *33* &ad1 &xc3 *34* &e6 &g7 *35* h6+! wins.

| 31 | &d2 | &a5 |

A useless excursion, but there was no good defense. Strangely enough, Black's difficulty stems from his third move and its consequent weakening on b6. If the pawn were still on a7 (preventing a later ♗b6) he might well hold.

On *31...♖ad8 32 ♖ad1 ♕f7 33 ♗b6 ♖b8 34 ♗c5 ♖bd8 35 ♕f3* picks up the d-pawn at leisure.

	32	**b3**		**♕d6**

Not *32...♖c8? 33 ♖xd3!*

	33	**♖ad1**		**♖e8**

On *33...♖ad8 34 ♖xd3 ♕xd3 35 ♖xd3 ♖xd3 36 ♗b6!*

	34	**♖xd3**		**♕xd3**

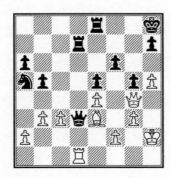

BISGUIER

Position after 34...♕xd3

FISCHER

Black is braced to give up his Queen for two Rooks and keep control of the crucial d-file.

	35	**♕xd7!**		**Black resigns**

A devastating X-ray. After *35...♕xd7 36 ♖xd7* it's just a matter of time. E.g., *35...♖e6 37 ♔h3* followed by ♔g4-f5, etc.

48 R. Byrne [U.S.A.] - Fischer

USA CHAMPIONSHIP 1963-4

GRUENFELD DEFENSE

The brilliancy prize

K. F. Kirby, editor of the South African Chess Quarterly, *summed up the astonishment and admiration of the chess world when he wrote:*
   "The Byrne game was quite fabulous, and I cannot call to mind anything to parallel it. After White's eleventh move I should adjudicate his position as slightly superior, and at worst completely safe. To turn this into a mating position in eleven more moves is more witchcraft than chess! Quite honestly, I do not see the man who can stop Bobby at this time..."
   And one can add nothing to Byrne's own words:
   "And as I sat pondering why Fischer would choose such a line, because it was so obviously lost for Black, there suddenly came 18...♘xg2. This dazzling move came as the shocker...The culminating combination is of such depth that, even at the very moment at which I resigned, both grandmasters who were commenting on the play for the spectators in a separate room believed that I had a won game!"

1	d4	♘f6
2	c4	g6
3	g3	c6
4	♗g2	...

In the 1962-3 US Championship we reached the same position, but Byrne continued *4 d5 b5! 5 dxc6 bxc4 6 cxd7+ ♘bxd7 7 ♗g2 ♖b8 8 ♘f3 ♗g7 9 0-0 0-0=* Black's weak c-pawn is compensated for by pressure on the open b-file.

| 4 | ... | d5 |
| 5 | cxd5 | ... |

5 ♕b3 maintains more tension.

| 5 | ... | cxd5 |

6	♘c3	♗g7
7	e3	...

Benko-Fischer, US Championship 1962-3, continued *7* ♘f3 0-0 *8* ♘e5 (if *8* 0-0 ♘e4!=) *8*...♗f5 *9* 0-0 ♘e4 *10* ♕b3 ♘c6 *11* ♕xd5 ♘xc3 *12* bxc3 ♕xd5 *13* ♗xd5 ♘xe5 *14* dxe5 ♗xe5 with a draw shortly.

7	...	0-0
8	♘ge2	♘c6
9	0-0	b6
10	b3	...

It's hard for either side to introduce an imbalance into this essentially symmetrical variation.

Deadeye equality also ensues after *10* ♘f4 e6 *11* b3 ♗a6 *12* ♖e1 ♖c8 *13* ♗a3 ♖e8 *14* ♖c1, etc. (Stahlberg-Flohr, Kemeri 1937.)

10	...	♗a6
11	♗a3	♖e8
12	♕d2	...

A good alternative is *12* ♖c1.

A kibitzer later suggested *12* f4?! to prevent ...e5. But after *12*...e6 followed by ...♗f8 and eventual doubling on the c-file, Black gets an advantage.

12	...	e5!

I was a bit worried about weakening my d-pawn, but felt that the tremendous activity obtained by my minor pieces would permit White no time to exploit it. *12*...e6 would probably lead to a draw.

13	dxe5	...

Passive is *13* ♖ac1 exd4 (if *13*...♖c8 *14* ♖fd1 e4 *15* f3! is tenable) *14* exd4 ♖c8 *15* f3 although Black has difficulty breaking through.

13	...	♘xe5

FISCHER

Position after 13...♘xe5

BYRNE

14   ♖fd1?   ...

Add another to those melancholy case histories entitled "the wrong Rook." Correct is *14* ♖ad1! Originally I gave the following "refutation": "*14...*♘e4 *15* ♘xe4 dxe4 *16* ♗xe4 ♕xd2 *17* ♖xd2 ♘c4 *18* ♗xa8 ♘xd2 *19* ♖d1 ♘c4 *20* bxc4 (best) *20...*♖xa8 regaining the Pawn with a big endgame advantage." But Averbakh found a hole in my analysis with *20* ♗c6! (instead of *20* bxc4 which I had carelessly given as "best"), *20...*♘xa3 *21* ♗xe8 ♗xe2 *22* ♖d7 and White is the one who wins instead of Black!

I spent an evening just staring at the position after *14* ♖ad1, trying everything, unwilling to let my brilliancy go down the drain. The more I looked, the more I liked White's game! For example, *14...*♖c8 (*14...*♘d3 is refuted by *15* ♕c2) *15* ♘xd5 ♘xd5 *16* ♗xd5 ♗d3 *17* ♗g2 ♖c2 *18* ♕xc2! *kaput.* No better is *14...*♕d7 *15* ♕c2 followed by ♖d2 and ♖fd1 (if *15...*♖ac8 *16* ♕b1!).

Another try which just falls short is *14* ♖ad1 ♕c7 *15* ♕c1! ♘e4!? (otherwise *16* ♕b1 consolidates) *16* ♘xd5! ♕xc1 *17* ♘xc1 ♗xf1 *18* ♗xe4 ♗h3 *19* ♘e7+ ♔h8 *20* ♗xa8 ♖xa8 *21* f4 keeping the extra Pawn. Indeed, how does Black even equalize, let alone sustain the initiative?

Finally I found *14...*♕c8! – the only move to keep the pressure. Now on *15* ♘xd5 ♘xd5 *16* ♗xd5 ♖d8 *17* f4 ♖xd5! *18* ♕xd5 ♗b7! *19* ♕d8+ (if *19* ♕d2 ♕h3! *20* ♘d4 ♘g4 *21* ♖fe1 [or *21* ♘c2 h5 with a strong attack] *21...*♘xe3! should win) *19...*♕xd8 *20* ♖xd8+ ♖xd8 *21* fxe5 ♗xe5 with a better ending. And on *15* ♖c1 ♕d7! *16* ♖cd1 ♖ad8 Black has finagled a precious tempo, since his Queen is on d7 instead of d8. After *14...*♕c8! relatively best is *15* ♗b2 (if *15* ♕c1 ♘e4 *16* ♘xd5 ♗xe2 *17* ♗xe4 ♔h8! wins the exchange. One possible line is *18* ♕xc8 ♖axc8 *19* ♘e7 ♖c7 *20* ♖c1 ♖d7 *21* ♖fe1 ♗f3!) although Black keeps the initiative with *15...*♕f5.

14	...	♘d3!
15	♕c2	...

There is hardly any other defense to the threat of ...♘e4.

A] *15* ♘d4 ♘e4 *16* ♘xe4 dxe4 *17* ♗b2 ♖c8 with a powerful bind.

B] *15* ♘f4 ♘e4 *16* ♘xe4 dxe4 (not *16...*♗xa1? *17* ♘d6) *17* ♖ab1 ♖c8 *18* ♘xd3 ♗c3! *19* ♕e2 ♗xd3 *20* ♕g4 f5 *21* ♕h3 ♗xb1! *22* ♖xd8 ♖exd8 *23* ♗f1 ♖d1 *24* ♔g2 ♗d3! *25* ♗xd3 exd3 wins.

C] *15* f3 ♗h6 *16* f4 (if *16* ♘f4? d4!) *16...*♗g7! resumes the threat of ...♘e4, only White has weakened himself in the interim.

15	...	♘xf2!

FISCHER

Position after 15...♘xf2!

BYRNE

The key to Black's previous play. The complete justification for this sac does not become apparent until White resigns!

16	♔xf2	♘g4+
17	♔g1	♘xe3
18	♕d2	...

Forced. Now on *18...*♘xd1 *19* ♖xd1 White is all right again.

18	...	♘xg2!

Removing this Bishop leaves White defenseless on his light squares.

19	♔xg2	d4!
20	♘xd4	♗b7+

The King is at Black's mercy.

| 21 | ♔f1 | ... |

Equally hopeless is *21 ♔g1 ♗xd4+ 22 ♕xd4 ♖e1+! 23 ♔f2 ♕xd4+ 24 ♖xd4 ♖xa1 25 ♖d7 ♖c8 26 ♖xb7* (if *26 ♗b2 ♖h1*) *26...♖xc3 27 ♖b8+ ♔g7 28 ♗b2 ♖xa2,* etc.

Or *21 ♔f2 ♕d7! 22 ♖ac1 ♕h3 23 ♘f3 ♗h6 24 ♕d3 ♗e3+ 25 ♕xe3 ♖xe3 26 ♔xe3 ♖e8+ 27 ♔f2 ♕f5!* finis!

| 21 | ... | ♕d7! |

FISCHER

Position after 21...♕d7!

BYRNE

White resigns

A bitter disappointment. I'd hoped for *22 ♕f2 ♕h3+ 23 ♔g1 ♖e1+!! 24 ♖xe1 ♗xd4* with mate to follow shortly. Also *22 ♘db5 ♕h3+ 23 ♔g1 ♗h6* and the curtain comes down.

49 Fischer - Steinmeyer [U.S.A.]

USA CHAMPIONSHIP 1963-4

CARO-KANN DEFENSE

A complex trap

While generally thought of as "one movers," some opening traps are deeper and more beautiful than others because falling into them requires a certain degree of skill. They might not attract and, if they did, might work for an amateur!

Steinmeyer's concept beginning with 13...♛f4+ is both subtle and novel. The only trouble is that it meets with a smashing refutation. Instead of simplifying, as Steinmeyer hopes, his variation enmeshes him in complications. The nail in the coffin is 16 ♞e5, after which Black's Queen can no longer be extricated without fatal loss of material.

1	e4	c6
2	d4	...

For 2 ♞c3 d5 3 ♞f3 see game 16.

2	...	d5
3	♞c3	dxe4
4	♞xe4	♝f5

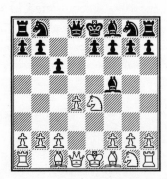

STEINMEYER

Position after 4...♝f5

FISCHER

5	♞g3	...

On tour (1964) I experimented with the weird 5 ♘c5!? Most of my opponents countered with 5...e5 6 ♘xb7 ♛xd4 (if 6...♛b6 7 ♘c5 ♝xc5 8 dxc5 ♛xc5 9 c3 White's better. Fischer-Petrosian, five-minute game, Bled 1961) 7 ♛xd4 exd4 8 ♝d3 with the better ending. Some replied with 5...b6 6 ♘a6 ♘xa6 7 ♝xa6 ♛d5! Still others played 5...♛c7 6 ♝d3 ♝xd3 7 ♘xd3 e6. White has more space, but only experience can tell whether he has the edge; however the Knight on d3 discourages the normal freeing maneuver ...c5 and/or ...e5. At least it's something to break the monotony.

| 5 | ... | ♝g6 |
| 6 | ♘f3 | ♘f6 |

More usual is the immediate ...♘d7 to prevent ♘e5.

| 7 | **h4** | ... |

7 ♝d3 (if 7 ♘e5 ♘bd7 8 ♘xg6 hxg6 Black is solid), 7...e6 8 0-0 ♝e7 9 c4 0-0 10 ♝xg6 hxg6 leads to equality. (Evans-Benko, US Championship 1962-3.)

| 7 | ... | h6 |
| 8 | ♝d3 | ... |

White can try to exploit the order of Black's moves by 8 ♘e5, but 8...♝h7 9 ♝c4 e6 10 ♛e2 ♘d5! (not 10...♛xd4? 11 ♘xf7!) followed by ...♘d7 equalizes.

8 h5 ♝h7 9 ♝d3 ♝xd3 10 ♛xd3 e6 11 ♝d2 ♘bd7 12 0-0-0 ♛c7 13 ♘e4 (Spassky-Petrosian, 13th match game 1966, continued 13 ♛e2 0-0-0 14 ♘e5 ♘xe5 15 dxe5 ♘d7 16 f4 with an edge) 13...0-0-0 14 g3! (Geller-Petrosian, Moscow 1967), and now 14...♘xe4 (instead of 14...♘g4?) 15 ♛xe4 ♝d6 holds White to a minimal pull.

8	...	♝xd3
9	♛xd3	e6
10	♝d2	♘bd7

Or 10...♛c7 11 c4 (if 11 0-0-0 ♝d6 12 ♘e4 ♝f4! 13 ♘xf6+ gxf6 is satisfactory) 11...♘bd7 12 ♝c3 (the whole idea is to prevent Black from swapping Bishops) 12...a5! 13 0-0!? (if 13 0-0-0 ♝b4!) 13...♝d6

14 ♘e4 (Tal suggested *14* d5!? mixing it up, but *14...*♗xg3! holds; not *15* dxe6? ♘e5; or *15* fxg3 cxd5 *16* cxd5 ♘xd5 *17* ♗xg7 ♖g8 *18* ♕h7 ♘7f6 *19* ♗xf6 ♘xf6 *20* ♕xh6 ♕xg3 *21* ♕d2=) *14...*♘xe4 *15* ♕xe4 0-0=. (Fischer-Donner, Varna 1962.)

11	**0-0-0**	♕**c7**
12	**c4**	...

STEINMEYER

Position after 12 c4

FISCHER

12	...	**0-0-0**

12...♗d6! *13* ♘e4 (if *13* ♘e2 0-0-0 *14* ♔b1 e5=) *13...*♗f4! leads to immediate simplifications.

13	♗**c3!**	...

Now Black no longer can force the exchange of Bishops.

13	...	♕**f4+?**

The start of a faulty concept. After *13...*♗d6 (on *13...*c5 *14* d5!) *14* ♘e4 ♗f4+ *15* ♔b1 ♘e5! *16* ♘xe5 ♗xe5 produces equality.

14	♔**b1**	♘**c5?**

He still has time to back out with *14...*♕c7.

15	♕**c2**	♘**ce4**

Now there is no turning back. On *15...♘cd7 16 ♘e5!* is very strong: e.g., *16...♘xe5 17 dxe5 ♘d7* (or *17...♘g4 18 ♖xd8+ ♔xd8 19 ♖d1+ ♔c8 20 ♖d4) 18 ♖d4 ♕xe5 19 ♖xd7!*, etc.

STEINMEYER

Position after 15...♘ce4

FISCHER

| 16 | ♘e5! | ... |

A clear refutation. The Queen's retreat is cut off and the ancient weakness on Black's f7 is etched more sharply than ever. Shamkovich-Goldberg, USSR 1961, continued with *16 ♗a5?* which won only against inferior defense.

| 16 | ... | ♘xf2 |

What else? *16...♘xg3* loses to *17 fxg3 ♕xg3 18 ♖d3 ♕f4 19 ♖f3 ♕e4 20 ♘xf7*. And *16...♘xc3+* is refuted by *17 bxc3! ♖g8* (if *17...♘g4 18 ♘h5! ♕f5 19 ♕xf5 exf5 20 ♘xf7) 18 ♖d3 h5 19 ♖f3 ♕h6 20 ♘xf7*, etc.

| 17 | ♖df1! | **Black resigns** |

Probably what Steinmeyer overlooked when he went into this whole mess. On *17...♕xg3 18 ♖xf2 ♕e3* (otherwise *♖f3) 19 ♖e2 ♕f4 20 ♘xf7* wins at least the exchange.

Motivated by my lopsided result (11-0!), Dr Kmoch congratulated Evans (the runner up) on "winning" the tournament ... and then he congratulated me on "winning the exhibition."

50 Fischer - Celle *[U.S.A.]*

CALIFORNIA 1964: Exhibition Tour

EVANS GAMBIT

Tour de force

As one of ten simultaneous clock games played on tour, at Davis College, this is a perfect example of the precept that if White makes a slip in the opening he is punished by loss of the initiative, while if Black makes a slip (since he is skating on thin ice from the very start) it is likely to be fatal. 6...d6 is the offender.

With 9 ♕h5 Fischer assumes a commanding control of space, but faces a strong defense which compels him to offer a piece in order to maintain pressure. Continuing with restraint and circumspection, he builds up the attack with a series of quiet developing moves — reminiscent of Morphy's famous victory over the Duke of Brunswick at the Paris opera. When the time is ripe, Fischer throws everything at Black's King, including the proverbial kitchen sink. His show of brute force is handsomely rewarded.

1	e4	e5
2	♘f3	♘c6
3	♗c4	♗c5
4	b4!?	...

The Evans was already analyzed to death by the 'nineties. But it still makes for enterprising chess.

4	...	♗xb4
5	c3	♗e7

Must be the trend. At least, on tour most players answered this way. For 5...♗a5 see game 44.

6	d4	d6?

A mistake is usually much more serious in these open games. Black must return the Pawn with 6...♘a5! 7 ♘xe5 ♘xc4 8 ♘xc4 d5!

7	**dxe5**	♘**xe5**

On *7...♘a5? 8 ♗xf7+! ♔xf7 9 ♕d5+ ♗e6 10 ♕xa5* wins a Pawn. *7...dxe5 8 ♕b3 ♘a5 9 ♗xf7+ ♔f8 10 ♕a4* is strong.

8	♘**xe5**	**dxe5**
9	♕**h5!**	**...**

In an earlier exhibition game I played *9 ♕b3* but got nothing after *9...♗e6! 10 ♗xe6 fxe6 11 ♗a3!?* (if *11 ♕xe6 ♕d6=*) *11...♕d3!*

9	**...**	**g6**
10	♕**xe5**	♘**f6**

On *10...f6 11 ♕b5+! c6? 12 ♕b3 ♔f8 13 ♗xg8!* wins.

11	♗**a3!**	**...**

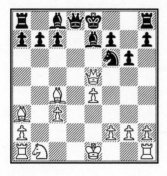

CELLE

Position after 11 ♗a3!

FISCHER

Incredible how Black is so completely immobilized by this one move!

11	**...**	♖**f8**

The only way to get relief. *11...♔f8?* works in all lines except *12 ♕xf6!*

12	**0-0**	♘**g4**

12...♘d7 followed by *...♘b6* might be better, but this certainly looked good at the time.

13	♕g3	♗xa3
14	♘xa3	♕e7!

Apparently Black has freed his game. If now *15* ♘c2 ♕e5 virtually forces an exchange of Queens. *15* ♘b5 is rendered harmless by ...♘e5. How's White to sustain the initiative?

15   ♗b5+!   ...

That's how. This forces Black to weaken himself on d6, although White must sacrifice a piece to exploit it.

15   ...   c6

On *15...*♗d7 *16* ♕xc7 (not *16* ♕xg4 c6!).

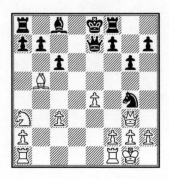

CELLE

Position after 15...c6

FISCHER

16   ♘c4!   ♕e6!

Some fascinating possibilities appear after *16...*cxb5 *17* ♘d6+ ♔d8 *18* ♖fd1 ♗d7 *19* ♘xb7+ ♔c8 *20* ♘d6+ ♔d8 *21* ♖d4! ♘e5 *22* ♖ad1 ♔c7 (if *22...*g5 *23* ♘f5 ♕e8 *24* ♕xe5! ♕xe5 *25* ♖xd7+ ♔e8 [if *25...*♔c8 *26* ♘e7+! wins] *26* ♖e7+! ♕xe7 *27* ♘g7 mate) *23* f4 ♘g4 *24* h3 ♘f6 *25* f5 ♔b6 *26* ♕e3 ♔c7 (after *26...*♔a6 *27* a4 smashes Black) *27* ♖c4+! bxc4 (if *27...*♔d8 *28* ♕c5 anyway) *28* ♕c5+ ♗c6 (if *28...*♔d8 *29* ♕a5 mate; or *28...*♔b8 *29* ♖b1+) *29* ♘b5+, etc.

Black may not have seen the mate, but he suspected the worst!

17   ♖ad1!   ...

Piling on the pressure. White mustn't amateurishly rush in with *17* ♕c7 ♕d7! forcing him to simplify by *18* ♘d6+ ♚e7 *19* ♘xc8+ ♖axc8 *20* ♕xd7+ ♚xd7, etc., and the advantage has evaporated.

17	...	**cxb5**

He might as well take it since after *17...*♗d7 *18* ♘d6+ ♚e7 *19* ♗c4 White wins a Pawn without any risk.

18	**♕c7**	**♗d7**

Forced.

19	**♘d6+**	**♚e7**
20	**♘f5+!**	...

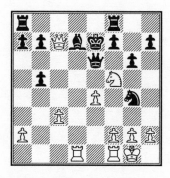

CELLE

Position after 20 ♘*f5+!*

FISCHER

The attack needs fresh fuel. Material is not what counts now, but open lines. Black is forced to capture against his will. *20...*♚e8 is out because of *21* ♘g7+. And *20...*♚f6 *21* ♖d6 gxf5 *22* ♕xd7! wins outright.

20	...	**gxf5**
21	**exf5**	**♖ac8**

On *21...*♕xf5 *22* ♕d6+ ♚d8 (*22...*♚e8 *23* ♖fe1+ ♗e6 *24* ♕d7 mate) *23* ♕xf8+ ♚c7 *24* ♕xa8 wins.

22	**♖xd7+!**	**♕xd7**

23	**f6+!**	...

Originally I intended *23 ♖e1+ ♘e5 24 ♖xe5+ ♔f6 25 ♕xd7 ♔xe5 26 ♕xb5+* with a won ending. But then I remembered Emanuel Lasker's maxim: "When you see a good move – wait – don't play it – you might find a better one."

23	...	**♘xf6**

Not *23...♔e8? 24 ♖e1+ ♕e6 25 ♕xc8* mate. On *23...♔xf6 24 ♕xd7.*

24	**♖e1+**	...

CELLE

Position after 24 ♖e1+

FISCHER

Note the amusing piece configuration. All Black's pieces are stepping on each other's toes.

24	...	**♘e4**

The only legal move!

25	**♖xe4+**	**♔f6**
26	**♕xd7**	**♖fd8**
27	**♕g4**	...

Here I forgot Lasker's maxim. *27 ♕e7+* would have forced mate in four.

27	...	**Black resigns**

51 Fischer - Smyslov *[U.S.S.R.]*

HAVANA 1965

RUY LOPEZ

Squeeze play

Fischer competed in this Capablanca Memorial Tournament by long-distance telephone, and his victory over the winner is reminiscent of the famous Lasker-Capablanca duel at St. Petersburg, 1914, where Black was also gradually constricted and strangled.

Taken by surprise with an antiquated line (5 d3), Smyslov soon gets into trouble. He finds a way out, although it burdens him with doubled King Pawns. After the subsequent exchange of Queens he apparently underestimates White's winning chances and permits himself to drift into a cramped ending. Applying persistent pressure, Fischer makes gradual inroads; the defensive task eventually proves too great and Smyslov buckles under the strain.

1	e4	e5
2	♘f3	♘c6
3	♗b5	a6
4	♗a4	♘f6
5	d3	...

Steinitz's favorite, long abandoned, and the first time I've employed it in a tournament game.

| 5 | ... | d6 |

A solid but passive reaction. An alternative is *5...b5 6 ♗b3 ♗e7 7 a4*, etc. Anderssen-Morphy, match 1858(!) continued: *5...♗c5 6 c3 b5 7 ♗c2 0-0 8 0-0 d5 9 exd5 ♘xd5 10 h3 h6* (Steinitz had a field day criticizing White's last two moves) *11 d4 exd4* with a satisfactory game for Black.

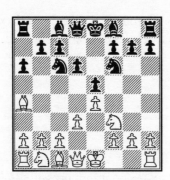

SMYSLOV

Position after 5...d6

FISCHER

6	**c3**	**♗e7**

On 6...g6 7 ♘bd2 (or Bronstein's 7 ♗g5) 7...♗g7 8 ♘f1 0-0 9 h4 opens fresh vistas.

7	**♘bd2**	**0-0**
8	**♘f1**	...

One facet of White's strategy is to defer castling and possibly institute a K-side attack with h3, g4, etc. Furthermore, this Knight can be deployed to e3 or g3 immediately without having to waste a tempo (after having castled) with ♖e1.

8	...	**b5**
9	**♗b3**	**d5**

Inconsistent, after having lost a tempo with ...d6. Right is 9...♘a5 10 ♗c2 c5 11 ♘e3 ♖e8 12 0-0 ♗f8 with equal chances.

10	**♕e2**	**dxe4**

Opens the position prematurely. No better would be 10...d4 11 ♘g3 dxc3 12 bxc3 b4 13 ♗d2. Black should keep tension in the center with 10...♗e6 11 ♘g3 (if 11 ♘g5 ♗g4 12 f3 ♗c8! 13 exd5 ♘a5!) 11...h6.

11	**dxe4**	**♗e6!**

I was surprised that Smyslov was prepared to saddle himself with doubled King Pawns, but surmised that it must be all right since he doesn't do such things lightly. Anyway Black's game, without this exchange, would remain permanently cramped.

| 12 | ♗xe6 | fxe6 |
| 13 | ♘g3 | ... |

This Knight is undeniably misplaced here, but White intends to castle and then regroup his pieces in order to bring maximum pressure to bear on the doubled Pawns.

| 13 | ... | ♕d7 |

Some annotators suggested the obvious *13...♗d6* (followed by ♘e7-g6, etc.) but Black has no time for such sophisticated strategy: e.g., *14* 0-0 ♘e7 *15* c4! c6 *16* ♖d1 winning material (if *16...♕c7 17* ♘g5).

| 14 | 0-0 | ... |

During the game I was kicking myself for allowing the subsequent exchange of Queens. Sharper is *14* a4 ♖ad8 (if *14...bxa4 15* ♕c4 a3 *16* b4) *15* axb5 axb5 *16* ♖a6 b4 *17* 0-0 and Black can no longer ease his burden with ...♕d3. So correct is *14...b4!*

| 14 | ... | ♖ad8 |

Suddenly Black's plan hit me! At first I thought he just wanted to control the d-file; but now I realized he was scheming to chop wood.

| 15 | a4 | ♕d3! |

Of course! With the Queens gone, it's that much harder to strike at Black's weaknesses.

16	♕xd3	♖xd3
17	axb5	axb5
18	♖a6!	...

Forcing Black's reply, and thus preventing the freeing maneuver with ...♗c5. *18* ♗e3 would be met by ...♘g4.

| 18 | ... | ℤd6 |

SMYSLOV

Position after 18...ℤd6

FISCHER

| 19 | ♔h1! | ... |

The threat was *19...♞d4* forcing a favorable series of exchanges.

| 19 | ... | ♞d7 |

19...b4 20 cxb4 ♞xb4 21 ℤa7 ℤc6 22 ♞xe5 ℤc2 would give Black active play for the Pawn.

| 20 | ♝e3 | ℤd8 |

20...b4 is still playable. Neither of us realized at this stage how essential this move was. I didn't want to weaken my c3 and c4 squares by playing b4 to prevent it; and Smyslov didn't want to commit himself yet.

| 21 | h3 | ... |

More accurate is *21 b4*, from which I abstained for the reasons already mentioned.

21	...	h6
22	ℤfa1	♞db8
23	ℤa8	ℤd1+
24	♔h2	...

On *24 ℤxd1 ℤxd1+ 25 ♔h2 ♝d6* holds (*26 ♝a7? ℤa1!*).

| 24 | ... | ℤxa1 |
| 25 | ℤxa1 | ... |

SMYSLOV

Position after 25 ♖xa1

FISCHER

25	...	♘d7?

When I spoke to Smyslov on the direct phone line immediately after the game, he congratulated me on a beautiful performance and attributed his loss to his reluctance to play ...b4 at some point – and this is his last chance. After *25...b4 26 cxb4 ♗xb4 27 ♘f1* Black obtains much more freedom than in the actual game, and eliminates a weakness (his b-pawn) as well. Perhaps Smyslov feared that in this line White could maneuver his Knight to c4; even so, this is hardly fatal.

26	b4!	...

Smyslov confessed that he felt Black was probably lost after this riposte. But the win is far from easy, and Black might later have improved upon his defense.

26	...	♔f7
27	♘f1	♗d6
28	g3	...

Once and for all negating all possible combinations with ...♘d4.

28	...	♘f6
29	♘1d2	♔e7
30	♖a6!	♘b8

Very uncomfortable is *30...♔d7 31 ♘e1 ♘b8 32 ♖a5 ♔c6.*

| 31 | ♖a5! | ... |

Now White strengthens his bind by forcing ...c6 which takes away another breathing space from Black's pieces.

31	...	c6
32	♔g2	♘bd7
33	♔f1	...

Preparing to bring the King to e2 where it can support the ♘e1-d3 maneuver.

SMYSLOV

Position after 33 ♔f1

FISCHER

33	...	♖c8?

A surprise! I had expected the much stouter defense with *33...♘e8!* (intending to exchange Rooks with ...♘c7 and ...♖a8). After *34 ♖a6 ♖c8 35 ♘b3 c5 36 bxc5 ♗xc5!* Black can hold. And there is no time for *34 ♘e1 ♘c7 35 ♘d3 ♖a8 36 ♘b3 ♖xa5 37 ♘xa5 ♘b8 38 ♗a7 ♘ca6 39 c4 ♗c7.*

The main line is *33...♘e8 34 ♘b3! ♘c7 35 ♖a7 ♖a8 36 ♘a5 ♘b8 37 ♖xa8 (if 37 ♖b7 ♔d7) 37...♘xa8 38 ♗a7 ♔d7 39 ♘b7.* It looks bad, but Black has chances to survive in the absence of a forced win.

34	♘e1!	♘e8

Too late now.

35	♘d3	♘c7
36	c4!	bxc4

36...♖a8? is refuted by *37 c5!* winning a piece.

37	♘xc4	...

The ideal position! Finally White has ganged up on Black's venerable weakness – his Pawn on e5.

37	...	♘b5

On *37...♖a8 38 ♖xa8 ♘xa8 39 ♘a5 ♘b8 40 ♗a7 ♔d7 41 ♘c4* picks off the e-pawn.

| 38 | ♖a6 | ... |

Keeping Black tied up some more.

| 38 | ... | ♔f6 |

38...♘b8 39 ♖a8 ♘c7 40 ♘xd6 ♔xd6 41 ♗c5+ wins.

| 39 | ♗c1! | ♗b8 |
| 40 | ♗b2 | ... |

Threatening f4.

| 40 | ... | c5 |

A desperate bid for counterplay.

| 41 | ♘b6! | ... |

41 ♖a5! also has a nasty sting; for if 41...cxb4 42 ♘cxe5! wins outright.

| 41 | ... | ♘xb6 |
| 42 | ♖xb6 | c4 |

On *42...♘d4 43 ♘xc5 ♗a7 44 ♘d7+ ♔g5 45 h4+ ♔h5 46 ♖b7 ♖c2 47 ♖xa7 ♖xb2 48 ♘xe5 ♖xb4 49 ♖xg7* is decisive.

| 43 | ♘c5 | **c3 and Black resigns** |

SMYSLOV

Final Position after 43...c3

FISCHER

White can win with *44 ♗c1 ♘d4 45 ♘d7+ ♔e7* (if *45...♔f7 46 ♖xb8 ♖xb8 47 ♘xb8 ♘b3 48 ♗a3 c2 49 ♘c6, etc.) 46 ♘xb8 ♘b3 47 ♖b7+ ♔d8 48 ♖d7+ ♔e8 49 ♖xg7!*

52 Fischer - Rossolimo *[U.S.A.]*

U.S.A. CHAMPIONSHIP 1965-6

FRENCH DEFENSE

Peekaboo strategy

The McCutcheon Variation gives rise to unusual positions where White is frequently obliged to forfeit the privilege of castling in order to try and wrest an advantage. After some slight but instructive opening inexactitudes on both sides, Rossolimo appears to achieve equality. Indeed, he is constantly on the brink of crashing through with a counter-attack against White's vulnerable King, although his own monarch is also stranded in the center. After 13...f5, which shores up his fortress, it's not clear just whose attack will come first.

In a theoretically important formation – a logical offshoot of this variation – Fischer unearths two fine moves (17 ♗b5+ and 19 ♘g1) to sustain his flagging initiative. Still, he is forced to wage a running battle, no sooner landing a blow than having to duck. Consequently, the outcome is in doubt until the very last punch.

1	e4	e6
2	d4	d5
3	♘c3	♘f6
4	♗g5	♗b4

The McCutcheon Variation, giving rise to immediate complications. 4...♗e7 or 4...dxe4 are tamer.

5	e5	h6
6	♗d2	...

6 exf6 hxg5 7 fxg7 ♖g8 leads to nothing.

6	...	♗xc3
7	bxc3	...

Against Petrosian, at Curaçao 1962, I tried the ridiculous *7 ♗xc3?*
♘e4 8 ♗a5?? (if *8 ♗b4 c5 9 dxc5 ♘xf2! 10 ♔xf2 ♕h4+*) *8...0-0*
(weaker is *8...b6 9 ♗b4 c5 10 ♗a3 cxd4 11 ♕xd4 ♘c6 12 ♗b5*) *9 ♗d3*
♘c6 10 ♗c3 ♘xc3 11 bxc3 f6 and Black already had the initiative.

7	...	♘e4
8	♕g4	g6

More risky is *8...♔f8 9 h4 c5 10 ♖h3.*

9	♗d3	♘xd2
10	♔xd2	c5

Producing a position well-known to theory, but never completely
worked out. Not *10...♕g5+ 11 ♕xg5 hxg5 12 g4!*

11	♘f3	...

ROSSOLIMO

Position after 11 ♘f3

FISCHER

11	...	♘c6

According to *Modern Chess Openings*, *11...♕c7* is more accurate; the
point being that *12 ♕f4* can be met by *12...f5!. 11...♗d7 12 dxc5*
deserves testing.

12	♕f4	...

Possibly better is *12 ♖ab1*, restraining the development of Black's
Q-side.

12	**...**		♕**c7**

Better is the natural *12*...♕a5 (if *12*...g5 *13* ♕f6! ♕xf6 *14* exf6 g4 *15* ♘e5 cxd4 *16* cxd4 ♘xd4 *17* h3 with a better ending) *13* ♖ab1 (if *13* ♖hb1 b6 *14* a4 ♗a6 *15* ♗b5 ♖c8 *16* dxc5 bxc5 *17* ♗xc6+ ♖xc6 *18* ♖b8+ ♖c8 holds) *13*...b6 *14* dxc5 ♕xc5 *15* ♘d4 ♘xd4 *16* cxd4 ♕a5+ with equality.

ROSSOLIMO

Position after 12...♕c7

FISCHER

13	**h4**	**...**

Sharper is *13* ♕f6! ♖g8 *14* h4 and if *14*...♕a5 (*14*...h5 looks practically forced) *15* h5! gxh5 *16* ♖xh5 cxd4 *17* ♖ah1 yielding good attacking prospects.

13	**...**	**f5!**

Re-establishing parity.

14	**g4**	**cxd4**
15	**cxd4**	♘**e7?**

After the game Rossolimo suggested *15*...♗d7 but White keeps the better of it after *16* gxf5 gxf5 (if *16*...exf5 *17* ♕g3 ♘e7 *18* e6! ♕a5+ *19* c3 ♗xe6 *20* ♖he1 gives a powerful attack) *17* ♖hg1 0-0-0 *18* ♖g6. At least Black's King reaches safety in this line.

16	**gxf5**	**exf5**
17	♗**b5+!**	**...**

ROSSOLIMO

Position after 17 ♗b5+!

FISCHER

| 17 | ... | ♚f8? |

On *17...♘c6* (if *17...♗d7 18 ♗xd7+ ♕xd7 19 e6!*) *18 ♗xc6+ bxc6* (*18...♕xc6* is again met by *19 e6! ♗xe6 20 ♘e5 ♕d6 21 ♘xg6 ♕xf4+ 22 ♘xf4* and the Knight beats the Bishop in the ending) *19 ♖hg1*, etc.

Black's best chance, however, is to try and reach sanctuary with *17...♚d8! 18 ♗d3 ♗e6*. White undoubtedly has the initiative, but it's hard to get at the King.

| 18 | ♗d3 | ... |

Mission accomplished. Now Black's King is pinioned to the K-side.

| 18 | ... | ♗e6 |
| 19 | ♘g1! | ... |

The key move. This Knight is headed for f4 where it can exert maximum pressure on the g-Pawn.

| 19 | ... | ♚f7 |
| 20 | ♘h3 | ♖ac8!? |

Quite rightly. Rossolimo prefers active defense. After *20...♖ag8* White eventually triples on the g-file (bringing his Knight to f4) with a crushing bind.

| 21 | ♖hg1 | ... |

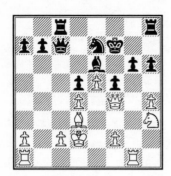

ROSSOLIMO

Position after 21 ♖hg1

FISCHER

21	...	b6

This takes a5 away from the Queen, eliminating any possible defenses there with check.

But Black also loses after *21...♕c3+ 22 ♔e3 ♘c6 23 ♖ab1 ♘b4 24 ♖xb4! ♕xb4 25 h5 ♖cg8 26 hxg6+ ♖xg6 27 ♖xg6 ♕e1+ 28 ♔f3 ♔xg6 29 ♕h4! ♕d1+ 30 ♔g2 ♖g8 31 ♔h2!*

22	h5!	♕c3+
23	♔e2	♘c6

On *23...♖cg8* (if *23...g5 24 ♘xg5+! hxg5 25 ♕xg5 ♔e8 26 ♕f6 ♔d7 27 ♗b5+! ♖c6 28 ♕xh8 ♕xc2+ 29 ♔f1* wins) *24 hxg6+ ♖xg6* (if *24...♘xg6 25 ♕f3*) *25 ♕h4* is decisive.

24	hxg6+	♔g7

No better is *24...♔e7 25 ♕h4+ ♔d7 26 ♖ad1! ♕xd4* (*26...♘xd4+? 27 ♕xd4!*) *27 ♘f4!*

25	♖ad1!	♘xd4+

On *25...♕xd4 26 ♔f1! ♕xe5 27 ♖e1 ♕xf4 28 ♘xf4 ♗d7 29 ♘h5+* wins.

26	♔f1	♖he8
27	♖g3	...

Overprotecting the Bishop. After the hasty *27 ♕h4 ♘f3! 28 ♕f6+ ♔g8 29 ♗xf5 ♘h2+ 30 ♔g2 ♕f3+ 31 ♔xh2 ♕xf5* holds!

| 27 | ... | ♘c6 |
| 28 | ♕h4 | ♘xe5 |

After *28...♕xe5 29 ♘f4* contains too many threats.

29	♘f4	♘g4
30	♘xe6+!	♖xe6
31	♗xf5	♕c4+
32	♔g1!	...

No credit for other moves!

ROSSOLIMO

Final Position after 32 ♔g1!

FISCHER

| 32 | ... | **Black resigns** |

If *32...♘xf2 33 ♕xc4 ♖xc4 34 ♔xf2 ♖f4+ 35 ♖f3*, etc.

A hard-fought game!

53 Portisch *[Hungary]* - Fischer

SANTA MONICA 1966

NIMZO INDIAN DEFENSE

Black magic

Here is one of the few instances when Fischer does not employ the fianchetto of his King's Bishop as a defense to the QP. By ignoring White's gambit on move nine he lays the groundwork for the positional trap (11...♕d7) into which Portisch falls (14 ♕xa8). Normally, two Rooks for the Queen is a good trade – better than good when it produces a setting in which the scope and power of the Rooks may be formidable. But Portisch's judgment is faulty, he fails to take into account the weakness of his Pawns. This is one of the rare occasions when the Queen can run rampant, and she does.

Still, the question remains: how did Black manage to weave his spell? To achieve a winning endgame within fifteen moves, against a specialist with White in this opening, is an almost unheard of feat.

1	**d4**	**♘f6**
2	**c4**	**e6!**

To throw White off balance. I felt Portisch was just too well-versed in the K's Indian.

3	**♘c3**	**♗b4**
4	**e3**	**...**

This has been fashionable for some time. Spassky's offbeat *4 ♗g5* leads to no advantage after *4...h6 5 ♗h4 c5 6 d5 d6 7 e3 ♗xc3+! 8 bxc3 e5*, etc. The two Knights are better than the Bishops in such closed formations.

4	...	**b6!**

Other moves have been analyzed to death.

5	♘ge2	...

Reshevsky-Fischer, US Championship 1966, continued: *5 ♗d3 ♗b7 6 ♘f3 0-0* (sharper is *6...♘e4! 7 0-0 f5* [or *7...♘xc3! 8 bxc3 ♗xc3 9 ♖b1 ♘c6!* and White hasn't got enough for his Pawn] *8 ♗xe4 fxe4 9 ♘d2 ♗xc3 10 bxc3 0-0 11 ♕g4 ♖f5!*= Gligorich-Larsen, Havana 1967. Not *12 ♘xe4? h5*) *7 0-0 ♗xc3* (*7...d5* is an alternative) *8 bxc3 ♗e4 9 ♕c2* and now *9...♗xf3!* (instead of *9...♗xd3*) *10 gxf3 c5* would lead to an exciting positional struggle – two Knights vs. two Bishops, but White's Pawn formation is shaky.

5	...	**♗a6**

Bronstein's active idea, trying to profit from White's last move. I had adopted it with success in the 1966 US Championship.

A very interesting try is *5...♘e4!?* as in the 1967 USSR Championship. Taimanov-Levin continued *6 ♕c2 ♗b7 7 f3* (*7 a3* is better), and now instead of *7...♗xc3+* (as in the game) *7...♘xc3! 8 ♘xc3* (*8 bxc3 ♗d6! 9 e4 ♘c6* with good play against White's doubled c-pawn) *8...♕h4+ 9 ♕f2 ♗xc3+ 10 bxc3 ♕xf2+ 11 ♔xf2 ♗a6!* threatening *...♘c6-a5* with at least equality.

FISCHER

Position after 5...♗a6

PORTISCH

6	♘g3	...

Somewhat inconsistent. The whole point is to play *6* a3 so that after *6...*♗xc3+ (if *6...*♗e7 *7* ♘f4 d5 *8* cxd5 ♗xf1 *9* ♔xf1 exd5 *10* g4! gives White a slight edge, as demonstrated in the 1954 Botvinnik-Smyslov match) *7* ♘xc3 White can avoid doubling his c-Pawn. After *7...*d5 *8* b3 0-0 *9* a4 ♘c6 I reached this position, as Black, twice in the 1966 US Championship. Addison played *10* ♗b2? and got the worst of it after *10...*dxc4 *11* bxc4 ♘a5 *12* ♘b5 c6 *13* ♘a3 ♕e7! *14* ♕c2 c5 *15* ♗e2 (finally) *15...*cxd4 *16* exd4 ♖fc8 *17* 0-0 ♖c6! *18* ♗f3 ♘d5 and White's c-Pawn falls. Evans chose *10* ♗e2 dxc4 *11* ♗a3! ♖e8 *12* b4 ♘e7 *13* 0-0? (*13* b5 ♗b7 *14* 0-0 permits White to regain his Pawn with a tiny pull) *13...*♘ed5 *14* ♖c1 c6! *15* ♗f3 b5 *16* a5 ♕c7 *17* ♕c2 ♖ad8 *18* ♖fd1 ♗b7 *19* ♖d2 ♘xc3 *20* ♕xc3 c5! *21* dxc5 ♗xf3 *22* gxf3 ♖xd2 *23* ♕xd2 ♖d8 *24* ♕e1 ♖d3 *25* ♗b2 ♘d5 and White soon collapsed.

6	...	♗xc3+!

Inferior is *6...*0-0 (not *6...*d5?? *7* ♕a4+) *7* e4 ♘c6 (White keeps his initiative also after *7...*c5 *8* d5 d6 *9* ♗e2 exd5 *10* exd5 ♗xc3+ *11* bxc3 ♘bd7 *12* 0-0 ♖e8 *13* ♕a4, etc. Portisch-Reshevsky, Santa Monica 1966) *8* ♗d3! d5 (*8...*♘xd4? *9* ♕a4 wins a piece) *9* cxd5 ♗xd3 *10* ♕xd3 exd5 *11* e5 ♘e4 *12* a3! with a clear advantage. Portisch-Spassky, Moscow 1967.

7	**bxc3**	**d5**
8	**♕f3**	...

The whole idea is dubious. No better is *8* ♗a3 dxc4! *9* ♕f3 ♕d5 *10* e4 ♕c6 and White hasn't got enough for the Pawn.

Simply *8* cxd5 leads to level play. It is White's insistence on seeking the initiative that lands him in trouble.

8	...	**0-0**
9	**e4!?**	...

Right is *9* cxd5 exd5 (not *9...*♗xf1? *10* dxe6!) *10* ♗xa6 ♘xa6 *11* ♕e2 ♕c8 *12* 0-0 c5 *13* dxc5 ♘xc5 *14* c4=. The text involves a gambit which Portisch probably had expected me to accept.

FISCHER

Position after 9 e4!?

PORTISCH

| 9 | ... | **dxe4!** |

An improvement over *9...dxc4!?* which I had played against Saidy in the 1966 US Championship: *10 ♗g5 h6 11 ♗d2?* (right is *11 h4! ♗b7! 12 ♗xf6 ♕xf6 13 ♕xf6 gxf6 14 ♗xc4* or White might try to continue the attack with *12 ♘h5!? ♘bd7!* – but not *12...hxg5? 13 hxg5 ♘xe4 14 ♘f6+!!* wins – Spassky) *11...♘bd7 12 e5 ♘d5 13 ♘f5* (if *13 ♘h5 ♕h4!*) *13...exf5 14 ♕xd5 ♖e8! 15 ♗xc4* (or *15 0-0-0 c5*) *15...♘xe5! 16 ♕xd8 ♘xc4+ 17 ♕xe8+ ♖xe8+ 18 ♔d1 ♘xd2 19 ♔xd2 ♖e2+* with an easily won endgame.

| 10 | ♘xe4 | ♘xe4 |
| 11 | ♕xe4 | **♕d7!!** |

The finest move in the game, far superior to the "natural" *11...♘d7 12 ♗d3 ♘f6 13 ♕h4* with two Bishops and a beautiful development despite the doubled Pawns.

Black can well afford to give up two Rooks for a Queen (after *12 ♕xa8? ♘c6*), as will soon become apparent. The text prepares ...♘c6-a5 hitting the "weakling," as Alekhine used to call that kind of a target.

| 12 | ♗a3 | ... |

White gets the worst of it after *12 ♗d3 f5 13 ♕e2 ♘c6*, etc. Still, this was a prudent choice.

| 12 | ... | **♖e8** |

FISCHER

Position after 12...♖e8

PORTISCH

| 13 | ♗d3 | ... |

13 0-0-0 seems more consistent, making a real fight of it. Such double-edged lines, however, are not to Portisch's taste.

| 13 | ... | f5 |
| 14 | ♕xa8? | ... |

Very bad judgment, White should resist temptation and try to hold on with *14* ♕e2. His doubled c-Pawn, though weak, is not fatal. As the game goes, however, it is.

14	...	♘c6
15	♕xe8+	♕xe8
16	0-0	♘a5
17	♖ae1	♗xc4

Too routine. Crushing is *17*...♕a4! E.g., *18* ♗b4 (if *18* ♗c1 ♗xc4 *19* ♗xc4 ♕xc4 should easily win) *18*...♗xc4 *19* ♗xc4 ♘xc4 *20* ♖xe6 a5 *21* ♗e7 ♘d2! *22* ♖fe1 ♘e4 *23* f3 ♕xa2! Curtains.

| 18 | ♗xc4 | ... |

If *18* ♗xf5? ♕a4 wins.

18	...	♘xc4
19	♗c1	c5
20	dxc5	...

White cannot hold the ending. If *20* d5? simply ...e5.

| 20 | ... | bxc5 |
| 21 | ♗f4 | h6! |

Preparing to expand on the K-side, which cannot be prevented.

22	♖e2	...

If *22 h4 e5! 23 ♗xe5 ♘xe5 24 f4 ♘f3+! 25 gxf3 ♕a4* and White's Pawns are too loose.

22	...	g5
23	♗e5	♕d8
24	♖fe1	...

On *24 f4 ♘d2! 25 ♖fe1 ♘e4* ties White up.

24	...	♔f7
25	h3	f4
26	♔h2	a6

Taking care of details, so that the Pawn will not be within the Bishop's reach after *26...♕d5 27 ♗b8*, etc.

27	♖e4	♕d5!

The Queen is boss.

FISCHER

Position after 27...♕d5!

PORTISCH

Black's superiority is obvious. He has some minor threats, and a major one which cannot be met. To the surprise of no one, *Sovietski Sport*, a Soviet magazine, reported that Portisch had blundered and thrown away a perfectly even endgame.

28	h4	...

After the comparatively better *28 ♖4e2*, Black wins more slowly with *28... f3! 29 gxf3* (or *29 ♖e4 fxg2* followed by *...♘d2 wins*) *29...♘d2*, etc.

| 28 | ... | ♘e3! |

Wins the exchange, as *29* f3 fails against *29*...♛d2 *30* ♖g1 ♛f2.

29	♖1xe3	fxe3
30	♖xe3	♛xa2
31	♖f3+	♚e8
32	♗g7	♛c4
33	hxg5	hxg5
34	♖f8+	...

A check before dying.

34	...	♚d7
35	♖a8	♚c6
	White resigns	

The ominous presence of Black's a-pawn is the deciding factor.

54 Fischer - Najdorf [*Argentina*]

SANTA MONICA 1966

SICILIAN DEFENSE

Najdorf's night off from the Najdorf

This game follows a loss (with Black) to Najdorf earlier in the tournament. Here, Najdorf adopts the Sicilian but not his Variation – perhaps because he had lost with it previously. (See game 40.) White soon launches a sharp line, a curious violation of principle involving three consecutive Bishop sorties before his other men have been developed. In relatively uncharted terrain, both players miss their way on move twelve. It then becomes a question of whether Najdorf's doubled center Pawns are a mass or a mess. Fischer proceeds to exploit his slight advantage with restraint, gradually building up pressure against Black's uncastled King. At the right moment he offers a stunning Pawn sacrifice (26 c5). Najdorf is compelled to decline, whereupon he lands in a hopeless endgame.

This forceful and resourceful performance typified Fischer's surge throughout the last half of the 2nd Piatigorsky Cup.

1	e4	c5
2	♘f3	♘c6

Najdorf avoids the Najdorf Variation.

3	d4	cxd4
4	♘xd4	e6

4...♘f6 obliges 5 ♘c3, which precludes the Maroczy Bind by c4. Ever since ways of combatting the "Bind" have been found, it has become almost an obsession to abstain from 4...♘f6, although the most that can be said for other moves is that some of them may be as good.

5	♘b5	...

Alekhine was of the opinion that *5* c4 is best, but it has since been discovered that White cannot maintain any advantage after *5*...♘f6 *6* ♘c3 ♗b4, etc.

| 5 | ... | d6 |
| 6 | ♗f4!? | ... |

Sharpest. Objectively speaking, it is probably best to establish an immediate Maroczy Bind with *6* c4.

| 6 | ... | e5 |

After *6*...♘e5!? *7* ♘1a3! (Bronstein's idea) is best. But not Euwe's suggestion to win a Pawn by *7* ♕d4 a6 *8* ♘xd6+?? ♗xd6 *9* ♗xe5 because of *9*...♕a5+! (ZUCKERMAN).

| 7 | ♗e3 | ♘f6 |

Black can avoid the doubling of his Pawns by *7*...a6 *8* ♘5c3 ♘f6 *9* ♗g5 ♗e7. However, Najdorf may have been worried about *9* ♗c4! Fischer-Badilles, Manila 1967, then continued: *9*...♗e7 *10* ♘d5! ♘xd5 *11* ♗xd5 0-0 *12* ♘c3 with absolute control of d5. After the text, *8* ♗c4 is met simply by *8*...♗e6! (but not *8*...♘xe4?? *9* ♕d5 ♗e6 *10* ♕xe4 d5 *11* ♗xd5! and wins) *9* ♗xe6 fxe6 *10* c4! ♗e7= (not *10*...♘xe4? *11* ♕g4).

| 8 | ♗g5!? | ... |

Another of Bronstein's ideas. The customary line was *8* ♘1c3 and after *8*...a6 *9* ♘a3 Black has 3 possibilities:

A] *9*...b5 *10* ♘d5 ♘xd5 (or *10*...♖b8 *11* ♘xf6+ ♕xf6 *12* ♘b1! with an edge for White) *11* exd5 ♘e7 *12* c4 with advantage.

B] Simagin gives *9*...♗e6 *10* ♘d5 ♗xd5! *11* exd5 ♘e7 *12* c4 ♘f5 with harmonious development for all of Black's pieces. Or *10* ♘c4 b5 *11* ♘b6 ♖b8 *12* ♘bd5 ♗xd5 *13* exd5 ♘e7 with a good game. But *13* ♘xd5!? (instead of *13* exd5) launches a promising gambit (*13*...♘xe4 *14* ♕f3 ♘c5 *15* 0-0-0).

C] Best is *9*...♖b8! *10* ♗g5 b5= Aronin-Taimanov, USSR Championship 1962. *11* ♘d5 is met by *11*...♕a5+ forcing *12* ♗d2 then *12*...♕d8 and White has made no progress. On *13* ♘xf6+ ♕xf6 *14* ♘b1 b4! and White must regroup his forces.

NAJDORF

Position after 8 ♗g5!?

FISCHER

The third consecutive Bishop sortie is well-motivated since White is threatening to double Black's f-Pawn.

8	...	♗e6?

Also weak is *8...a6 9 ♗xf6 gxf6 10 ♘5c3 f5? 11 ♕h5! ♘d4 12 ♗c4 ♕c7 13 ♘d2 ♘xc2+ 14 ♔e2 ♘xa1* (Bronstein-Polugayevsky, USSR Championship 1964) and now simply *15 ♖xa1!* must win out. Another try is *11...♗g7!?* (instead of *11...♘d4*) *12 ♗c4 0-0 13 exf5 ♘d4 14 ♗d3 ♖e8 15 ♗e4!* (not *15 f6?* as in Estrin-Tcherepkov, Leningrad 1964). For instance, *15...d5 16 ♘xd5 ♗xf5 17 ♗xf5 ♕xd5 18 ♘c3 ♕xg2? 19 ♗e4 ♘xc2+ 20 ♔e2 ♘d4+ 21 ♔e3*, etc.

But Black could equalize immediately with *8...♕a5+! 9 ♕d2* (or *9 ♗d2 ♕d8 draws) 9...♘xe4 10 ♕xa5 ♘xa5 11 ♗e3* (R.Byrne suggests *11 ♘c7+? ♔d7 12 ♘xa8 ♘xg5 13 ♗b5+*, but after *13...♔d8! 14 ♘c3 ♗d7 15 0-0-0 ♗e7* White's straying Knight is soon lost) *11...♔d7 12 ♘xa7 d5*, etc.

9	♘1c3	...

After *9 c4 h6! 10 ♗xf6 gxf6* Black's position is excellent.

9	...	a6
10	♗xf6	gxf6
11	♘a3	♘d4

Other possibilities (all favoring White) are:

A] *11...b5 12 ♘d5!*
B] *11...♗e7 12 ♗c4!*
C] *11...f5? 12 ♗c4 ♗xc4 13 ♘xc4 fxe4 14 ♘xe4 d5 15 ♕xd5!*

12   **&c4?**   ...

Correct is *12 ♘c4* and if *12...♖c8 13 ♘e3 ♗h6* (if *13...♕b6* simply *14 ♖b1*) *14 ♗d3 ♖g8 15 ♕h5!* snuffs out Black's initiative.

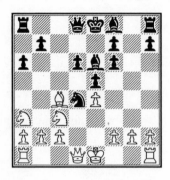

NAJDORF

Position after 12 ♗c4?

FISCHER

12   ...   **b5**

Sharper is *12...d5! 13 ♘xd5* (if *13 exd5 ♗xa3 14 bxa3 ♕a5*) *13...♗xa3 14 bxa3 ♕a5+ 15 ♔f1* (or *15 c3 ♗xd5 16 ♗xd5 ♕xc3+ 17 ♔f1 ♖c8!* with advantage) *15...0-0-0* with active play: e.g., *16 c3*, then *...♘b5*, etc.

13   **♗xe6**   ...

Of course not the tempting *13 ♗d5? b4*.

13   ...   **fxe6**

All in all this exchange benefits Black since it enables him to protect his weak squares (d5 and f5). However if (as in the sequence) his central Pawn mass can be restrained, then it becomes merely a fixed target subject to constant pressure.

14   **♘e2**   **♘c6**

Black should get some scope for his pieces by *14...♘xe2! 15 ♕xe2 d5*. The check looming on h5 is not to be feared.

15   **♘g3**   ...

15 c4 at once is met by *15...♕a5+*

15	...	♕d7?

Dr. Kmoch recommends *15...d5!* Or *15...♕a5+!* *16* c3 b4 and if *17* ♘c4 ♕c5.

16	**c4**	♘d4
17	**0-0**	**b4**

"Castling Q-side is a risk Black's insurance company would not permit him to take." (R.Byrne)

The text later enables White to use this b-Pawn to pry open the a-file (after a3). Better is *17...♗g7*.

18	♘c2	♘xc2
19	♕xc2	**h5**
20	♖fd1	**h4**
21	♘f1	♖g8?

Better is *21...h3 22* g3 ♕c6 with reasonable play.

22	**a3!**	**h3**
23	**g3**	**bxa3**
24	♖xa3	♕c6
25	♕e2!	**f5**

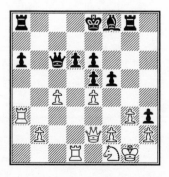

NAJDORF

Position after 25...f5

FISCHER

Hoping to trade his h-Pawn for the e-Pawn in the event of *26* ♕h5+. But White now is ready to exploit Black's poor development.

26	**c5!**	**...**

More than a glancing blow. Black can know nothing about the imminent destruction of his compact mass of center Pawns.

26	**...**	♕**xe4**

26...dxc5 (if 26...♕xc5 27 ♕h5+ followed by exf5, etc.) 27 ♕h5+ ♔e7 28 ♖ad3 fxe4 29 ♖3d2 is quite hopeless for Black.

27	♕**xe4**	**fxe4**
28	**cxd6**	**...**

Black's game is in ruins – note his pathetic triplets on the e-file. The rest is technique.

28	**...**	♗**h6**

To prevent ♘e3-c4.

29	♖**a5**	♔**d7**
30	♖**xe5**	♗**g7**
31	♖**xe4**	♗**xb2**
32	♘**e3**	**a5**

A last gasp. Different people feel differently about resigning.

33	♘**c4**	♖**gb8**
34	♖**h4**	♔**c6**
35	♖**h7**	♗**d4**
36	♖**c7+**	♔**d5**
37	**d7**	**a4**

NAJDORF

Position after 37...a4

FISCHER

38	♘b6+	...	

Najdorf was probably hoping for *38* ♖c8! ♖xc8 *39* ♘b6+ ♔c5 *40* dxc8=♕+? ♖xc8 *41* ♘xc8 a3 with some practical chances. But we both overlooked the neat *Zwischenzug 40* ♖c1+! ♔xb6 *41* ♖xc8! breaking all further resistance.

The text is good enough, but prolongs the game.

38	...	♖xb6
39	♖c8	...

The point: on *39...*♖bb8 the Pawn queens with check.

39	...	♖d6
40	♖xa8	♖xd7
41	♖xa4	e5
42	♔f1	♖b7
43	f4!	♔e6
44	fxe5	♖f7+
45	♔e2	♖f2+
46	♔d3	♗xe5
47	♖e1!	**Black resigns**

NAJDORF

Final Position after 47 ♖e1!

FISCHER

After *47...*♖f5 *48* ♖a5 (win by pin!) *48...*♔f6 *49* ♖exe5 ♖xe5 *50* ♖xe5 ♔xe5 *51* ♔e3 ♔f5 *52* ♔d4! (but not *52* ♔f3 ♔g5 *53* g4?? ♔h4! and draws) *52...*♔g5 *53* ♔e5 ♔g4 *54* ♔e4 ♔g5 *55* ♔f3 ♔f5 *56* g4+ followed by ♔g3 wins.

55 Fischer - Bednarsky [Poland]

HAVANA OLYMPIC 1966

SICILIAN DEFENSE

The price of incaution

Once more Fischer rehabilitates his pet move (6 ♗c4) against his favorite Najdorf Variation, and it is remarkable that he should continue to win with such ease. In fact, his opponents do not seem to offer serious resistance. Young Bednarsky apparently is caught napping, improvises, and loses in just 22 moves!

Seeking active counterplay, Bednarsky blunders through bravado. He takes a tainted Pawn (9...♘fxe4) and impetuously pursues the attack only to find himself in an ambush which, ironically, he had helped to construct. By move 12 Fischer obtains a formation at which he had had success even as a child. Naturally he wins, but the economy with which he does so is delightful.

1	e4	c5
2	♘f3	d6
3	d4	cxd4
4	♘xd4	♘f6
5	♘c3	a6
6	♗c4	...

Here we go again!

6	...	e6

Probably best. White's Bishop is made to "bite on granite."

7	♗b3	...

Too slow is Bronstein's idea *7* a3. E.g., Robatsch-Fischer, Havana 1965: 7...♗e7 *8* ♗a2 0-0 *9* 0-0 b5 *10* f4 ♗b7 *11* f5 e5 (Black is healthy as long as White can't exploit his hole on d5) *12* ♘de2 ♘bd7 *13* ♘g3 ♖c8 *14* ♗e3 (if *14* ♗g5 ♖xc3! *15* bxc3 ♘xe4 with advantage —

Gligorich) *14...♘b6 15 ♗xb6 ♕xb6+ 16 ♔h1 ♕e3!* (to prevent ♘h5) with the better game for Black.

White would of course like to get in f4-f5 as swiftly as possible, but he must exercise some caution. The text is essentially a waiting move which narrows Black's options. After *7 f4* Black has a choice of *7...d5, 7...b5,* or *7...♘xe4 8 ♘xe4 d5.*

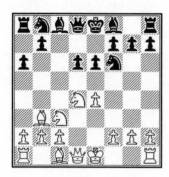

BEDNARSKY

Position after 7 ♗b3

FISCHER

7   ...   ♘bd7

In order to reach c5 with an attack on the Bishop as well as the e-Pawn. But *7...b5!* is better (see game 17). An example of static White play is Garcia-Fischer, Havana Olympic 1966: *8 a3 ♗e7 9 ♗e3 0-0 10 0-0 ♗b7 11 f3 ♘bd7 12 ♕d2* (*12 ♗xe6!?* leads to rough equality) *12...♘e5 13 ♕f2 ♕c7 14 ♖ac1 ♔h8! 15 ♘ce2 ♖g8! 16 ♔h1 g5! 17 h3 ♖g6 18 ♘g3 ♖ag8* (White is curiously helpless against the threat of ...h5 and ...g4. His normal break with f4 is restrained by the silent Bishop on b7) *19 ♘xe6? fxe6 20 ♗xe6 ♘xe4! 21 ♘xe4 ♖xe6* White resigns.

After *7...b5* recent analysis indicates that Black's best plan is rapid development on the Q-side: *8 f4 ♗b7 9 f5 e5 10 ♘de2 ♘bd7 11 ♗g5 ♗e7.* Now on *12 ♘g3?* (Correct is *12 ♗xf6 ♘xf6 13 ♕d3 ♖c8* with even chances – Fischer-Zuckerman, US Championship 1966) *12...♖c8! 13 0-0 h5!* White's in trouble, as indicated by the following examples:

A] *14 h4 b4 15 ♗xf6 ♗xf6 16 ♘d5 ♗xh4 17 ♘xh5!? ♕g5 18 f6 g6 19 ♘g7+ ♔d8 20 ♖f3 ♗g3 21 ♕d3 ♗h2+ 22 ♔f1 ♘c5 23 ♖h3!? ♖h4! 24 ♕f3 ♘xb3 25 axb3 ♖xh3 26 ♕xh3 ♗xd5 27 exd5 ♕xf6+ 28 ♔e1 ♕f4* and since there's nothing left – but emptiness – White resigns. (R.Byrne-Fischer, Tunisia Interzonal, 1967)

B] *14* ♗xf6 ♘xf6 *15* ♘d5 h4 *16* ♘xf6+ gxf6 *17* ♘e2 ♗xe4 *18* ♗d5 ♕b6+ *19* ♔h1 ♗xd5 *20* ♕xd5 ♖xc2 *21* ♕d3 ♕c6 *22* ♖ac1 h3! (Ciocaltea-Gheorghiu, Bucharest 1967.)

8	**f4!**	**♘c5!?**

Too passive is *8...*♗e7 *9* ♕f3 0-0 *10* g4.

Bad is *8...*b5 *9* f5! e5 *10* ♘c6! ♕c7 *11* ♘b4! and White is ready to sit on Black once he occupies the hole on d5.

9	**f5!**	**...**

Thematic. Bednarsky told me after the game he had reached this position before, as White, and he had continued *9* e5 dxe5 *10* fxe5 ♘fd7 *11* ♗f4 vs. Bogdanovich, East Germany 1964. Obviously that approach is too tame.

9	**...**	**♘fxe4!?**

Playing with fire.

The question is whether *9...*e5 is sufficient. Apparently not, after *10* ♘de2 ♘xb3 (not *10...*♘cxe4? *11* ♘xe4 ♘xe4 *12* ♕d5 ♘g5 *13* h4) *11* axb3 h6 *12* ♘g3 followed by ♘h5 with a bind. R.Byrne-Bogdanovich, Sarajevo 1967.

9...♗e7 is steadier than the text (for *9...*♘xb3 *10* axb3 see note to White's 7th move in game 58). But White stays on top after *10* ♕f3 0-0 *11* ♗e3. Now on *11...*d5 *12* exd5 ♘xb3 *13* ♘xb3! exf5 (if *13...*♘xd5? *14* 0-0-0 wins a Pawn) *14* 0-0-0, etc.

10	**fxe6!**	**...**

BEDNARSKY

Position after 10 fxe6!

FISCHER

10	...	♕h4+?

Tempting, but suicidal. Black had two better tries:

A] *10...♗xe6 11 ♘xe4 ♘xe4 12 ♘xe6 fxe6* (not *12...♕h4+ 13 g3 ♘xg3 14 ♗g5! ♕e4+ 15 ♔d2 ♘xh1 16 ♘c7+ ♔d7 17 ♘xa8* wins) *13 ♕g4 ♘c5 14 ♗e3!* with a strong initiative.

B] *10...fxe6! 11 ♘xe4 ♘xe4 12 0-0 ♕e7!* (weaker is *12...♘c5 13 ♕g4* – if *13...♘xb3 14 axb3 e5 15 ♕f3*). White has good play for the Pawn, but no forced win in view.

11	g3	♘xg3
12	♘f3!	...

This twist is well known: e.g., from the Vienna *1 e4 e5 2 ♘c3 ♘f6 3 f4 d5 4 fxe5 ♘xe4 5 d3 ♕h4+ 6 g3 ♘xg3 7 ♘f3*, etc.

Only not *12 exf7+? ♔d8 13 ♘f3 ♕e7+!*

12	...	♕h5
13	exf7+	♔d8
14	♖g1	♘f5
15	♘d5!	♕xf7

Black's attack has boomeranged. Now his King gets caught in a merciless crossfire.

On *15...h6 16 ♘f4!* picks off the Queen. No better is *15...♘xb3 16 ♗g5+ ♔d7* (or *16...♗e7 17 ♘xe7! ♘xe7 18 ♕xd6+*) *17 ♘e5+!*

16	♗g5+	♔e8
17	♕e2+!	...

By now I was hunting for bigger game than the paltry win of a Queen after *17 ♘f6+ gxf6 18 ♗xf7+.*

17	...	♗e6
18	♘f4	♔d7
19	0-0-0	...

BEDNARSKY

Position after 19 0-0-0

FISCHER

One threat of course is *20 ♘e5+*.

| 19 | ... | ♛e8 |

Black is helpless. After *19...♘xb3+ 20* axb3 ♛e8 *21* ♖ge1 ♝g8 *22* ♛d3 it's also quits. The only way for Black to last is to give up his Queen with *19...♝xb3 20 ♘e5+ ♚c7 21 ♘xf7 ♝xf7*.

| 20 | ♝xe6+ | ♘xe6 |
| 21 | ♛e4! | ... |

Centralization with a vengeance!

| 21 | ... | g6 |
| 22 | ♘xe6 | **Black resigns** |

On *22...♛xe6 23* ♛xb7+ ♚e8 *24* ♖ge1! wins everything.

56 Fischer - Gligorich [*Yugoslavia*]

HAVANA OLYMPIC 1966

RUY LOPEZ

The Fischer continuation

Fischer's surprising 4 ♗xc6, a revival of Emanuel Lasker's Exchange Variation – the one he used at St. Petersburg in 1914 to defeat Alekhine and Capablanca, but which subsequently fell into desuetude because ways to equalize were rapidly discovered – drew from his opponent the obligatory response. However, Fischer's next move, regarded as inferior, and his sixth (the customary follow-up) prepared no one for the gambit which he introduced on move seven. Gligorich reacted with innocent appropriateness until move seventeen, then made a startling blunder that met with speedy retribution. Because, in the course of the tournament, Fischer had played and won two other games with this very same line (demonstrating in each case White's hitherto unsuspected potential), it was promptly dubbed "The Fischer Variation." Of course, sticklers will insist that it should be called the Fischer continuation of the Barendregt Variation.

1	e4	e5
2	♘f3	♘c6
3	♗b5	a6
4	♗xc6!	...

A surprise! I had introduced this in an earlier game against Portisch (see note to Black's 6th). After sizing up Gligorich over-the-board, I decided he was ripe for a repeat performance.

4	...	dxc6

This recapture is so automatic that most annotators fail to comment on it. After 4...bxc6 5 d4 exd4 6 ♕xd4 White maintains an enduring initiative, If 6...♕f6 7 ♕d3! (but not 7 e5 ♕g6 8 0-0 ♗b7 9 e6? fxe6 10 ♘e5 ♕xg2+! 11 ♔xg2 c5+ – an old trap.)

5	0-0!	...

GLIGORICH

Position after 5 0-0!

FISCHER

"The text poses more problems for Black than does an immediate 5 d4 and Nimzovich is once more proved right in his pronouncement that the threat is stronger than its execution. Though White has sold his strong Bishop for a Knight, a Bishop which is usually Black's main strategical problem in many variations of the Lopez, there is no basic flaw in White's tactics. He has gained a tempo for development, somewhat spoiled Black's Pawn structure and revived the threat on Black's e-Pawn." (GLIGORICH).

The text was favored by Emanuel Lasker, Bernstein and also, in recent years, by the Dutch master Barendregt. I had been pondering it for a long time before deciding to include it in my arsenal.

5   ...   **f6!**

"This position has not been seen frequently in the modern grandmaster praxis and, thanks to imaginative Fischer, we have to go back to the 19th century to find the alternatives for Black. It is not clear, however, that Black has any better way of defending the e-Pawn." (GLIGORICH).

Black can defend his e-Pawn in numerous ways. Let's look at the lemons first.

A] 5...♗e7? (played by Reshevsky) 6 ♘xe5! ♕d4 7 ♘f3 ♕xe4 8 ♖e1 (instead of 8 d3? as in Malesich-Reshevsky, Maribor 1967) and it's doubtful Black can get out of the opening with equality. One example, 8...♕f5 9 b3! ♘f6 10 ♗a3 (or 10 ♖e5!) 10...♗e6 11 ♘d4, etc.

B] The ballet dancer Harmonist showed good sense by trying 5...♕f6 with the threat of ...♗g4 (against Schallopp in Frankfurt 1887) but after 6 d4 exd4 7 ♗g5! ♕g6 8 ♕xd4 White can get a clear initiative.

C] 5...♗d6? 6 d4 exd4 (not 6...f6? 7 dxe5 fxe5 8 ♘xe5! – or 6...♗g4 7 dxe5 ♗xf3 8 ♕xf3 with a comfortable K-side Pawn majority, as in Schallopp-Blackburne, Frankfurt 1887) 7 ♕xd4 f6 8 ♘bd2! ♘e7 9 ♘c4, etc.

D] A reasonable try is Bronstein's *5...♕d6!? 6 d3 (6 ♘a3?* works well against *6...♗e6? 7 ♘g5* but *6...b5!* strands the Knight) *6...f6 7 ♗e3 c5 8 ♘bd2 ♗e6 9 ♕e2 0-0-0=*. White has possibilities of breaking on the Q-side after a3 followed by ♖fb1 and b4, but Black can probably prevent this expansion.

So best is *5...♕d6 6 d4 exd4 7 ♘xd4*, etc.

E] The most ambitious continuation is *5...♗g4!? 6 h3 h5!?* (Em. Lasker used to win such positions for White after *6...♗xf3 7 ♕xf3*. Hort-Kolarov, Poland 1967, continued: *7...♕f6 8 ♕g3 ♗d6 9 d3 ♕g6 10 ♗e3!? ♕xg3 11 fxg3* and White managed to grind out a win in the ensuing endgame) *7 d3!* (On *7 c3 ♕d3! 8 hxg4 hxg4 9 ♘xe5 ♗d6! 10 ♘xd3 ♗h2+* draws. A fantasy variation occurs after *8 ♕b3? ♗xf3 9 ♕xb7 ♔d7 10 ♕xa8 ♗xg2! 11 ♔xg2 ♖h6! 12 ♖g1 ♖g6+ 13 ♔h2 ♖xg1 14 ♔xg1 ♗c5* with a winning attack) *7...♕f6 8 ♘bd2!* (Keres in his old book on the open games wrongly praises this whole line for Black, having considered only *8 hxg4? hxg4 9 ♘g5 ♕h6 10 ♘h3 ♕h4 11 ♔h2 g6 12 ♘c3 gxh3 13 g3 ♕e7* with advantage) *8...♘e7* (now *8...g5* is met by *9 ♘c4! ♗xf3 10 ♕xf3 ♕xf3 11 gxf3 f6 12 h4! gxh4 13 f4* with promising play for the Pawn. But not *9 ♖e1? ♗e6 10 d4 g4 11 ♘xe5 gxh3 12 g3 h2+ 13 ♔g2 h4* with initiative) *9 ♖e1!* (or *9 ♘c4! ♗xf3 10 ♕xf3 ♕xf3 11 gxf3 ♘g6 12 ♗e3 c5 13 a4!* White stands better and eventually won. Hort-Sliwa, Poland 1967) *9...♘g6 10 d4! ♗d6 11 hxg4 hxg4 12 ♘h2 ♖xh2! 13 ♕xg4! ♖h4 14 ♕f5* and White is slightly better.

6   **d4**   **♗g4!**

Best. In our earlier game Portisch had tried *6...exd4 7 ♘xd4! c5* (Portisch played the more sensible *7...♗d6* in a subsequent event but it's still inferior after *8 ♕h5+! g6 9 ♕f3 ♗xh2+? 10 ♔xh2 ♕xd4 11 ♖d1!) 8 ♘b3 ♕xd1* (now *8...♗d6?* is met by *9 ♘xc5!) 9 ♖xd1 ♗d6* (the queer-looking *9...b6* as a defensive try scored an unmerited success in a Soviet women's tournament due to White's passive play. But *10 ♗f4 ♖a7! 11 ♘c3 ♘e7 12 a4!* followed by a5 is almost decisive. (*12...a5?* is impossible because of *13 ♘b5!* Polugaievsky's *9...♗d7* offers defensive prospects) *10 ♘a5! b5* (amusing is *10...♗g4? 11 f3 0-0-0?? 12 e5!* and Black resigns. Hort-Zelandinow, Havana 1967. Keres tried *10...♘h6* but also failed to equalize after *11 ♗xh6 gxh6 12 ♘c4 ♗e7 13 ♘c3 ♗e6 14 ♘d5*. Bagirov-Keres, Moscow 1967) *11 c4 ♘e7 12 ♗e3 f5 13 ♘c3 f4 14 e5! ♗xe5 15 ♗xc5* and Black's disorganized position soon crumbled.

GLIGORICH

Position after 6...♝g4!

FISCHER

| 7 | c3! | ... |

The text involves a gambit.

Curiously, this was Gligorich's own published suggestion when he annotated his game against Lee at Hastings 1965-6, which had continued *7* dxe5 ♕xd1 *8* ♖xd1 ♝xf3! (Fischer-Smyslov, Monaco 1967, went *8...fxe5? 9* ♖d3! ♝xf3 *10* ♖xf3 ♘f6 *11* ♘c3 ♝b4 *12* ♝g5! ♝xc3 *13* bxc3! [was Black playing for the cheap trap *13* ♝xf6? ♝xb2 *14* ♝xg7?? ♝xa1 *15* ♝xh8 0-0-0!] *13...*♖f8 *14* ♝xf6 ♖xf6 *15* ♖xf6 gxf6 *16* ♖d1! and White should have won the ending) *9* gxf3 fxe5 *10* f4 ♘f6 and now *11* ♘c3! (instead of *11* fxe5? ♘xe4 *12* ♝e3 ♝c5 *13* ♘d2 ♘xd2 *14* ♝xc5 0-0-0 as in the game) *11...*♝d6 *12* fxe5 ♝xe5 *13* ♘a4! gives White the better of a probable draw.

So the best is *7* dxe5! ♕xd1 *8* ♖xd1 ♝xf3! *9* gxf3 fxe5 *10* ♝e3! followed by ♘d2-c4 with pressure. If *10...*♘e7 *11* f4! keeps the initiative.

| 7 | ... | exd4 |

An alternative is *7...*♝d6 holding the center.

| 8 | cxd4 | ♕d7 |

Black dares not accept the Pawn. *8...*♝xf3 *9* ♕xf3 ♕xd4 *10* ♖d1 ♕c4 *11* ♝f4, etc. However, Gligorich said (in *Chess Review*) he had completely forgotten his Hastings analysis, which indicated Black's best as *8...c5! 9* d5 ♝d6.

| 9 | h3! | ... |

"Putting the question to the Bishop." Nimzovich, Steinitz, Evans, and other theoreticians have pointed out the enormous value of kicking this Bishop before the pin becomes really troublesome. Here, White must exercise care since his h-Pawn could easily become a potential target.

9 ... ♗e6

This natural retreat, which releases the tension, gives White too free a hand and is the subsequent cause of Gligorich's difficulties. Better is 9...♗h5! as played against me by Jimenez in a later round. After 10 ♘e5! ♗xd1 (bad is 10...♕xh3 11 gxh3 ♗xd1 12 ♖xd1 fxe5 13 dxe5 ♗c5 14 ♔g2 with a dangerous preponderance of center Pawns) 11 ♘xd7 ♔xd7 12 ♖xd1 Black should hold the ending, although he found a way to lose: 12...♖e8 13 f3 (13 ♘c3 is more accurate) 13...♘e7 14 ♘c3 ♔c8 15 ♗e3 f5 16 ♖ac1 fxe4 17 fxe4 g6? (17...♘g6 is correct) 18 ♗f4! ♗g7 19 d5! ♖d8 20 ♘a4! ♖hf8 21 g3 g5? (cracking under the pressure – 21...♖f7 is more sensible) 22 ♗xg5 ♖f7 23 ♔g2 cxd5 24 exd5 ♔b8 25 ♖e1 ♗f8 26 ♖f1! ♗g7 27 ♗f6 ♖g8 28 ♖ce1 ♖d7 29 d6! cxd6 30 ♗xe7 ♗xe7 31 ♖f7 resigns (if 31...♖e8 32 ♘b6 ♖c7 33 ♘d5).

10	♘c3	0-0-0
11	♗f4!	...

GLIGORICH

Position after 11 ♗f4!

FISCHER

11 ... ♘e7?

More solid is *11...♗d6! 12 ♗xd6 ♕xd6.*

The critical line is *11*...g5!? *12* ♗g3 h5 *13* d5! cxd5 *14* ♖c1! and now:

A] *14*...♗d6 *15* ♘a4! ♔b8 *16* ♘c5 ♕e7 *17* ♘xa6+! bxa6 *18* ♘d4 ♗d7 *19* ♕b3+ ♔a7 *20* ♖xc7+!! ♗xc7 *21* ♗xc7 ♗b5 (if *21*...♕c5 *22* ♕e3! is the simplest win) *22* ♘c6+! (Palacio) *22*...♗xc6 *23* ♕b6+ and mate next.

B] The fantastic win is *14*...dxe4 *15* ♘a4! ♔b8 *16* ♖xc7!! ♕xd1 *17* ♖c8+!!! ♔a7 (or *17*...♔xc8 *18* ♘b6 mate) *18* ♗b8+ ♔a8 *19* ♘b6 mate.

12	♖c1	♘g6

Black has lost time in order to reach this inferior square.

13	♗g3	♗d6
14	♘a4!	♗xg3?

Yielding his c5 permanently to the Knight.
Correct is *14*...♔b8 *15* ♘c5 ♕e7.

15	fxg3	♔b8

Bad is *15*...b6 *16* d5! ♗f7 (*16*...cxd5? *17* ♘xb6+) *17* ♕e2!, etc.

16	♘c5	♕d6
17	♕a4!	...

GLIGORICH

Position after 17 ♕a4!

FISCHER

17	...	♔a7??

Catastrophic. After *17*...♗c8 *18* ♖c3 (*18*...♕xg3? *19* ♘e5 ♕h4 *20* ♘xc6+), Black might have hung on with *18*...♘f8!

| 18 | ♘xa6! | ... |

The finishing stroke.

| 18 | ... | ♗xh3 |

Desperation! *18...bxa6 19 ♖xc6* costs Black's Queen to prevent mate.

| 19 | e5! | ... |

The most forceful method.

| 19 | ... | ♘xe5 |

Sheer desperation!! After *19...fxe5 20 ♘c5+ ♔b8 21 ♖c3!* followed by ♖a3 is most persuasive.

20	dxe5	fxe5
21	♘c5+	♔b8
22	gxh3	e4

Never say die!

23	♘xe4	♕e7
24	♖c3	b5
25	♕c2	...

Time to consolidate. *25 ♕a6* also does the trick.

According to a Havana newspaper, some casual spectators who had just wandered in thought White had merely won two pieces for a Rook. Nobody could believe that Gligorich was playing on two pieces behind! The rude awakening came when –

| 25 | ... | **Black resigns** |

57 Larsen *[Denmark]* - Fischer

MONACO 1967

KING'S INDIAN DEFENSE

Change of pace

*Larsen, uncharacteristically, forces an early exchange of Queens so
that he can spring a surprise in the resulting endgame. Fischer beats
him to it (13…b6) and proceeds to defend with meticulous care.
It looks as if a draw must ensue, but Larsen presses. He is rebuffed,
and again a draw seems imminent. Larsen senses no danger and,
as if by inertia, continues to play for a win. As the game simplifies,
the self-inflicted dark square weaknesses in the Dane's position
gradually reveal themselves. By move thirty it becomes Fischer's turn
to assume the initiative, and he probes these flaws judiciously.
Thrown on the defensive, Larsen makes one or two reckless moves out
of which Fischer constructs elegant combinations. Thus, what begins
as a barren endgame is transformed into an exhibition of chess
sensibility and virtuosity.*

1	d4	♘f6
2	c4	g6
3	♘c3	♗g7
4	e4	d6
5	♗e2	…

Larsen had won some good games with *5 ♘f3 0-0 6 ♗e3* but after
6...e5! (which no one seems to have played) White gets no advantage.
7 ♗e2 ♘c6 transposes into well-known modern lines. And *7 d5 ♘g4
8 ♗g5 f6 9 ♗h4 ♕e8* gives Black dynamic play. Now *10 h3 ♘h6
11 g4!? f5* is too risky for White. Finally on *7 dxe5 dxe5 8 ♕xd8 ♖xd8
9 ♘d5(?) ♘a6!* gives Black the better ending.

5	…	0-0
6	♘f3	e5
7	0-0	♘c6

FISCHER

Position after 7...♘c6

LARSEN

| 8 | ♗e3 | ... |

A bit of a surprise. I had expected *8* d5 ♘e7 *9* ♘e1 ♘d7 *10* ♘d3 f5 *11* ♗d2. Now I had in mind *11...c5! 12* f3 f4! (but not *12...♘f6? 13* g4! f4 *14* h4! and Black's K-side counterplay is completely stymied) with active chances. Larsen-Najdorf, Santa Monica 1966, had continued *11...♘f6? 12* f3 f4 *13* c5! g5 *14* ♖c1 ♘g6 *15* cxd6 cxd6 *16* ♘b5 ♖f7 *17* ♕c2! ♘e8 *18* a4 and White came first on the Q-side since Black's attack never got off the ground.

| 8 | ... | ♖e8! |

The cleanest way to equalize. Najdorf found this move after some painful experiences with *8...♘g4* in his match vs. Reshevsky. The main point if that *9* d5 ♘d4! levels.

| 9 | dxe5 | dxe5 |
| 10 | ♕xd8 | ♘xd8 |

A dubious improvement over *10...♖xd8!* as played by Reshevsky in his match with Benko. After *11* ♗g5 Black must not play *11...♖d7?* (after which Benko's *12* ♗d1!! followed by ♗a4 was very strong) but *11...♖f8!* solves all his problems.

11	♘b5	♘e6
12	♘g5	♖e7
13	♖fd1	...

Larsen is attempting to improve on Reshevsky-Fischer, Santa Monica 1966, which continued: *13* ♘xe6 ♗xe6 *14* f3 c6 *15* ♘c3 ♖d7 *16* ♖fd1 ♗f8 *17* ♔f2 b6 *18* b3 ♖b7 *19* ♘a4 ♘d7 *20* ♘b2 b5 with an eventual draw.

FISCHER

Position after 13 ♖fd1

LARSEN

| *13* | ... | **b6!** |

In my 9th match game with Reshevsky, 1961, I tried *13...c6!?* Larsen told me he had intended *14* ♘xa7!? (instead of *14* ♘xe6 ♗xe6 *15* ♘c3 ♖d7=) *14...*♗d7 *15* ♘xe6 ♗xe6 *16* f3. But after *16...*♖d7! (threatening ...♖d4) Black has fair play for the Pawn, considering that the Knight is stranded on a7.

The book text was an improvement that I had hatched some time ago.

| *14* | **c5!?** | ... |

Typically, Larsen adopts an enterprising continuation. He should settle for *14* ♘xe6 ♗xe6 *15* f3 with a draw in view. By overestimating his chances, he gradually drifts into a losing position.

| *14* | ... | ♘xc5 |

Naturally not *14...*bxc5? *15* ♘xe6 ♗xe6 *16* ♗xc5 ♖d7 *17* f3 wins.

| *15* | ♖d8+ | ♗f8 |

No better is *15...*♖e8 *16* ♖xe8+ ♘xe8 *17* ♗xc5 bxc5 *18* ♗c4! Or *15...*♘e8? *16* ♗xc5 bxc5 *17* ♘xc7 ♖xc7 *18* ♖xe8+ ♗f8 *19* ♘xh7!

| *16* | ♘xa7 | ♖xa7 |

On *16...♗b7 17 ♖xa8 ♗xa8 18* f3 White has a slight pull despite his misplaced Knight. After *18...c6 19 ♘c8 ♖b7 20 ♖d1* maintains some pressure.

	17	♖xc8	...

White recovers his pawn with even chances.

FISCHER

Position after 17 ♖xc8

LARSEN

	17	...	♔g7

Black wisely resists the temptation of *17...♘cxe4?? 18 ♘xe4 ♘xe4 19 ♗h6*. But even more accurate than the text is *17...h6! 18 ♘f3 ♔g7 19 ♗xc5 bxc5 20 ♗d3* completely neutralizing any initiative for either side.

	18	f3	♘e8
	19	a3(?)	...

Larsen's reluctance to simplify will soon backfire. Correct is *19 ♗xc5! bxc5 20 ♖b8* with theoretical winning chances because of the passed a-Pawn. But it would be difficult to make headway because of the opposite colored Bishops.

	19	...	♘d6
	20	♖d8	...

Optimistic as ever! *20 ♖b8 ♘d7 21 ♖d8 ♘b7 22 ♖c8 ♘d6* would lead to a draw by repetition.

	20	...	h6

21	♘h3	♘e6
22	♖b8	♖e8
23	♖xe8	♘xe8

FISCHER

Position after 23...♘xe8

LARSEN

"Now White's initiative is over and the position is even but by no means drawish. There is a lot of play." (KMOCH)

White's dark squares, notably his d4, are weak. But it's still not too serious.

| 24 | ♗b5 | ... |

Pointless. White should start bringing his Knight into the game via f2. He can't prevent ...♗c5, gaining control of the dark squares. Of course not *24* b4? ♗xb4.

24	...	♘d6
25	♗f1	♘b7!
26	♘f2	♗c5!
27	♗xc5	♘bxc5
28	♖d1	h5!

To keep the Knight out of g4. This "prophylactic" thrust would have gladdened Nimzovich's heart. Not *28...♘d4? 29 ♘g4 f6 30 f4!*

| 29 | ♖d5 | ... |

Larsen still has illusions, but his game is fast deteriorating. More prudent is *29 ♘d3 ♘xd3 30 ♗xd3 ♘d4 31 ♔f2*. White probably should hold the ending despite Black's creeping pressure.

29	...	♔f6
30	h4	♔e7!
31	♗c4	...

The Pawn is poisoned: *31* ♖xe5? c6 followed by ...♘d7 (or ...f6). The mission of the Rook has failed, but no serious harm has been done.

| 31 | ... | c6 |
| 32 | ♖d2 | ♘d4! |

Finally the Knight has gained this dominant outpost.

| 33 | ♔f1 | ... |

The more active *33* ♘d3 is preferable. Now Black's tactical threats begin to proliferate.

| 33 | ... | f5! |
| 34 | b4 | ... |

Meets with a still sharper counter thrust. *34* ♘d3 offered a better chance for survival. After the text White's a-Pawn is weakened.

Not *34* exf5 ♘xf5 with the double threat of ...♘e3+ or ♘xh4 (and if *35* ♖e2? ♘g3+).

| 34 | ... | b5! |
| 35 | ♗g8 | ... |

35 bxc5 bxc4 clearly wins for Black. And *35* ♗xb5? is refuted by *35*...♘cb3.

| 35 | ... | fxe4! |

FISCHER

Position after 35...fxe4!

LARSEN

Fixing White with another weakness.

	36	**fxe4**	...

Not *36* bxc5 e3 *37* ♖xd4 (if *37* ♖d3 exf2 *38* ♔xf2 ♖a8 *39* ♗a2 b4 –
or *37* ♖a2? exf2 *38* ♔xf2 ♔f8!) *37*...exd4 *38* ♘d3 ♖xa3 *39* ♔e2 ♖c3,
etc.

36	...	♘d7
37	♖d3	♖a6!

Threatening ♘c2 which, if played immediately, could have been met
by *38* ♖c3.

38	♖c3	c5!

FISCHER

Position after 38...c5!

LARSEN

This surprising combination apparently confused Larsen, who was in
time-pressure.

39	**g4?**	...

The last blunder. On *39* bxc5 b4! *40* ♖c1! (not *40* axb4 ♖a1+) there's
still a lot of fight. If *40*...♖xa3 (or *40*...bxa3 *41* ♗a2) *41* c6 ♘b6.

39	...	c4

This protected passed Pawn is just too strong. Not *39*...♘f6 *40* ♖xc5!

40	gxh5	gxh5
41	♗d5	♘f6
42	♖g3	♘xd5

| 43 | exd5 | ♖f6 |
| 44 | ♔g2 | ... |

The sealed move. White is completely tied up. On *44 ♔g1?* ♘e2+ wins. Or if *44 ♔e1* ♖f4 mops up.

44	...	♘f5
45	♖h3	♖g6+
46	♔f3	♘d4+

FISCHER

Position after 46...♘d4+

LARSEN

| 47 | ♔e3 | ... |

On *47 ♔e4 ♔d6* White is in *zugzwang*. If *48 ♖h2* (to prevent ...♖g2) *48...♖g3*.

47	...	♖g2
48	♖h1	♔d6
49	♘e4+	♔xd5
50	♘c3+	♔e6
51	♖c1	...

White has to prevent ...♖c2 as then the Knight cannot move because of ...♖e2 mate.

51	...	♖h2
52	a4	♖h3+
53	♔f2	♘b3
54	♔g2	♘xc1
55	♔xh3	bxa4
56	♘xa4	♘e2

57	**b5**	**c3**
58	**b6**	**c2**
59	**♘c5+**	**♚d5**

FISCHER

Position after 59...♚d5

LARSEN

| 60 | *♘b3* | ... |

White can choose his own end. If *60 ♘d3* (or *60 b7 c1=♕ 61 b8=♕ ♕h1 mate*) *60...♘f4+ 61 ♘xf4+ exf4 62 b7 c1=♕ 63 b8=♕ ♕h1 mate*.

60	...	**♚c6**
61	**♚g2**	**♚xb6**
	White resigns	

58 Fischer - Geller [U.S.S.R.]

SKOPJE 1967

SICILIAN DEFENSE

Flawed masterpiece

After Fischer dropped this miniature (his third loss in a row to Geller) Kurajica concluded: "He just cannot play against Geller." Another Yugoslav, Trifunovich, opined at greater length:

> *Geller is one of the best-prepared players in the world as to opening theory, and Fischer cannot be superior in that respect...Fischer [as White] chose a very sharp and modern variation...playing to win in the early stage of the game, as he usually does, and successfully, against weaker opponents. Fischer played better and attained a superior position, but it was very difficult to find the right solution over-the-board...There was his mistake...He has to impose a hard positional game, playing without pretensions for a win in the very opening.*

Nowhere but in the notes that follow have the above errors been answered. Were it not for a momentary lapse (a3?), Fischer would have won this little gem on move twenty – despite his critics.

1	**e4**	**c5**
2	**♘f3**	**d6**
3	**d4**	**cxd4**
4	**♘xd4**	**♘f6**
5	**♘c3**	**♘c6**
6	**♗c4**	**e6**

There is no apparent refutation to Benko's roguish 6...♕b6!? Saidy ventured it against me in the 1967 US Championship. After *7* ♘b3 e6 *8* 0-0 ♗e7 *9* ♗e3 ♕c7 *10* f4 0-0 *11* ♗d3 it's a mutually hard game. Also see game 11.

GELLER

Position after 6...e6

FISCHER

7   ♗e3   ...

7 ♗b3 cuts down Black's options. Fischer–Dely, Skopje 1967, continued: *7...a6 8 f4!* ♕*a5 (8...*♘*a5 9 f5!* ♘*xb3 10 axb3* ♗*e7 11* ♕*f3 0-0 12* ♗*e3* ♗*d7 13 g4 e5 14* ♘*de2* with a crush in sight: Fischer–Bielicki, Mar del Plata 1960. *8...*♕*c7 9 f5!* ♘*xd4 10* ♕*xd4 exf5 11 exf5* ♗*xf5 12 0-0* yields a strong attack) *9 0-0!* ♘*xd4?* (a better try is *9...d5* but after *10* ♘*xc6! bxc6 11 f5!* White's on top. If *11...d4? 12* ♘*e2 e5* either *13* ♘*g3* or *13* ♕*d3* retains the advantage. Also on *11...*♗*e7 12 e5* ♘*d7 13 fxe6 fxe6* [or *13...*♘*xe5 14* ♗*f4!*] *14* ♕*g4.* Finally, *11...*♗*c5+ 12* ♔*h1 0-0* may be tenable) *10* ♕*xd4 d5 (10...*♕*c5 11* ♕*xc5 dxc5 12 a4!* puts Black in an excruciating bind) *11* ♗*e3!* ♘*xe4* (if *11...*♘*g4 12* ♔*h1!* ♘*xe3 13* ♕*xe3 dxe4 14* ♕*xe4!* ♗*e7 15* ♖*ae1* and mate is lurking in the wings: e.g., *15...g6 16* ♘*d5!* ♗*d8 17* ♕*e5 0-0 18* ♘*e7+!* wins. Slightly more accurate, but still bad, is *11...dxe4 12* ♘*xe4* ♗*e7 13* ♘*d6+,* etc.) *12* ♘*xe4 dxe4 13 f5!* ♕*b4* (if *13...exf5 14 g4!* ♗*e6* [*14...*♕*b4 15* ♗*a4+! b5 16* ♕*d5!* wins] *15 gxf5* ♗*xb3 16 axb3* ♕*b4 17* ♖*a4!* ♕*xd4 18* ♖*xd4* and Black is in a curiously hopeless predicament: e.g., *18...*♗*e7 19* ♖*xe4* ♔*f8 20 f6!!* ♗*xf6 21* ♖*xf6! gxf6 22* ♗*h6+* and mates) *14 fxe6* ♗*xe6 15* ♗*xe6! fxe6 16* ♖*xf8+!* ♕*xf8 17* ♕*a4+!* resigns. On *17...b5 18* ♕*xe4* ♖*d8 19* ♕*c6+!* ♖*d7 20* ♖*d1* ♕*e7* and now *21* ♗*b6* (Dely). (About the only move that doesn't win is *21* ♗*g5? 0-0!*)

7   ...   ♗e7

Too routine. Black should start quicker action on the Q-side. More reasonable is *7...a6 8* ♗*b3* ♕*c7 9* ♕*e2* (or *9 f4*) *9...b5 10 0-0-0* ♘*a5* (*10...*♗*b7* is also possible, whereupon White might reply *11 f3*).

8 &b3 ...

Against Pascual, in a clock exhibition game at Davao (Philippines) 1967, I essayed *8* ♕e2 a6 *9* 0-0-0 ♕c7 *10* &b3 &d7 *11* g4 ♘xd4 *12* &xd4 (Fishy. Better is *12* ♖xd4) *12*...e5 *13* g5 exd4 *14* gxf6 dxc3 *15* fxe7 cxb2+ *16* ♔b1 ♔xe7? (*16*...&e6 equalizes) *17* ♕h5! g6 *18* ♕h4+ f6 *19* e5! dxe5 *20* f4 e4 *21* ♕h6 ♖ae8 *22* ♖d4 ♔d8 *23* ♖hd1 ♔c8 (the beauty part is *23*...♖e7 *24* &e6!! ♖xe6 *25* ♕g7, mopping up) *24* ♖xd7 ♕xd7 *25* ♖xd7 ♔xd7 *26* ♕g7+ ♔d6 *27* ♕xb7 e3 *28* ♕b6+ resigns.

8 ... 0-0
9 ♕e2 ...

Preparing Q-side castling and disallowing the reply ...♘g4 which would be the case after *9* ♕d2.

GELLER

Position after 9 ♕e2

FISCHER

9 ... ♕a5

Geller's attempt to improve on the customary *9*...a6 *10* 0-0-0 ♕c7 *11* g4 ♘xd4 *12* ♖xd4! b5 (Tal gives *12*...e5 *13* ♖c4! ♕d8 *14* g5 ♘e8 *15* ♖xc8! ♖xc8 *16* h4 ♘c7 *17* ♕g4 followed by h5, with a terrific attack) *13* g5 ♘d7 *14* ♕h5 ♘e5 *15* f4 ♘c6 *16* ♖d3 ♘b4 *17* ♖d2 ♖d8 *18* f5 g6 *19* fxg6 hxg6 *20* ♕h4 ♘c6 *21* ♕g3 ♘e5 *22* h4 &b7 *23* h5 b4 *24* hxg6 ♘xg6 *25* ♖dh2 bxc3 *26* &d4 e5 *27* ♖h8+!! ♘xh8 *28* g6! &f6 *29* gxf7++ ♔f8 *30* ♖h7! and White wins (Velimirovich-Nikolich, Belgrade 1964.)

10	**0-0-0**	...

10 0-0 also comes into consideration.

10	...	♘xd4

Apparently Geller rejected *10*...♗d7 *11* ♘db5! ♘e8 *12* ♗f4 a6 *13* ♘xd6 ♘xd6 *14* ♗xd6 ♗xd6 *15* ♖xd6 ♕g5+ *16* ♕d2 ♕xg2 *17* ♖hd1 ♗e8 *18* ♕f4 with good pressure.

11	♗xd4	♗d7

Black cannot afford to go Pawn-snatching with *11*...♕g5+? *12* ♔b1 ♕xg2? *13* ♖hg1! ♕h3 (if *13*...♕xh2 *14* ♖h1 ♕f4 *15* ♖dg1! e5 [or *15*...g6 *16* ♗e3 ♕e5 *17* ♖g5] *16* ♗e3 ♗g4 *17* ♕e1 ♕f3 *18* ♖g3 wins the Queen) *14* e5 ♘e8 (on *14*...dxe5 *15* ♕xe5 carries too many threats) *15* exd6 ♗xd6 *16* ♗xg7! ♘xg7 *17* ♖xd6 and it's not a game any more. But interesting is *12*...e5 (instead of *12*...♕xg2) *13* h4 ♕xg2 *14* ♖dg1 ♗g4 *15* ♖xg2! ♗xe2 *16* ♘xe2 exd4 *17* ♘xd4 with advantage (if *17*...♘xe4 *18* f3! followed by ♘f5).

12	♔b1	...

GELLER

Position after 12 ♔b1

FISCHER

A critical position. White's immediate threat is *13* ♗xf6.

12	...	♗c6

In a later round Sofrevsky tried to improve against me with *12*...♖ad8, but got into trouble after *13* ♕e3! Black now rejected a dangerous Pawn sac which must be examined very carefully: *13...b5!?* But *14* a3! (not *14* Bxa7 Ra8 with active play) *14...b4 15* axb4 Qxb4 *16* Bxa7 Qb7 *17* Qb6! Qa8 *18* f3 and Black has no good way to prosecute his attack. Consequently, Sofrevsky chose *13...b6 14* Bxf6! gxf6? (Black should reconcile himself to the loss of a Pawn after *14...Bxf6 15* Rxd6 Bc8) *15* Nd5!! Rfe8 (if *15...exd5 16* Rxd5 Qa6 *17* Rh5! wins – *17...Bg4 18* Qg3, etc.) *16* Nxe7+ (*16* Qh6! is a quicker kill) *16...Rxe7 17* Rxd6 Rc8 *18* Qd4 Be8? *19* Qxf6 resigns.

13	f4	Rad8

If *13...e5 14* Be3! Bxe4 (not *14...Nxe4? 15* Nxe4 Bxe4 *16* Bd2 wins) *15* Nxe4 Nxe4 *16* Qf3 with advantage.

14	Rhf1	...

I already had in mind the ensuing sacrifice. Also strong is *14* g4 – not to mention Trifunovich's post-mortem suggestion *14* f5! exf5 (not *14...e5 15* Bf2 d5? *16* exd5 Nxd5 *17* Nxd5 Bxd5 *18* Qxe5 wins a piece) *15* exf5 Rfe8 *16* Qf2 with positional pressure.

14	...	b5

On *14...d5 15* e5 Ne4 *16* f5! maintains the initiative.

15	f5!!	...

The die is cast. I didn't want to lose a tempo playing it safe with *15* a3.

15	...	b4
16	fxe6!	bxc3
17	exf7+	Kh8

Not *17...Rxf7 18* Bxf7+ Kxf7 *19* Qc4+ d5 *20* Qxc6, etc.

18	Rf5!	Qb4

On *18...Qc7* I had intended *19* Rdf1 (threatening Rxf6). If then *19...Nd7* (or on *19...Nxe4 20* Qg4 is bitter) *20* Rh5! (threatening Rxh7+) is decisive.

| 19 | ♕f1! | ... |

A hard move to find – it took around 45 minutes. The threat of ♖xf6 must be attended to.

| 19 | ... | ♘xe4 |

A fighting defense. *19...♘d7* loses immediately to *20 ♖h5 ♘e5 21 ♕f5 h6 22 ♕g6!!* ♖xf7 (*22...♘xg6* allows *23* ♖xh6 mate) *23* ♗xe5, etc. On *19...♖xf7 20* ♗xc3 wins. And *19...♗xe4* gives White the pleasant choice of *20* ♖xf6 or *20* ♖b5.

Objectively best is *19...♘g4*. But after *20* ♗xc3 (*20* ♖h5 ♗d7! holds) *20...♕b7* (if *20...♕xe4 21* ♖d4!) *21* ♕f4 with three Pawns for the piece and a winning attack in the offing.

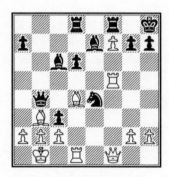

GELLER

Position after 19...♘xe4

FISCHER

| 20 | a3? | ... |

Losing! A couple of hours after the game it occurred to me that White has a problem-like win after *20* ♕f4!! (with the threat of ♖h5). Black has no adequate defense.

A] *20...d5 21* ♕e5 ♘f6 *22* ♖xf6 ♗xf6 *23* ♕xf6!

B] *20...♘d2+ 21* ♖xd2 cxd2 *22* c3!! ♕xb3 *23* ♗xg7+! ♔xg7 *24* ♕g4+ ♔h8 *25* ♕d4+ and mates.

C] *20...cxb2 21* ♖h5! (threatening ♗xg7+) *21...♘c3+* (if *21...♗f6 22* ♕f5 h6 *23* ♖xh6+! gxh6 *24* ♕g6!! forces mate) *22* ♔xb2 ♘xd1+ (or *22...♖xf7 23* ♕xf7 ♘xd1+ *24* ♔b1!! ♕xd4 *25* ♖xh7+!! ♔xh7 *26* ♕h5 mate) *23* ♔c1 ♖xf7 (forced) *24* ♗xf7! (*24* ♕xf7?? ♗g5+) and Black has no satisfactory answer to the threat of *25* ♖xh7+ ♔xh7 *26* ♕f5+ and mates. If *24...♗d7 25* ♗xg7+ wins Black's Queen.

| 20 | ... | ♛b7 |
| 21 | ♛f4 | ♝a4!! |

I didn't see it! Moreover, the strength of this resource didn't become fully apparent to me for another two moves.

| 22 | ♛g4 | ... |

Also futile is *22 ♛h6 ♝f6 23 ♖xf6 ♝xb3*.

| 22 | ... | ♝f6! |
| 23 | ♖xf6 | ♝xb3! |

GELLER

Position after 23...♝xb3!

FISCHER

At long last I saw the point of Geller's clever defense. As I was studying *24 ♖f4*, it suddenly dawned on me that *24...♝a2+* was curtains. So –

White resigns

After *24 cxb3 ♘xf6!* is the quietus. It is not enough to be a good player, observed Dr Tarrasch; you must also play well.

59 Kholmov *[U.S.S.R.]* - Fischer

SKOPJE 1967

KING'S INDIAN DEFENSE

The erring Bishop

In order to restrain Black from creating complications, Kholmov employs an unpretentious system. But he posts his Bishop prematurely on a3, then penetrates ambitiously with 11 ♗d6. Fischer, with the routine 11...♕a5, promptly refutes. It is instructive to observe how, from now on, he creates an unhealthy climate wherever the Bishop seeks lodging. His Queen returns to a3 on no less than three separate occasions, prompting one annotator to inquire, dryly, whether he was perhaps inventing perpetual motion. As early as move twelve it became apparent to both players that White was lost. However, Kholmov did his best to avert the inevitable for another twenty moves.

Fischer (with White) had lost to Kholmov in their only previous encounter, played via telephone to Havana in '65. Here, Fischer's victory brought him first place, a half point ahead of Geller.

1	d4	♘f6
2	♘f3	g6
3	g3	♗g7
4	♗g2	0-0
5	0-0	d6
6	♘c3	...

A straightforward but essentially passive development. The idea is to avoid creating a weakness with c4; however, a drawback is White can no longer dominate the center with a Pawn-wedge.

6	...	♘bd7

More flexible than 6...d5 which I adopted against Ivkov at the Piatigorsky Cup, 1966. That game continued 7 ♘e5 c6 8 e4 and now Black could have equalized easily with 8...dxe4 (instead of 8...♗e6?) 9 ♘xe4 ♘xe4 10 ♗xe4 ♗h3 (not 10...c5? 11 ♕f3!) 11 ♖e1 ♘d7, etc.

7	**b3**	...

A normal continuation, although it is dubious that White's Bishop is effective once posted on b2 or a3. This system is characterized by Pawn symmetry and quiet play with drawing tendencies. But a draw is precisely what I could not afford in this crucial encounter.

7 e4 e5 also presents Black with no opening problems.

7	...	**e5**
8	**dxe5**	...

Dissipating the central tension. Black has no trouble getting play after 8 e4 exd4 9 ♘xd4 ♖e8.

8	...	**dxe5**
9	**e4**	...

"The turbulent complications of the normal K's Indian can hardly arise, and the position can already be evaluated as even." (TRIFUNOVICH).

9	...	**♖e8**
10	**♗a3**	...

Better is *10* a4 a5 *11* ♗a3; whereupon the Bishop will be immune from eventual attack after ...♕a5.

"Even so early, White is on the wrong track. The Bishop has nothing to seek on the a3-f8 diagonal. Yet, while it is easy now to condemn this move, till now it has often been adopted by White with never a harsh word. The punishment which ensues, however ... is more severe than any this commentator has observed hitherto. *10* ♗b2 is correct." (TRIFUNOVICH).

10	...	**c6**

Black invites the Bishop to seize a strong position." (TRIFUNOVICH).

11	**♗d6?**	...

Kholmov consumed over half an hour on this mistake. The idea is to keep Black bottled up while exerting pressure on the e-Pawn. The only trouble with the move, however, is that it loses. As Tarrasch wrote: "When you don't know what to do, wait for your opponent to get an idea – it's sure to be wrong!" *11* ♕e2 was indicated.

11   ...   ♕**a5!**

This normal freeing maneuver is now devastating.

12   ♕**d3**   ...

What else? *12* b4 ♕a3 leaves White in the same predicament.

FISCHER

Position after 12 ♕*d3*

KHOLMOV

Black now has a shot which wins two pieces for a Rook; or, as it turns out, a lowly Pawn (which proves fatal).

12   ...   ♖**e6!**

Springing the trap! White cannot avoid material loss. Geller, who was tied with me for the lead, had displayed great interest in my game – up to now. When he saw this position, he smiled wryly. I never noticed him looking at the game again.

13   **b4**   ...

No matter how White wriggles and squirms, he cannot escape the fate in store for him. After *13* ♘e2 Black has the pleasant choice of either ...♘xe4 or ...♘e8 – both of which win a Pawn.

After the game Kholmov told me he had originally intended *13* ♘g5 ♖xd6 *14* ♕xd6 ♕xc3 *15* ♕e7 with active play. However, he saw (too late) that simply *14*...h6! squelches all such illusions.

| 13 | ... | ♕a3! |

Renewing the ancient threat of ...♖xd6.

| 14 | ♗c7 | ... |

The wandering Bishop hopes to receive succor. But, in so doing, it must abandon protection of the b-pawn.

| 14 | ... | ♕xb4 |

Perhaps White was hoping for *14...♘e8 15 ♗a5 b6 16 ♖ab1! bxa5 17 ♖b3 ♘c5! 18 bxc5 ♕xc5 19 ♖fb1* where Black's technical difficulties are great.

| 15 | ♖ab1 | ♕e7! |

A cute tactical point. *15...♕f8?* loses the exchange after *16 ♘g5* (if the Rook retreats, then White's Bishop returns to d6). Now *16 ♘g5* is refuted by *16...♘c5*. For all practical purposes the game is over.

| 16 | ♖fd1 | ♘e8 |
| 17 | ♗a5 | ... |

No rest for the weary.

17	...	♖d6
18	♕e2	♖xd1+
19	♕xd1	♗f8
20	♘d2	...

Bad – as is everything else. *20 ♗b4 ♕f6 21 ♗xf8 ♘xf8* leaves White a Pawn behind with his weak squares still showing.

| 20 | ... | ♕a3! |

Winning even more material.

21	♘c4	♕c5
22	♗f1	b5
23	♘d2	...

23 ♗b4 drops a piece to *23...♕d4*.

| 23 | ... | ♕a3! |

This curious shuttle has proved White's undoing.

24	♘b3	♘c5
25	♗xb5	...

Desperation. After *25* ♗d8 ♘e6! *26* ♗a5 ♘d6, Black wins as he pleases.

25	...	**cxb5**
26	♘xb5	**♕a4**

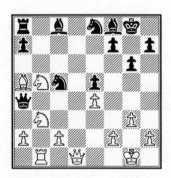

FISCHER

Position after 26...♕a4

KHOLMOV

27	♘xc5	...

Perhaps White had intended *27* ♕d5, but *27...*♕xe4! spells *finis*.

27	...	**♕xa5**
28	**♕d5**	**♖b8**
29	**a4**	**♗h3!**

Quickest.

30	**♕xe5**	**♖c8**
31	**♘d3**	**♕xa4**
32	**♘e1**	**a6**
	White resigns	

The Knight has no good square. If *33* ♘d4 ♗g7. Or *33* ♘c3 ♕c4. Finally, *33* ♘a7 ♖c7 *34* ♖a1 ♕d7 *35* ♖xa6 ♖xa7 *36* ♖xa7 ♕xa7 *37* ♕xe8 ♕a1 delivers the mate.

Afterwards, Geller tried to offer my opponent some sympathy. I overheard a dismayed Kholmov telling him that I had "seen everything!" This game was particularly sweet because it was my first win against a Russian in almost a dozen tries (since game 52) – and my first with Black since 1962 (Korchnoi at Curaçao).

60 Fischer - Stein *[U.S.S.R.]*

INTERZONAL, SOUSSE 1967

RUY LOPEZ

When champions meet

On his ninth turn Black varies the routine sparring but the game proceeds innocuously until Fischer veers with 14 b4, intensifying the struggle. If, in the ensuing slugfest, Stein can be said to have made an error, it is the strategic one of so pressing on the Q-side as to allow White to become entrenched on the opposite wing. Fischer's prosecution of the attack is crowned by a brilliant offer of a piece (29 ♗xf5) which the Soviet champion declines. Had Fischer then renewed the sacrifice, the end would have come sooner. In his detailed notes Fischer refers to this oversight, reveals some important thoughts on the Ruy, pinpoints "the losing move" (21...♘b6), criticizes a second subtle mistake of his own (26 ♘f3), and offers a possible defense for Stein (28...♗f6), which other commentators have failed to note.

It is unfortunate that this interesting and most instructive game was expunged from the official records due to Fischer's withdrawal before having completed half his playing schedule.

| 1 | e4 | ... |

I have never opened with the d-pawn – on principle.

| 1 | ... | e5 |

I had expected the Sicilian, with Stein's favorite accelerated Dragon (2...g6). I suspect that the Russians "group-think" before important games to decide which openings will upset their opponents psychologically.

| 2 | ♘f3 | ♘c6 |
| 3 | ♗b5 | a6 |

Possibly Stein was braced for *4 ♗xc6*, as in game 56.

4	♗a4	...

Relieving the suspense.

4	...	♘f6
5	0-0	♗e7
6	♖e1	b5
7	♗b3	d6

In the event the reader is interested in what I may have had in mind against the Marshall Attack, he is referred to my game against Spassky at the Piatigorsky Cup, 1966, which continued: *7*...0-0 *8* c3 d5 *9* exd5 ♘xd5 *10* ♘xe5 ♘xe5 *11* ♖xe5 c6 *12* g3!? ♗d6 *13* ♖e1 ♘f6 *14* d4 ♗g4 *15* ♕d3 (*15* f3 might be better) *15*...c5 and now *16* ♗c2! (instead of *16* dxc5?) allows Black insufficient compensation for his Pawn.

8	c3	0-0
9	h3	...

For *9* d4 see game 36.

STEIN

Position after 9 h3

FISCHER

9	...	♗b7

A rare side line. *9*...♘a5 *10* ♗c2 c5 is a better-known sequence. The text is somewhat passive and commits the Bishop perhaps prematurely. Usually Stein continues *9*...♘d7 *10* d4 ♗f6; then *11* a4 is slightly better for White.

The line chosen in the game comes to resemble Breyer's Defense (9...♘b8 10 d4 ♘bd7 11 ♘bd2 ♗b7 12 ♗c2! ♖e8 13 b4 exd4 14 cxd4 a5 15 bxa5 c5) – see note to White's 17th move.

| 10 | **d4** | ♘a5 |

Believe it or not, this Knight is headed for d7! Black may prefer the shorter route with 10...♘b8; but experience has shown that after 11 dxe5 dxe5 12 ♕xd8, Black is obliged to recapture with his Bishop, which interferes with his development and produces endgame difficulties.

| 11 | **♗c2** | ♘c4 |

Unsound is 11...exd4 12 cxd4 d5 13 e5 ♘e4 14 ♘c3 f5 15 exf6 *e.p.* ♗xf6 16 ♘xe4 dxe4 17 ♗xe4 ♗xe4 18 ♖xe4 c5 19 d5 and Black remains a Pawn down.

Another possibility is 11...exd4 12 cxd4 c5 but White holds the edge with 13 ♘bd2. On 11...c5 immediately, White replies 12 ♘bd2, retaining the option of d5, locking in Black's Bishop on b7.

| 12 | **b3** | ♘b6 |
| 13 | **♘bd2** | ... |

Not 13 dxe5 dxe5 14 ♕xd8 ♖axd8 15 ♘xe5 ♘xe4!=.

| 13 | **...** | ♘bd7 |

Black's 5th move with this Knight! 13...exd4 14 cxd4 c5 seems more active.

Stein-Lutikov, Moscow 1966 continued 13...♖e8? 14 ♘f1? and Black equalized easily. However, White should vary with 14 dxe5 dxe5 15 ♘xe5 ♗d6 16 ♘ef3 ♗xe4 (16...♘xe4 17 ♘xe4 ♗xe4 18 ♗g5! busts Black) 17 ♘xe4 ♘xe4 18 ♕d3! (White can't win a piece because his Queen hangs at the end after ...♗h2+), with initiative.

| 14 | **b4!** | ... |

Prevents ...c5 and prepares a dominating build-up with 15 ♗b2 followed by c4. The routine continuation 14 ♗b2 (Keres-Gligorich, Zurich 1959) gives nothing.

STEIN

Position after 14 b4!

FISCHER

14	...		exd4

Stein makes his bid for active counterplay even though it involves abandoning his "strong point" (e5-Pawn). If *14...a5 15 ♘b3!* and Black might find himself in straightened circumstances after the Knight reaches a5.

15	cxd4		a5

On *15...c5 16 bxc5 dxc5 17 d5* White's steamroller in the center is more formidable than Black's Q-side majority.

16	bxa5		c5

Inferior would be *16...♖xa5 17 d5! c5 18 dxc6 e.p. ♗xc6 19 ♘d4*, after which White, among other things, goes to work on the isolated b-Pawn.

17	e5!		...

This identical position was reached by transposition, with Black's Rook on e8, in Cirich-Robatsch, Beverwijk 1967, which continued: *17 ♗b2 ♕xa5 18 a4 b4 19 ♘c4 ♕c7 20 e5 dxe5 21 dxe5 ♘d5 22 ♘fd2 ♘7b6* and now Spassky's recommendation of *23 e6!* is unpleasant for Black. (See note to Black's 9th move.)

17	...		dxe5

Another line of defense is *17...♘e8* with the idea of eliminating both of White's center Pawns. "The consequences are very ramified, and there is some danger that Black may fail to recover White's Pawn on its a5 or may lose his own on b5, or both. The text is more active but also more dangerous for Black's King." (KMOCH).

| 18 | dxe5 | ♘d5 |
| 19 | ♘e4 | ♘b4! |

The idea is to force the Bishop to retreat and thereby hem in White's QR. On *19...♖xa5 20 ♘eg5! h6 21 ♕d3! g6 22 ♘e6!* wins.

| 20 | ♗b1 | ♖xa5 |
| 21 | ♕e2! | ... |

Increasing the pressure. Not *21 e6 fxe6 22 ♘eg5?* (or *22 ♘fg5 ♗d5 23 ♘xh7 ♖f5!* holds) *22...♗xf3! 23 ♘xf3 ♗f6* wins.

STEIN

Position after 21 ♕e2!

FISCHER

One can sense the storm looming against Black's King.

| 21 | ... | ♘b6? |

Quite possibly "the losing move." It is better to reserve this Knight for the defense of the K-side. More prudent is *21...♖e8!* with *...♘f8* in the offing. *22 ♖d1 ♕c7* leads to nought. And *22 e6* leads to no demonstrable advantage after *22...fxe6 23 ♘eg5 ♗xg5 24 ♘xg5 ♘f8 25 ♕h5 g6*, etc.

| 22 | ♘fg5! | ... |

Now the threats are beginning to jell.

| 22 | ... | ♗xe4! |

Forced, because if *22...h6 23* ♘h7!! stands Black up. On *23...*♖e8
(*23...*♔xh7 *24* ♘xc5 dis.+ followed by ♘xb7 leads to a small fork)
24 ♘hf6+! ♗xf6 (*24...*gxf6 *25* ♕g4+ ♔h8 *26* ♘d6! ♗xd6 *27* ♕f5!
♔g7 *28* ♗xh6+ leads to mate) *25* ♘xf6+ ♕xf6 (again if *25...*gxf6
26 ♕g4+ ♔f8 *27* ♗xh6+ ♔e7 *28* e6! ♔d6 *29* ♕g3+ ♔c6 *30* ♗e4+
♘4d5 *31* exf7 ♖h8 *32* ♗xd5+ wins) *26* exf6 wins the exchange.

Also insufficient is *22...*g6 *23* e6! f5 *24* ♘f7! followed by ♗b2 with
a crushing attack.

23	♕xe4	g6
24	♕h4	h5
25	♕g3!	...

Now White threatens *26* ♘e6! ♗h4! *27* ♘xd8 ♗xg3 *28* ♘b7 ♖a7
29 ♘xc5. After Black's next move, this variation fails against
29...♗xe5.

Impetuous would be *25* g4?? ♕d4.

| 25 | ... | ♘c4! |
| 26 | ♘f3? | ... |

More forcing is *26* e6! f5 *27* ♘f3 (not *27* ♘f7 ♖xf7! *28* exf7+ ♔xf7
29 ♗xf5! gxf5 *30* ♕f3 ♔g6 *31* g4 ♕d5 and a draw appears likely)
27...♔g7 *28* ♕f4 ♖h8 transposing into the game (but not *27...*♖f6
28 ♗g5 ♔h7 *29* ♗xf6 ♗xf6 *30* ♗xf5! gxf5 *31* ♖ad1 ♘d5 *32* e7! ♗xe7
33 ♖xd5 is decisive.). This order of moves would prohibit the defense
mentioned in the note to Black's 28th; after being forced to play *26...*f5,
Black loses his options.

At this stage the power failed. In the dark I began to worry about
26...♘d3! (if *27* ♖d1 ♘xc1! and White has nothing). Then the lights
came on again and I saw clearly that *26...*♘d3? was crushed by
27 ♗xd3! ♕xd3 *28* ♗g5! and White penetrates decisively on the weak
dark squares.

26	...	♔g7
27	♕f4	♖h8
28	e6!	...

"This blow rocks the remnants of the tower around the Black King." (GLIGORICH).

STEIN

Position after 28 e6!

FISCHER

| 28 | ... | **f5** |

Much stiffer resistance (taking advantage of White's inaccurate 26th move) is offered by *28...♗f6!* (not *28...f6 29 ♘h4*) *29* exf7 ♗xa1 (*29...♛d6? 30* f8=♛+! ♔xf8 *31* ♛e4 ♛d7 *32* ♗g5! ♖a6 *33* ♗xf6 ♖xf6 *34* ♘e5! winning a Pawn and eventually the game) *30* f8=♛+! ♛xf8 *31* ♛c7+ ♔g8 *32* ♗xg6 ♘d5 (if *32...♖a6 33* ♖e8!) *33* ♛b7 ♘f6 *34* ♗f4 (threatening *35* ♘g5 and ♗f7+) *34...♖h7!* White now appears to have nothing better than *35* ♗xh7+ ♘xh7 *36* ♛d5+ ♛f7 (worse is *36...♔h8? 37* ♛xh5!) *37* ♛xf7+ ♔xf7 *38* ♖xa1 with chances by virtue of the extra Pawn. But this would be a tough ending to win!

| 29 | ♗xf5! | ♛f8 |

The only reasonable way to decline the sacrifice. On *29...♗d6 30* e7! ♗xf4 (or *30...♗xe7 31* ♛g3 ♖a6 *32* ♘g5, etc.) *31* exd8=♛ ♖xd8 *32* ♗xf4 gxf5 *33* ♗c7! (R.Byrne).

Kmoch suggests that "Leonidas might even have better taken a chance and faced the storm by playing *29...gxf5.*" But the Bishop is tabu, for White wins quickly with *30* ♛g3+. Black now has two defenses which fail:

A] *30...♔f8 31* ♛g6 ♛e8 (if *31...♘d6 32* ♘e5!) *32* ♗h6+ ♖xh6 *33* ♛xh6+ ♔g8 *34* ♘g5.

B] *30...♔h7 31* ♘g5+! ♗xg5 *32* ♗xg5 ♛d3 (if *32...♛b8 33* ♛h4! ♔g6 *34* ♗f6 – or *32...♛e8 33* ♖ad1 ♖a7 *34* ♖d8! ♛xd8 *35* ♗xd8 ♖xd8

36 e7 ♖e8 37 ♖e6! ♖exe7 38 ♕g6+ ♔h8 39 ♕f6+ ♗g7 40 ♕h6+ and mates) 33 ♕c7+ ♔g6 34 ♕f7+! ♔xg5 35 ♕g7+ ♔f4 36 ♖ad1!, etc.

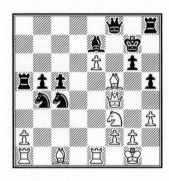

STEIN

Position after 29...♕f8

FISCHER

30	♗e4?	...

Littlewood indicates *30 ♘h4!* as a quick win for White. He's right. The main line is *30...♗xh4 31 ♕xh4 ♕xf5 (if 31...♕f6 32 ♕g3! – or 31...gxf5 32 ♕g5+ ♔h7 33 e7 ♕e8 34 ♖e6!) 32 ♕e7+ ♔g8 33 ♕d8+ ♔g7 34 ♕c7+ ♔g8 35 e7*, etc.

30	...	♕xf4
31	♗xf4	♖e8?

Stein's post-mortem suggestion of *31...♖a6* is met by *32 ♖ad1 ♖xe6 33 ♖d7* (threatening ♘g5), etc.

But the best try is *31...♖xa2!* On *32 ♖ad1 ♖a7* holds. And if *32 ♖xa2 ♘xa2 33 ♘e5 g5 34 ♗g3* maintains the initiative, but Black has drawing chances.

Black, however, was in extreme time-pressure.

32	♖ad1	♖a6
33	♖d7	...

Even more convincing is *33 ♗b7! ♖a7 34 ♖d7.*

33	...	♖xe6
34	♘g5	♖f6

Costs the exchange. But no better is *34...♖a6 35 ♗b1 ♔f6 36 ♘e4+ ♔f7 37 ♘xc5*, etc.

35	♗f3!	♖xf4

Of course *35...♔f8* is refuted by *36 ♘h7+*.

36	♘e6+	♔f6
37	♘xf4	♘e5
38	♖b7	♗d6
39	♔f1	...

Puts an end to all effective resistance. White's material superiority must tell.

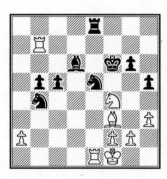

STEIN

Position after 39 ♔f1

FISCHER

39	...	♘c2

A pretty point is revealed after *39...♘xf3 40 ♖xe8 ♘d2+ 41 ♔e2 ♗xf4 42 ♖f8+ ♔g5 43 ♖xf4 ♔xf4 44 ♔xd2*, resigns.

40	♖e4	♘d4
41	♖b6	♖d8
42	♘d5+	♔f5
43	♘e3+	...

The sealed move seals Black's fate. Not only is White an exchange ahead, but his attack still rages.

43	...	♔e6

Equally hopeless is *43...♔f6 44 ♗e2 b4 45 f4* followed by *♗c4*.

44	♗e2!	...

"The double threat of *45* f4 and *45* ♗xb5 clears the last stone from the road to victory." (KMOCH).

44	...	♚d7
45	♗xb5+	♘xb5
46	♖xb5	♚c6
47	a4	♗c7
48	♚e2	g5
49	g3	♖a8
50	♖b2	♖f8
51	f4	...

The beginning of the end.

51	...	gxf4
52	gxf4	♘f7
53	♖e6+	♘d6

If *53*...♗d6 *54* ♖f6! is powerful.

54	f5	♖a8
55	♖d2!	♖xa4
56	f6	**Black resigns**

On *56*...♖f4 *57* ♘d5 wins the house. A stubborn fight!

BOBBY FISCHER'S TOURNAMENT AND MATCH RECORD

(BORN: MARCH 9, 1943)

Event	Year	Place
Brooklyn Chess Club Championship	1955	3rd-5th
USA Amateur Championship, New Jersey	1955	minus score
USA Junior Championship, Nebraska	1955	10th-20th
Greater New York City Championship	1956	5th-7th
Manhattan Chess Club, "A" Reserve	1956	1st
USA Amateur Championship, New Jersey	1956	21st
USA Junior Championship, Philadelphia	1956	1st
USA Open Championship, Oklahoma	1956	4th-8th
Canadian Open Championship, Montreal	1956	8th-12th
Eastern States Championship, Washington	1956	2nd
Rosenwald Trophy Tournament, New York	1956-7	8th
Log Cabin Open Championship, New Jersey	1957	6th
Western Open Championship, Milwaukee	1957	7th
USA Junior Championship, San Francisco	1957	1st
USA Open Championship, Cleveland	1957	1st
Eight-game match with Cardoso, New York	1957	6-2 (won)
New Jersey Open Championship	1957	1st
North Central Championship, Milwaukee	1957	6th
USA Championship, New York	1957-8	1st
Interzonal, Portoroz	1958	5th-6th
Four-game match with Matulovich, Belgrade	1958	2½-1½ (won)
USA Championship, New York	1958-9	1st
Mar del Plata, Argentina	1959	3rd-4th
Santiago, Chile	1959	4th-7th
Zurich, Switzerland	1959	3rd-4th
Candidates' Tournament, Yugoslavia	1959	5th-6th

USA Championship, New York	1959-60	1st
Mar del Plata, Argentina	1960	1st
Buenos Aires	1960	13th
Reykjavik, Iceland	1960	1st
Olympic Team Tournament, Leipzig 1st board	1960	high scorer (finals)
USA Championship, New York	1960-1	1st
Sixteen-game match with Reshevsky, New York and Los Angeles (unfinished)	1961	5½-5½
Bled, Yugoslavia	1961	2nd
Interzonal, Stockholm	1962	1st
Candidates' Tournament, Curaçao	1962	4th
Olympic Team Tournament, Varna 1st board	1962	high scorer (prelims)
USA Championship, New York	1962-3	1st
Western Open, Michigan	1963	1st
New York State Open Tournament	1963	1st
USA Championship, New York	1963-4	1st
Capablanca Memorial, Havana, Cuba	1965	2nd-4th
USA Championship, New York	1965-6	1st
Piatigorsky Cup, Los Angeles	1966	2nd
Olympic Team Tournament, Havana 1st board	1966	2nd high scorer
USA Championship, New York	1966-7	1st
Monaco	1967	1st
Skopje, Yugoslavia	1967	1st
Interzonal, Sousse	1967	withdrew while leading
Israel	1968	1st
Yugoslavia	1968	1st